CROP INTERNATIONAL STUD

This book is the winner of the 2015 In[...] awarded by the Comparative Research Programme on Poverty (CROP) and Zed Books. This prize is awarded to book projects that challenge the dominant thinking and knowledge about poverty and provide sound contributions to the eradication and/or prevention of poverty in our world.

For more information, see: www.crop.org

About CROP

CROP, the Comparative Research Programme on Poverty, is a response from the academic community to the problems of poverty. The programme was initiated by the International Social Science Council in 1992, and the CROP Secretariat was officially opened in June 1993 by the Director General of UNESCO, Dr Federico Mayor.

In recent years, poverty-related issues have moved up on the international agenda, with poverty eradication now defined as the greatest global challenge facing the world today. In cooperation with its sponsors, the International Science Council (ISC) and the University of Bergen (UiB), CROP works with knowledge networks, institutions and scholars to establish independent and critical poverty research in order to help shape policies for long-term poverty prevention and eradication.

The CROP network comprises scholars engaged in poverty-related research across a variety of academic disciplines. Researchers from more than 100 different countries are represented in the network, which is coordinated by the CROP Secretariat at the University of Bergen, Norway.

The CROP series on International Studies in Poverty Research presents expert research and essential analyses of different aspects of poverty worldwide. By promoting a fuller understanding of the nature, extent, depth, distribution, trends, causes and effects of poverty and poverty-related issues, this series will contribute to knowledge concerning the prevention and eradication of poverty at global, regional, national and local levels.

For more information, contact:
CROP Secretariat
PO Box 7800, 5020 Bergen, Norway
Phone: +47 55 58 97 44
Email: crop@uib.no
Visiting address: Jekteviksbakken 31
www.crop.org

Series editors

Juliana Martínez Franzoni, Associate Professor of Political Science at the University of Costa Rica.

Thomas Pogge, Leitner Professor of Philosophy and International Affairs at Yale University.

CROP INTERNATIONAL STUDIES IN POVERTY RESEARCH
Published by Zed Books in association with CROP.

David Gordon and Paul Spicker (eds), *The International Glossary on Poverty*, 1999.

Francis Wilson, Nazneen Kanji and Einar Braathen (eds), *Poverty Reduction: What Role for the State in Today's Globalized Economy?* 2001.

Willem van Genugten and Camilo Perez-Bustillo (eds), *The Poverty of Rights: Human Rights and the Eradication of Poverty*, 2001.

Else Øyen et al. (eds), *Best Practices in Poverty Reduction: An Analytical Framework*, 2002.

Lucy Williams, Asbjørn Kjønstad and Peter Robson (eds), *Law and Poverty: The Legal System and Poverty Reduction*, 2003.

Elisa P. Reis and Mick Moore (eds), *Elite Perceptions of Poverty and Inequality*, 2005.

Robyn Eversole, John-Andrew McNeish and Alberto D. Cimadamore (eds), *Indigenous Peoples and Poverty: An International Perspective*, 2005.

Lucy Williams (ed.), *International Poverty Law: An Emerging Discourse*, 2006.

Maria Petmesidou and Christos Papatheodorou (eds), *Poverty and Social Deprivation in the Mediterranean*, 2006.

Paul Spicker, Sonia Alvarez Leguizamón and David Gordon (eds), *Poverty: An International Glossary*, 2nd edn, 2007.

Santosh Mehrotra and Enrique Delamonica, *Eliminating Human Poverty: Macroeconomic and Social Policies for Equitable Growth*, 2007.

David Hemson, Kassim Kulindwa, Haakon Lein and Adolfo Mascarenhas (eds), *Poverty and Water: Explorations of the Reciprocal Relationship*, 2008.

Ronaldo Munck, Narathius Asingwire, Honor Fagan and Consolata Kabonesa (eds), *Water and Development: Good Governance after Neoliberalism*, 2015.

Abraar Karan and Geeta Sodhi (eds), *Protecting the Health of the Poor: Social Movements in the South*, 2015.

Alberto D. Cimadamore, Gabriele Koehler and Thomas Pogge (eds), *Poverty and the Millennium Development Goals: A Critical Look Forward*, 2016.

Alberto D. Cimadamore, Gro Therese Lie, Maurice B. Mittelmark and Fungisai P. Gwanzura Ottemöller (eds), *Development and Sustainability Science: The Challenge of Social Change*, 2016.

Einar Braathen, Julian May and Gemma Wright (eds), *Poverty and Inequality in Middle Income Countries: Policy Achievements, Political Obstacles*, 2016.

Julio Boltvinik and Susan Archer Mann, *Peasant Poverty and Persistence: Theories, Debates, Realities and Policies*, 2016.

ABOUT THE AUTHOR

Andrew Martin Fischer is Associate Professor of Social Policy and Development Studies at the Institute of Social Studies (ISS). He is also the founding editor of the book series of the UK and Ireland Development Studies Association, published by Oxford University Press, entitled *Critical Frontiers of International Development Studies*, and editor at the journal *Development and Change*. He won the 2015 International Studies in Poverty Prize, awarded by the Comparative Research Programme on Poverty (CROP) in 2016.

He has been involved in development studies and work in developing countries for over 30 years. This started with time spent in India and Nicaragua in the late 1980s, followed by seven years living and working with local communities in northern India and Nepal. He subsequently started his PhD at the London School of Economics (LSE) in 2002, which dealt extensively with issues of poverty, inequality and social exclusion within the context of rapid economic growth in the Tibetan areas of western China. This included two years of fieldwork in the region. His work became well-known for its critical engagement with concepts of social exclusion and marginalisation, as elaborated in his first two books: *State Growth and Social Exclusion in Tibet: Challenges of Recent Economic Growth* (NIAS Press, 2005), and *The Disempowered Development of Tibet in China: A study in the economics of marginalisation* (Lexington Books, 2014).

More generally, he has led teaching on poverty and social policy at LSE and the ISS and has worked with and/or advised various multilateral agencies and NGOs, including UNRISD, UNW, UNDP, UNICEF, UNECOSOC, Amnesty International and Human Rights Watch.

Fischer's current research is focused on the role of redistribution in development at local, regional and global scales and its interaction with finance and production. Since 2015, he has been leading a European Research Council Starting Grant on the political economy of externally financing social policy in developing countries, under which he completed this book.

POVERTY AS IDEOLOGY

RESCUING SOCIAL JUSTICE FROM GLOBAL DEVELOPMENT AGENDAS

Andrew Martin Fischer

ZED

Poverty as Ideology: Rescuing Social Justice from Global Development Agendas
was first published in 2018 by Zed Books Ltd., The Foundry, 17 Oval Way,
London SE11 5RR, UK.

www.zedbooks.net

Typeset in Plantin and Kievit by Swales & Willis Ltd, Exeter, Devon
Index by Ed Emery
Cover design by Kika Sroka-Miller

A catalogue record for this book is available from the British Library

ISBN 978-1-78699-045-7 hb
ISBN 978-1-78699-044-0 pb
ISBN 978-1-78699-046-4 pdf
ISBN 978-1-78699-047-1 epub
ISBN 978-1-78699-048-8 mobi

Printed and bound by CPI Group (UK) Ltd, Croydon, CR0 4YY

To our two daughters, Amiya and Éva,
in the hope that they inherit a better earth.

CONTENTS

ILLUSTRATIONS

Figures

Table

ABBREVIATIONS

BMI	body mass index
BMR	basal metabolic rate
CCTs	conditional cash transfers
CPI	consumer price index
DHS	demographic and health survey
FAO	Food and Agriculture Organization
FDI	foreign direct investment
GDP	gross domestic product
GNI	gross national income
HDI	Human Development Index
HDR	Human Development Report
IFI	international financial institution
ILO	International Labour Organization
IMF	International Monetary Fund
INGO	international non-governmental organisation
MDGs	Millennium Development Goals
MPI	Multidimensional Poverty Index
NGO	Non-governmental organisation
OECD	Organisation for Economic Co-operation and Development
PPP	purchasing power parity
SAP	structural adjustment programme
SDGs	Sustainable Development Goals
UNDP	United Nations Development Programme
UNICEF	United Nations International Children's Emergency Fund
UNRISD	United Nations Research Institute for Social Development
WB	World Bank
WDR	World Development Report

ACKNOWLEDGEMENTS

This book has been long in the making and even longer in conception, and I am indebted to many people who shared parts of the journey. First are those people we might categorise as relatively poor if we must, who have generously shared their time, thoughts and experiences with me through the course of my own forays into engagement, exchange and research. I am humbly grateful to them for having given me insights and richness in so many ways, about and far beyond the subject of poverty.

More specifically, my foremost acknowledgement is to my wife, Mary Zsamboky, who is always an incredible source of support and inspiration. She helped me through many of the deep moments of discouragement with this book and through the numerous convoluted knots I had woven with the text. As two full-time working parents, much of her support has also been in the form of patience and in distracting our two very rambunctious young daughters while I have been absorbed with writing and rewriting this book, although the moments she engaged with the text and the ideas within it have shaped me and the book profoundly.

Other friends and colleagues have also been of great support. In particular, Andy Sumner has been a wonderful source of encouragement and is exemplary in his generosity with feedback, comments and general sharing, right up to the last finishing touches of the book. He also emboldened my initial steps towards this book in the late 2000s and I owe him much of the scholarly attention that was brought to my initial work beyond the subject of Tibet and China. Ben Radley and Charmaine Ramos provided extremely useful comments in the final revisions of the book, as did the anonymous reviewers and Maria Gabriela Palacio Ludeña on an earlier draft. Emma Cantal Dadap provided much-needed assistance in the preparation of the manuscript and, together with Ana Lucía Badillo Salgado and Benedict Yiyugsah, the three have proven to be a wonderful team of PhD researchers with whom to explore some of the ideas in this book, particularly around the subject of social protection. Thanks are also due more generally to the numerous colleagues and students, inside and outside of ISS and previously LSE, who shared with me parts of my intellectual and research meanderings that contributed to different tangents of the book. They are too numerous to list here, although I trust that they will recognise themselves if and when they read this.

With regard to earlier influences, I remain indebted to Kari Polanyi Levitt for her depth of knowledge and breadth of vision in the field of development economics, which have undoubtedly shaped the ways that I started approaching the study of poverty when I returned to academia for my PhD. James Putzel, my PhD supervisor at LSE, has remained an incredible source of support and friendship ever since, and always reminds me to keep my eye on the ball, in terms of the strategic political significance of our scholarship in the current context. The person who at first contributed most to my more technical understanding of poverty measurement was Athar Hussain, my other PhD supervisor at LSE, as well as Tim Dyson, on matters pertaining to demography and population studies. Tim's example as a consummate social scientist, in the true sense of the word 'scientist', as well as a wonderfully gracious person, continues to provide me with a role model. The work of Thandika Mkandawire has also greatly influenced me and I feel privileged to have been able to cross paths and exchange ideas with him over the past ten years or so.

Finally, thanks are also due to Ashwani Saith for having given me the opportunity to dig my teeth into teaching poverty at LSE, where I first taught on his course and then took it over from him when he left. The meeting of many like minds at ISS also provided fertile ground for developing the ideas of this book, notably Murat Arsel, Arjun Bedi, Erhard Berner, Jun Borras, Bram Büscher, Amrita Chhachhi, Anirban Dasgupta, Arjan de Haan, Wendy Harcourt, Roy Huijsmans, Rosalba Icaza, Mahmoud Messkoub, Jos Mooij, Susan Newman, Howard Nicholas, Bridget O'Laughlin, Auma Okwany, Robert Sparrow, Max Spoor, Servaas Storm, Ben White and Marc Wuyts, among others.

Special thanks are also due to the editors at Zed Books, who have been incredibly patient with my delays at delivering this manuscript, in particular Kim Walker and more recently Dominic Fagan. Other people involved with them on the production side have also been a pleasure to work with, namely Megan Symons. The people working at or with CROP have also had endless patience with me, namely Jakob Horstmann, Maria Sollohub and Charlotte Lillefjære-Tertnæs. I am of course honoured to have been selected for the 2015 International Studies in Poverty Prize, which was a huge boost of encouragement to finally complete this book project, which I had been working on since 2008. I sincerely hope that the result honours this award.

Infinite gratitude is reserved for my parents, Phyllis and Conrad Fischer, who impressed on me a deep commitment to peace and social justice that I can only hope to mimic. My mother in particular remains an inspiration in the depth, breadth and durability of her commitment, with a humility and wisdom that I have simply never encountered in the many years that I have now spent studying and working in academia. Whenever I write, I think of her discerning gaze over the relevance of whatever I manage to transcribe and of her example as to how to live the values we profess.

Finally, it should be noted that much of the work on this book has been completed under the auspices of the AIDSOCPRO project (Aiding Social Protection: The Political Economy of Externally Financing Social Policy in Developing Countries), which has received funding from the European Research Council (ERC) under the European Union's Horizon 2020 research and innovation programme (grant agreement No 638647).

1 | INTRODUCTION: POVERTY, IDEOLOGY AND DEVELOPMENT

It has become widely accepted, even among more critical scholars, that global poverty has fallen over the last several decades, as the one silver lining in an otherwise tumultuous world. The reiteration of this conventional wisdom has even achieved the status of a platitude, a perfunctory preamble that must preface every speech about the state of the world in multilateral fora. But what does this actually mean, in particular for poor people? Has global poverty actually fallen? According to whose authority, by what measures and to what effect? These questions are especially important given the ways that global poverty statistics have been marshalled to legitimise the reigning international economic order, particularly since the advent of global goal-setting exercises in the new millennium.

For much of the first decade after the Millennium Development Goals (MDGs) were agreed in the early 2000s, the consensus was that the progress on the various goals, if any, had been slow, particularly with respect to Goal One on income poverty. The strong improvements in China and South Asia stood out as the exceptions and accounted for most of the aggregate progress, in contrast to stagnation elsewhere. Global growth then ticked upwards during the decade and more general improvements came to be registered, even despite the financial crisis in 2007–2009. These included sub-Saharan Africa, which had erstwhile been the most ailing region. The improvements were in large part facilitated by broader macroeconomic factors such as commodity and financial 'super-cycles'. Among other things, these provided some fiscal space for many governments to re-invigorate development strategies that had been shelved for years under the exigences of austerity and adjustment. It also allowed them to dabble in policies that addressed the targets of the MDGs, such as cash transfers, millennium schools or primary health care. Such cycles, however, massively unsettled the structures of relative prices that inform income poverty analysis, such as with respect to the relative costs of urban housing, transport or food. The conventional wisdom nonetheless settled on the narrative that income poverty had fallen, as informed by World Bank data. With the arrival of the Sustainable Development Goals (SDGs), it was therefore time for the global community to cement the gains and make more progress while also newly focusing on sustainability and inequality, however these were to be understood.

All of this assumes, of course, that gains were made. They probably were made in the most minimalist sense, although even this is notoriously difficult to evaluate in a manner that can be objectively compared across time and space. Most contemporary work on the subject of global poverty defers – whether with fidelity or reluctance – to the authority of the World Bank production of global poverty statistics. The latest are usually invoked, drawn from the most recent rendition of World Bank data based on the most recent revisions of purchasing power parity (PPP) poverty lines applied to the latest available survey data. I have refrained from reciting such rituals in this book because, in all honesty, we probably do not know. An understanding of the highly contrived processes of producing such statistics erodes any confidence in their feigned scientific accuracy. Deferring to them as if they are accurate carries the risk of being coopted into the political projects that they have been designed to serve.

This is not to deny that global poverty – understood in a minimalist 'absolute' sense – has probably fallen over the past decades, despite many hiccups and patchy regional concentrations. Global productivity has definitely been increasing in recent decades, in dramatic and revolutionary ways. The world as a whole has been producing and consuming more and more stuff per person than ever before in the history of this planet, and this despite relatively rapid population growth. The common trope that 'trickle-down economics' does not work is not entirely accurate. Trickle-down does occur, although in quite unequal ways, and wide swathes of the global population have shared in the spoils of increasing consumption, as they nibble along the value chain of growing productivity and accumulation. Whether or not this has made them better off – materially, humanly, ecologically, spiritually or in terms of security, quality of life or happiness – is a different question. Indeed, we must be very careful not to make simplistic associations between various objective dimensions of economic or human development and subjective states such as happiness (however understood). Nonetheless, even if we restrict ourselves to the objective states, our ability to be certain about what, precisely, has been going on at global, regional, national or local scales is difficult to pin down as soon as we start to scratch beneath the veneer of official certitude.

Uncomfortable questions

Part of the problem relates to the politics of representation. This refers to struggles over controlling the narrative about how we are to interpret and remember the legacy of the most recent phase of global capitalism. Has it been one of progress, even liberation, as proposed by many, such as the editors of *The Economist*, who have been among its foremost cheerleaders? (Images might be conjured of people being 'pulled out' of poverty, as is commonly alluded.) Or has it been one of increased subordination, exploitation and/or oppression, as suggested by many on the political left, such as Li (2017)? To put it more crudely, has the world become better or worse off since the early 1980s or, as seemingly preferred by various global agendas, since the end of the Cold War from 1990 onwards? The reality – which is already very difficult to assess – is regularly obscured by the smoke of ideological warfare.

Poverty has definitely fallen in OECD countries from a long-term perspective of a century or so. But does this hold for the last 40, 30, 20 or 10 years? The question is particularly pertinent in light of the common observation that average real wages in the US, UK and other rich countries have been more or less stagnant since the 1970s, counterbalanced by the radical changes in typical consumption profiles over the same period (e.g., think of mobile phone expenses, which were effectively non-existent for most people 25 to 30 years ago but are now considered essential needs for even poor people in rich and even middle-income countries). Stagnant wages have been compensated by increasing work, especially in the US, which does increase household incomes, but at what cost? Appropriately, some have started to talk about time poverty in such contexts of overwork.

These questions are equally pertinent in poorer countries, particularly in light of the rise of so-called 'emerging economies'. Debates raged even in rapidly growing China until the 2000s concerning the stagnation of real wages at the lower end of urban employment, particularly among urban migrants (although even such stagnant urban wages would have represented a significant increase over the previous earnings of rural migrants, hence driving up incomes overall). A Lewisian turning point was declared by some when these wages appeared to be rising in real terms towards the end of the 2000s. Yet, the turning point was also contested by others given the equally if not more rapidly rising costs of living in urban areas, which possibly were not being accurately reflected in price and cost-of-living indices. Beyond the exceptional case of China, our understanding of realities within other rapidly changing contexts remains far more tenuous, in terms of whether modest increases in income or wages are *really* real, or simply reflections of changes in poorly measured consumption patterns, changing relative prices, new dependencies and so forth.

In other words, consumption has definitely been changing around the world. Yet if we measure such changes incorrectly, then at least part of what is registered as improving real incomes or living standards might in fact represent inadequately measured changes in prices and costs of living, or else in the baseline of minimally acceptable needs for survival and functioning in rapidly changing contexts. Much of what we cognise as economic growth and rising incomes is based on a real creation of new value by the same amounts of labour (i.e., productivity). But much might also be due to adding more workers to production at the same or even lower levels of productivity, or by making workers work longer and harder (i.e., the intensification of labour). Some might also simply reflect the appropriation or expropriation from people through increased exploitation or other forms of extracting value. To use the term coined by David Harvey (adapting Marx's conception of primitive accumulation), how much of growth is actually a reflection of accumulation by dispossession? Given biases in practices of accountancy, dispossession might actually appear as growth, particularly in contexts of rapid structural change where dispossession can be disguised as the creation of new value.

With or without dispossession, standard measures of growth in this sense can reflect the monetisation[1] and commodification[2] of already-existing livelihoods that, prior to monetisation, were poorly reflected by household income surveys or national accounts. For instance, in situations commonly described as 'subsistence', much of the functional value of household production and consumption is often significantly underestimated by surveys, as discussed in Chapter 3. As such households start to derive more of their income through selling their labour and more of their consumption through purchasing commodities with cash, they come to conform more with the conceptions of conventional surveying. The transition might therefore be registered as an increase in incomes and consumption, even though this might simply represent the fact that surveys reflect more of the consumption that was already taking place. Such processes of commodification and monetisation might involve increasing exploitation or they might not; standard household surveys generally provide little guidance on such matters. The point is that tangible changes in people's livelihoods or quality of life in poor countries can be very difficult to decipher in such processes of transformation. This is particularly the case when the processes become financialised, that is, when consumption becomes increasingly mediated through borrowing, allowing the burden of current consumption to be postponed into the future. These questions are so difficult to pinpoint precisely because they involve so many changing elements, such that the measurement of poverty is at best a moving target.

Similar questions can also be asked with regard to the rationale for aggregating various dimensions of poverty beyond the purely economic, such as with so-called multidimensional measures of poverty. Although seemingly noble in intention, is it appropriate to aggregate health and education with income or consumption proxies, thereby allowing trade-offs between them to disguise deteriorations or improvements in one of them? In particular, health and education have been generally improving across the world, even in contexts of stagnant income and persistent poverty (at least in terms of crude measures such as enrolments, not necessarily in terms of outcomes such as literacy). As noted by much work in contemporary demography (and also by Deaton 2013), the reason for the dissonance is that substantial improvements in these human development dimensions can be achieved cheaply, with relatively few resources, and hence in quite poor settings. As a result, as argued by Dyson (2001, 2011), health and demographic transitions, along with urbanisation, are taking place throughout the world to a considerable extent independent of economic performance or even levels of income.[3] In light of these insights, should we disguise through aggregation the persistence of income or consumption poverty with these improvements in human development indicators? This was a crucial question to ask in the 1980s and 1990s, when the dissonance was in the direction of improving health despite worsening poverty in many countries. Since then, in many instances the question has reversed, with rising incomes contrasting with much more sluggish improvements in health and education.

This understanding of the production and consumption of global poverty statistics as an inherently political beast runs against the depoliticising tendencies in poverty studies, which is also apparent in much of the recent literature on inequality. There is a tendency to view poverty (alongside ideas such as human rights) as occupying an innately moral higher ground, in contrast to the dirtier world of politics and ideologies. Indeed, some might even hold that various policy positions (e.g., liberalisation, privatisation, etc.) should ultimately be judged by the way they deliver on poverty (and other higher moral standards, such as human rights), as if the two are possible to untangle. However, they are not possible to untangle. Or else, if they are, we need to start with the politics that are imbued within poverty representations in order to have a clearer view of what these representations actually represent.

Deconstructing the politics of poverty measures

The primary purpose of this book is to pry open these implications of poverty conception and measurement. The task is important given the central ideological role that this particular set of social statistics plays in contemporary development policy and in representations of the most recent and particularly virulent phase of global capitalism. The aim is to strip back the increasingly sophisticated technicality of poverty studies in order to demystify the fundamental political and normative choices that are implied by various methods and measures, and how the resulting political constructs obscure or reveal the changing nature of social needs within the evolution of capitalist development. In this manner, we can examine how the ways we conceive and measure poverty instil propensities towards ideologically formed views of poverty, anti-poverty policies and broader social and development policies

The exercise is not meant as a rejection of the empirical project of social scientific measurement, as is common in some corners of post-structuralist and post-development scholarship. The arguments of this book will nonetheless carry resonance with many of the critiques of mainstream development in these more critical literatures, such as with respect to the subjective, ideational and govermentality aspects of poverty studies and policies, and how poverty is constituted as a problem, represented and territorialised.[4] However, most of this literature is thin in its examination of actual methods in poverty studies and is hence weak in terms of locating critique within a technical understanding of poverty concepts and measures on their own terms.[5] Instead, the technical is left to the continued dominance of economists (in contrast to the past, when the study of poverty tended to be led by sociologists, such as the late Peter Townsend).

Much of post-development scholarship also appears to conflate critique of neoliberal policies with critique of development more generally. This leads to much confusion about whether the issue at hand is the failure of various state projects of development and how they instrumentalise poverty as part of their logic of governmentality, or the failure of development under neoliberalism more specifically. It also leads to confusion as to whether, in rejecting the latter, one is also rejecting the former on the basis that they share certain commonalities, such as the perceived need to render poor populations legible as a means to regulate and discipline them, even despite their diametrically opposed modalities for doing so.

Instead of engaging in such conflations, the exercise of this book starts from a methodological appreciation of the empirical project – indeed, of the necessity of empirics to support modern forms of social provisioning and public policy. It nonetheless examines the ideological biases that are inherent to such projects, with the understanding that social sciences are invariably and intrinsically interpretative and normative. All social statistics must be understood as institutional constructs, as institutionally mediated attempts to cognise social realities. They are therefore shaped by the power relations and ideologically informed ways of seeing the world that permeate their institutional origins.

Ideological, in the sense used here, does not necessarily refer in a strict sense to formally defined political ideologies and sets of ideas, although it includes these. Rather, it is used here in a more general sense. Drawing from Curtis White (2013), who himself draws from the sense of the term used by Karl Marx, ideology can be understood as the stories and ideas that we live out as members of particular communities in order to establish ways of understanding about how to best live together, in our case within complex modern societies. In an interview with Heumann (2014), he clarifies that the 'pejorative sense of the term comes from the idea that structures of power and privilege can and do manipulate and enforce these stories in order to support their own interests ... Telling stories that you want everyone to see themselves in, but that really favor only one group, requires dishonesty.' As he elaborates along the lines of his own work on science, 'the primary ideological story told by science is that it has no relation to ideology ... [which can] become the covering [fiction] for stupendous destruction and cruelty.'

Poverty statistics are no exception to this rule. More precisely, they prove the rule on steroids given the political sensitivity associated with them and the central role that the idea of poverty has come to play in contemporary ideologies about capitalist development. Indeed, poverty statistics are often even marshalled to legitimise oppression, as is common in the occasional publications that seek to defend colonial legacies on the basis of health and education improvements in many colonies in the late nineteenth and first half of the twentieth century.[6] (While this was the case, it is arguably reflective not of colonialism but of the fact that late colonialism occurred at a time when these human development transitions were happening throughout the world, with or without colonies, as part of a global process.) Poverty statistics are also often used to justify occupation and forced incorporation, as I have studied at length in my work on Chinese regional development strategies in the Tibetan areas of western China (e.g., see Fischer 2005, 2014a). Similarly, global poverty statistics have been marshalled in various ways to legitimise the reigning international economic order. The global goal-setting exercises of the new millennium have been more specifically oriented towards legitimising the recent and particularly virulent phase of capitalism variously coined as 'neoliberalism' or more euphemistically as 'globalisation'. (See the end of this Introduction for a clarification on the use of these two terms in this book.)

Understanding poverty as ideology

With these implications in mind, three central arguments run throughout this book. All three are built on a structuralist and political economy approach to understanding modern poverty as fundamentally relative to changing social norms in contexts of structural transformation. The reproduction of poverty within a context of development arguably cannot be appreciated without this foundation.

The first argument is quite simply that the very conception of poverty is inherently political, insofar as it involves choices about norms and standards that cannot be determined empirically, even though they must be empirically informed. Technocratic renderings of poverty analysis tend to veil such politics with the chimera of scientific objectivity, thereby tending to de-politicise the policy debates concerning poverty. This in turn serves to veil underlying agendas and allows paradigmatic shifts in theory and practice to be hidden behind principles of charity and altruism.

This point resonates strongly with similar recent arguments made by Angus Deaton. For instance, in his Lionel Robbins Memorial Lecture at the London School of Economics in 2014, he also argued that poverty and inequality measurement depends on politics as well as theory, and discussed why and how the politics of poverty is so often disguised as science.[7] This book definitely owes a huge debt to the massive contributions that this seminal scholar has made to the field over decades and up to the present, including on these points. However, the political dimension is pushed further in this book, perhaps beyond where he would be willing to go, into a more explicit engagement and critique of the orthodoxy that has dominated development economics and policy since the late 1970s.

For instance, as I have argued in Fischer (2010a, 2013a), the heavy reliance in the MDGs on a raft of absolute poverty targets, both money-metric and multidimensional, is not only riddled with methodological quagmires, it has also arguably lent weight to these orthodox agendas. The more 'participatory' character of the SDGs has been celebrated – at least officially – in contrast to the more technocratic approach to determining the MDGs, although this interpretation remains contested (e.g., Esser 2014, 2017). Nonetheless, the SDGs have similarly shrouded these more politicised aspects of poverty conception and measurement, and their implicit policy biases towards orthodoxy.

The apparent apolitical framing and universalist appeal of these agendas hides this fact, while the stifling of political debate though the performance of consensus in global development agendas has arguably lent the upper hand to the institutionally and politically more powerful voices within these agendas. In this sense, they can be appropriately described as depoliticising projects, purportedly setting ethical guidelines that transcend the deadlock of endless ideological disputes that have rocked development since the early 1980s. However, they have not actually been explicit about any particular policy agenda – due to necessity, of course, because then no consensus would have ever been reached. Nonetheless, they have thereby been used rhetorically to support a wide range of policy agendas, many contradictory, providing cover for very political choices to be made on matters that are central to determining patterns of social integration. In this respect, they might well amount, ironically, to a Trojan Horse for progressive agendas inspired by genuine universalism, while also serving to reinforce dominant narratives of the recent past as one of tentatively progressive emancipation.

Second, and more specifically in relation to orthodoxy, the emphasis of absolute measures in these global development agendas – including so-called multidimensional measures – is both a reflection of a policy bias towards targeting in social provisioning, and in turn instils biases towards targeting in a reinforcing manner, as against more universalistic or cross-class solidaristic forms of provisioning. This is partly because these absolute poverty measures and related indicators are inspired and designed as targeting devices. However, a more subtle reason is that absolute conceptions and measures are poorly suited to reflect the value of more universalistic forms of provisioning and they also encourage a policy priority of expediency over equality, in terms addressing the poorest first rather than addressing the institutional implications brought into play in the process.

Obviously, absolute conceptions of poverty and targeting in policy derive from a sense of ethical obligation to address extreme deprivations such as hunger and famine. However, it is precisely this moral imperative that has made them such effective vehicles for coopting social justice concerns into orthodox mainstream agendas that, in many respects, have been quite antithetical to social justice. It has allowed for the generalisation of what might be called a humanitarian imperative – meaning the urgency of reaching the poorest of the poor in the most expedient manner possible – into the broader and more regularised systems of social provisioning, at a time when many of these systems have been under rapid construction. The rapid construction has nonetheless been occurring within legacies of highly stratified and segregated societies, which targeting modalities reinforce and entrench rather than attenuate.

These biases are reinforced by the above-mentioned depoliticisation. Indeed, the subtle but powerful shift towards top-down technocratically controlled targeting systems as the accepted best practices within these agendas is another instance of how the depoliticising tendencies in contemporary poverty studies are, in fact, fundamentally political at the level of practice. This is more than simply an issue about targeting. Rather, it is about the institutional modalities through which targeting is practised and their political consequences – such as the severing of practices of rights-claiming and contestation by beneficiaries from processes of beneficiary selection – which have been hugely neglected by scholarship. Notably, such modalities have been facilitated by the ease of econometric technologies and are often favoured because they place less pressure on limited local administrative resources, both human and financial. They are also often advocated in the name of empowerment. However, empowerment is usually evoked in reference to the policy interventions that result from poverty identification, such as cash transfers giving women extra monetary resources that purportedly enhance their intra-household bargaining power, rather than in terms of how these interventions actually strengthen (or weaken) political systems of representation and accountability.

The third central argument running through this book is a more fundamental critique of absolute conceptions of poverty – again, both money-metric and multidimensional. Such absolute measures have a secular tendency to underestimate the reproduction of poverty over time, given their abstraction of fundamental aspects of relativity associated with modern poverty, particularly in relation to modern processes of structural transformation, which are here understood as the essence of development. These are most fundamentally expressed as movements of people out of agrarian-based rural societies and into more urban-industrial ones, or else associated processes such as demographic transition.

This transformative emphasis is important because, even within the minority view in support of using relative poverty approaches for poor countries, the notion of 'relative' is mostly used with reference to social norms. However, the idea that poverty is relative to structural transformations is arguably more fundamental. The reason is that profiles of essential social needs – or what I refer to as compelling social needs – generally change, often quite radically, within such transformations. This is especially the case within contexts of urbanisation, but also with respect to increases in baseline norms such as literacy and schooling levels, or morbidity and mortality rates.[8] This is not necessarily the same as an upward shift in subjective preferences, such as when people start to expect more as they become more affluent. Rather, it is a question of the minimum requirements for functioning in modern societies and economies, short of which the options are generally exclusion or exploitation (or both).

While this third point is fundamental, it has been neglected in scholarship. It is worth elaborating further in this Introduction because it is the foundation on which the rest of the arguments of the book are built.

The fundamental relativity of modern poverty

An essential issue that lurks in the uncomfortable questions of poverty studies is the fundamentally relative nature of modern poverty. This refers not only to the fact that poverty must always be judged relative to prevailing social norms, even in very poor societies, which is more or less along the lines of Peter Townsend's definition of relative poverty or deprivation (e.g., Townsend 1979 or 1993). It also refers to the fact that these social norms change within the context of modern capitalist development and demographic transition, and along with them essential social needs also change. They must therefore be judged in relation to the broader processes of social and economic structural transformation associated with development, in terms of how social needs are situated within, conditioned by and evolve alongside such transformations. It is in this sense that the reproduction of modern poverty needs to be understood as fundamentally relative.

Conventional 'absolute' measures of poverty, in contrast, are used to try to fix absolute minimum standards that are applicable in all places and all times, usually expressed in terms of minimum food requirements. For instance, the poverty targets of the MDGs and SDGs – of lowering the global poverty rate by half from its 1990 level, measured by a 1.25 purchasing-power-parity dollar-a-day poverty line in the case of the MDGs – are goals that restrict our notions of economic wellbeing to an absolute minimum level of subsistence, below which one would essentially starve. In other words, this poverty line has been roughly associated with the idea of 'absolute poverty', meaning that a person's daily income is insufficient to be able to procure around 2100 to 2400 calories a day in addition to some minimal amounts of non-food essentials.

Pogge and Reddy (2002a, 2002b) have contended that, in fact, this poverty line does not provide an accurate or consistent assessment of absolute basic needs. Other criticisms include the problematic issues of measurement (e.g., see Saith 2005 or Fischer 2010a, 2013a), issues of converting income to food (as per Amartya Sen's entitlement and subsequent capability approach) or else questions of consumer sovereignty (i.e., that poor people – like everyone else – might prefer to spend extra income on entertainment rather than food, as highlighted in the behavioural work by Banerjee and Duflo 2011).

However, a more fundamental critique is that such absolute conceptions are so minimally defined that they essentially become obsolete over time through the course of the structural transformations that are associated with development, especially but not only urbanisation. This thereby results in a secular tendency to underestimate the reproduction of poverty over time given that these fundamental aspects of relativity associated with modern poverty are abstracted from the calculus of these standard measures. In other words, much of falling poverty rates might actually be a reflection of the fact that these standard measures are increasingly falling behind the evolution of what can be referred to as the compelling social needs of poor people.

Social needs, in the sense used here, must be differentiated from the more general idea of socially constructed or conditioned relative norms and subjective preferences, in that they produce very real and hard constraints that can involuntarily drive people into objective states of deprivation if not met. Examples include access to necessary and available health care; meeting the educational needs of employment, especially in post-primary schooling; housing and transport; financial needs such as interest and principle payments on debt; or any other necessity for participating in society with a minimal degree of functionality, let alone dignity. The point is that needs of this nature cannot be foregone without excessively adverse consequences, raising the question of freedom or agency within choice.

These contrast with subjective preferences. Preferences might also be to a large extent socially conditioned, but without necessarily involving severe consequences to livelihood if foregone (except, of course, when they overlap with essential needs, that is, when preferences are an expression or reflection of such needs). Examples include feeling deprived if one does not own a television, or feeling deprived of any other non-essential item relative to the expectations of one's perceived social position. Norms and preferences can also have strong compelling effects on people, such as through expectations of normality or dignity, and might through these effects also have an impact on various aspects of poverty by influencing consumption choices. But these choices are not necessarily taken out of hard constraints of survival. Nor are the associated compulsions restricted to those experiencing objective deprivations, in the sense that they are also experienced by relatively wealthy people attempting to keep up with the Joneses, so to speak.

The distinction is at times subtle, but essential. Much of the behavioural research in poverty studies, for instance, as best represented by Banerjee and Duflo (2011), is implicitly focused on preferences, that is, consumption of what are considered to be non-essential goods and services. Banerjee and Duflo also consider the more structural factors that constrain the ability of people to get out of poverty traps, which they refer to as the economic environment of the poor, which needs to be unpacked in specific cases. This is similar to the idea of social needs, although more generally the behavioural tangent of scholarship has lost sight of how compulsion is structurally and institutionally conditioned through needs, and how this conditioning changes through the course of contemporary structural transformation. The blind spot is in part because of the excessively narrow focus of the behavioural scholarship on very micro descriptions of poor people, implemented through randomised control trials and such, while relegating to far more superficial treatment the more macro, structural and institutional contexts that condition the lives of such people and within which they behave and make their choices. Indeed, this is a more general problem with the assertion of 'microfoundations' in economics, as discussed further in Chapter 6.

Crucial in this regard is the relation between compulsion and social needs, or the distinction between compulsions that are driven by the imperatives of survival, versus compulsions that are more generally driven by socially conditioned preferences and consumer choices that are not necessarily taken within a calculus of survival. The former function as hard, binding constraints on people. They can either keep those already below a conventionally defined poverty threshold in that position, or else they can force people who are otherwise above the threshold below it. Compulsions that keep people in poverty are often referred to as poverty traps, although the use of this term is again often associated with behavioural research, for instance, in the examination of how the behaviour of poor people keeps them in poverty, rather than an examination of broader structural issues that constrain or condition such behaviour.

Compulsions that effectively bring people below a poverty threshold include, for instance, the need to secure health insurance in the US, which often compels people to accept otherwise substandard minimum-wage employment that is insufficient to keep a family above the US poverty line, and/or compels them to remain in that employment. In other countries that similarly do not have effective universalistic forms of health care,[9] such as in most developing countries, health expenses are a major cost factor that can drive families deep into absolute deprivation even if their incomes are well above the absolute poverty line, as studied, for instance, in the innovative work by van Doorslaer (2005) and discussed further in this book. Similarly, people might forsake food consumption or other necessary expenditures in order to afford the transport required for urban employment. In this sense, even if people have incomes that are well above the value of food required to avoid hunger and starvation, as is the rough measure of absolute poverty lines, they can still face strong compulsions in their lives in relation to a broader range of social needs that are dependent on context and are not necessarily or at all reflected by such absolute lines. One effect is that food consumption might be constrained as a result, not only towards an under-consumption of basic calorie needs, but also towards the consumption of the cheapest calories available, which in turn might be associated as much with rising obesity rates among the poor as it is with hunger.

Social needs and development

Simply considering the social norms of a particular context in time is therefore not enough, given that contexts change and, hence, social needs are not fixed over time, particularly during the course of the social and economic transformations typically associated with development. Indeed, as eloquently put by Peter Townsend,

'Relativity' applies to both resources and to material and social conditions. Societies are passing through such rapid change that a poverty standard devised at some historical date in the past is difficult to justify under new conditions. People living in the present are not subject to the same laws and obligations as well as customs that applied to a previous era. Globalization is remorselessly interrelating peoples and their standards of living at the same time as inequalities are growing in most countries. There are, therefore, major objections to merely updating any historical benchmark of poverty on the basis of some index of prices. (Townsend 2006, p. 21)

Accordingly, conceptions of poverty require an understanding of the evolution of compelling social needs within development. Amartya Sen's work has mostly eclipsed that of Townsend's in the field of development studies (that is, the study of poverty in 'developing' countries), given that Townsend's own empirical work has been more associated with the UK and Europe (despite important contributions such as Townsend 1993). Sen's theorisation of development, however, is not particularly helpful for understanding development as structural transformation, as argued in Chapter 4. The following therefore elaborates on some ways that we might conceive of this relation between changing social needs and development.

Perhaps one of the most fundamental expressions of the social and economic transformations associated with development has been the shift over the last century in most parts of the world from what might be called the sufficiency of subsistence to scarcity amidst abundance. Keeping in mind the problematic caricatures of the idea of subsistence, as discussed in the Chapter 3, the main concern of subsistence sufficiency at a societal level is to produce enough food to eat and to provide for other basic needs, in addition to the distributional questions regarding how such production is divided among classes and other groupings. Indeed, this was the major concern with 'food availability decline' explanations for famine that Sen famously contested (e.g., Sen 1977), although it is ironic that Townsend (1985) subsequently criticised Sen's conception of an 'absolutist core' of poverty as perpetuating a narrow subsistence-standard conception of poverty.

Nonetheless, if we accept an essential understanding of subsistence at a societal level as having sufficient supplies of food for meeting minimum food consumption needs, the last hundred years of capitalist development have definitely seen a large proportion – perhaps the majority – of an increasingly large global population emerge from conditions that might be characterised as subsistence in this sense. The main concern that remains is one's position relative to the norms operating in the society and economy. Distributional issues are also a major concern, although these are freed from the constraints of the overall product that a society needs for achieving subsistence. The poor in the latter situation might nonetheless appear to be still abiding in an insufficient state of subsistence, not having gone through any process of 'structural transformation'. However, the structural processes underpinning such appearances have utterly transformed. The double irony is that they increasingly occur amidst levels of abundance that are far more generalised than in the recent past.

Central in this regard is how the integration of poor people into broader systems imposes austerity on their consumption through various mechanisms. The most essential is in terms of how their labour is valued relative to other values in the system. Subsistence levels of consumption are presumably the lower bound of such valuation. Indeed, this is the predicament posited by classical economists such as Malthus, Ricardo and Marx, who assumed that workers' wages would always be squeezed down to a level of subsistence defined by the price of food, whether through the forces of population growth (à la Malthus), or through class conflict (à la Marx). However, for them, this was a generalised condition for the population. Only a minority of capitalists or landed elites (aka 'rentiers') would rise above it. Theirs was arguably a fairly accurate assessment of early to mid-nineteenth-century Europe, when wages were stagnant despite the rising levels of wealth generated by the early phases of industrial revolution (e.g., cf. Braudel 1979; Wrigley 1999, 2004). Indeed, Arthur Lewis (1954) classically drew on this stylised fact from the economic history of England as a conceptual starting point for his famous model of economic growth with unlimited supplies of labour. Similar conditions would have prevailed elsewhere in the world, exacerbated by various colonial processes of suppressing labour value and syphoning wealth from the colonised societies. As a result, pre-modern per-capita incomes across different world regions, as estimated by Angus Maddison (2001), for instance, were more or less equivalent up to around 1820, reflective of the subsistence (or labour productivity) conditions in each region. Maddison's estimates for Western Europe were slightly higher, which, if accurate, would reflect the slightly greater productivity in England in particular, and the superiority of the region in commerce and conquest, and the subsequent accumulation of wealth from colonisation and empires.

In the shift from subsistence sufficiency to scarcity amidst abundance, the limits to mass consumption become less binding. Correspondingly, the processes of depreciating the value of labour or otherwise syphoning the value that labour creates become relatively more dominant, if only because the floor of subsistence becomes less constraining. To use the Marxist terminology, there is more potential for relative surplus extraction, which becomes proportionately more important than absolute surplus extraction. Scarcity is nonetheless reasserted through these processes of extraction to the extent that the value of labour can still be pushed back down to a level of subsistence, and the social relations and class struggles that permit or prevent this are a core concern of Marxist political economy. While these processes might manifest as if the poor are still residing in a state of traditional subsistence, they are fundamentally different because of their co-existence with and interdependence on modern capitalist forms of accumulation and circulation. However, such co-existence also becomes increasingly subtle and difficult to identify as economies become more complex and more densely integrated into larger systems. This facilitates the naïve illusions among what John Kenneth Galbraith (1992) called the 'contented classes' that their contentment does not have anything to do with the trials of the poor.

An additional consideration of structural transformation is that the requirements of subsistence also transform. The most obvious of these transformations is urbanisation. When populations urbanise and move away from agriculture, this utterly changes the livelihood, consumption and provisioning profiles of people involved in such transitions, particularly with respect to housing and transport. Livelihoods also become mostly commoditised, in the sense that food 'self-provisioning' mostly disappears as a possibility for maintaining basic subsistence.

Other new and emerging social needs also compound these transformations. Educational transitions shift the boundaries of what is considered a minimal standard for participating in relatively decent, increasingly urban employment. For instance, when the social norm is increasingly based on a floor of full primary enrolment and increasing levels of secondary education, this raises the minimal threshold for socially acceptable schooling qualifications in labour markets. Health and demographic transitions also change the spectrum of health care needs, particularly with ageing populations and the so-called 'double burden' of chronic diseases becoming more prominent even as infectious diseases are still prominent, as is the case in many poorer countries. They also change the range of possibilities in health provisioning, thereby having a formative influence on demand for such services.

Industrial transformations in many cases can be more difficult to discern among the poor and in non-industrialised contexts. Nonetheless, where consumption is increasingly 'industrialised', in the sense of passing through industrial processes, it creates stronger dependencies in peoples' reliance on such forms of consumption, in contrast to self-provisioning or local artisanal production. Celso Furtado (1983) called this the modernisation of consumption within 'industrial civilisation', referring to the structuring of an entire economy, including the consumption patterns of its poorer and more marginalised members, around industrial processes and technologies, even if large parts of the economy are not involved in industrial production *per se* and/or become progressively marginalised from the wealth generated through industrial processes. Indeed, as argued by Furtado, a key condition of postwar development has been that developing countries access modern 'industrial civilisation' through consumption, not production. The rising productivity of industrial systems can therefore reinforce these dependencies, even while marginalising people from the production of what they consume. This is especially the case as consumption becomes increasingly integrated into regional and global systems of production and/or distribution, which further severs the link between the consumption of industrial goods by poor people and the production of such goods.

Shifting policy, institutional and ideological orientations within reform agendas, as discussed in the next chapter, can also accentuate many of the changing cost structures and consumption profiles involved in such transformations, such as with respect to service provisioning. Examples include increasing 'cost-recovery' or commoditisation in health and education services, or removal of subsidies for transport prices, particularly in contexts where such services are increasingly privatised. Similarly, financial needs can also intensify in such contexts, such as interest and principle payments on debt, student loans, credit card debt or mortgage payments. Even the relative costs associated with corruption can rise, such as the oft-noted rapid increase of corruption in China, in contrast to the more austere socialist times when corruption was very muted and muzzled.

In many settings where various absolute poverty measures are declining, aspects of relative poverty (in the sense discussed above) can be exacerbated through these new forms of compelling social need that are not necessarily captured by conventional approaches of absolute poverty measurement, even though they have an effect on the experience of absolute poverty. Even without entering the realm of multidimensional poverty measures, the thresholds that would allow for a sufficient level of income or expenditure to meet such compelling social needs and that would also reflect a substantive sense of inclusion into decent employment (without exploitation or bondage) are generally much higher than those that are currently used in the various 'absolute' poverty measures. The trends might also be divergent, in contrast to the comparison of various 'purchasing-power-parity' dollar-or-more-a-day poverty rate trends, which essentially reflect each other (see Chapter 3). Indeed, the incongruence between various recent urban protests over issues such as rising bus fares (such as those in Brazil in 2013) and observations of falling (absolute) poverty rates in the same settings is notable in this regard (to the extent that such protests are related to poverty, which is discussed in Chapter 5). In these situations, increased fares might be experienced as a straw too much for the backs of many people who would be many times above the absolute poverty line and yet still struggling to meet essential social needs, including in urban transport.

In this respect, the proliferation of poverty measures under both the MDGs and SGDs provide little insight in the evolution of compelling social needs given that they refer to a very restrictive sense of achievement within a range of multidimensional absolute poverty targets, with the exception of a few inequality targets in the SDGs.

Indeed, the MDGs exclusively focused on absolute targets, while absolute targets remain at the core of the Sustainable Development Goals (SDGs). There is an urgent necessity to widen our scope in ways that embrace a more complex understanding of evolving social needs and how these relate to the inherent relativity of modern poverty. As discussed in Chapter 4, this is not necessarily achieved through an emphasis of multidimensional poverty. Insofar as the various dimensions of multidimensional poverty are also conceived in terms of absolute minimal attainments fixed over time, they succumb to the same incapacity to provide insight into the evolution of compelling social needs as the money-metric measures they are meant to criticise, such as income poverty measures.

Moreover, the proliferation of measures have distracted attention away from broader development processes that shape present and future manifestations of poverty. Rather, they arguably contribute to a tendency to under-evaluate the dynamic reproduction of poverty within contexts of substantial structural and institutional change, as discussed further in Chapter 3. They are also unable to distinguish between changes that are genuinely progressive and those that are immiserating or due to intensifications of work and effort. The latter could include, for instance, cases where people urbanise due to dispossession and eviction, rather than through a voluntary choice to diversify livelihoods or to take advantage of wage differentials, but where such urbanisation gives the appearance of improving livelihoods according to these conventional measures. Or else, it can include cases where increasing incomes or other multidimensional indicators occur through longer working hours, worsening conditions of work, holding multiple jobs, delaying retirement or not taking necessary sick or maternity leave. More generally, absolute measures are unsuited to understanding broader processes of social integration, stratification, segregation and subordination.

In particular, when compulsions derived from social needs result in strong labour market dependence – that is, when people are not free to not engage with labour markets – this enhances the possibilities for exploitation. In other words, turning the inclusion discourse on its head, a lack of freedom to be able to exclude oneself from markets (rather than to be included) is an important condition of exploitation. Inversely, autonomy from such dependence is an important subjective economic value, serving both symbolic cultural as well as instrumental economic functions. However, as discussed in Chapter 3, these more subtle but nonetheless powerful dimensions are poorly reflected by standard absolute poverty measures, particularly within transitions from agrarian to non-agrarian settings.

Moreover, if labour is not free to not work, then we must fundamentally question the extension of a simple 'micro-foundation' market logic to employment. For instance, Heintz (2008, p. 13) cites empirical studies documenting an increase in labour force participation – particularly among women – when average real earnings fall, suggesting that labour supply and earnings may be negatively correlated, particularly among low-income households. The reason is that households increase their labour supply when faced with lower earnings in order to make ends meet. This makes sense to anyone who has been in such situations, even though it is contradictory with standard microeconomic theory that would predict a decline in labour supply in response to falling wages, thereby equilibrating the labour market. The only way of rationalising this conventional logic is if we assume that workers are free to not engage with labour markets, in other words, that they have sufficient economic security to not work – generally a privilege of the relatively wealthy who can genuinely think in terms of work and leisure substitutions.

It is in this sense that we might even suggest that a sufficient level of economic security is required for markets to function in the ways they are conventionally postulated in neoclassical economic theory. In other words, liberalism arguably needs socialism in order to be actualised. This being said, compulsions need not only emerge from the classical condition of people barely subsisting at survival wages. Compulsions that discipline labour can also operate in more affluent conditions, as noted above, particularly given that social needs also evolve relative to changing structural contexts and social status. This last point will be taken up further in Chapter 5 on social exclusion, as well as in the Conclusion of the book.

Three dominant approaches and a framework

The aim of this book is not to conduct an exhaustive survey of poverty concepts and methods, but instead to focus on some of the most dominant and influential in order to demonstrate their fundamentally political and ideological nature and, more particularly, how they have been coopted by mainstream agendas as described above.

Three main poverty approaches are chosen for this purpose, given their centrality to various global development agendas, especially the MDGs and SDGs, and also because they have stood the test of time and of personalistic fads. The first is the standard money-metric approach (often known as the 'income', 'expenditure' or 'monetary' approach). The second is the multidimensional approach, building off the entitlement, capability and human development approaches. The third is the social exclusion approach. The social exclusion approach is chosen because it informs the commonplace references to 'inclusive development' or 'inclusive growth' throughout the current global development agendas. The meaning of inclusion is vague and ambiguous in these agendas, although attempts at specification usually mirror the attempts to define and specify social exclusion in the 1990s and early 2000s. Through these channels, the approach continues to bear influence on contemporary agendas. Given the centrality of these three approaches to the MDGs, SDGs and other agendas, they are sufficient to establish the main arguments of this book.

A specific chapter has not been dedicated to gender, or what is often known as gender approaches to poverty, parallel to these three poverty approaches. The reasons for this choice are three-fold. The first is one of deference. Formative contributions have already been made in this area, such as by Naila Kabeer, Diane Elson and others, which to a large degree approach the question of poverty from similar perspectives as in this book, and to which this book does not add much extra value. If anything, I am indebted to their contributions. The second is conceptual. Having taught and researched poverty for many years, it is not clear to me that gender itself offers an alternative concept or measure to the study of poverty, as it is often presented in contrast to a monetary or capability approach. Rather, it offers a crucial perspective that needs to be taken into account within all poverty measures. Indeed, following from this, the third reason stems from my preference to integrate gender perspectives throughout rather than segregating gender into a separate chapter, represented as a specific approach, to which only those interested might choose to concern themselves.

The analysis of these three dominant approaches is preceded by the following chapter, which elaborates on the aspects of politicisation and ideology discussed above in order to make clearer what, precisely, is at issue. This is boiled down to the politics of representation, the politics of prioritisation and the politics of conception and production. The last two chapters before the conclusion then return to these broader theoretical and conceptual issues.

Chapter 6 proposes a schematic framework for building a structuralist and institutionalist political economy approach for what we might call critical poverty studies. The aim is to place the study of poverty within a broader holistic perspective of the creation and division of wealth within and across societies, particularly within the context of modern capitalist development. This also includes a consideration of the theoretical debates and the normative and ideological assumptions that are built into paradigmatic conceptions of poverty and development.

For this purpose, I propose a framework that is based on two conceptual dimensions that are implicit in much of the ideas and policies relating to poverty and social needs. The first dimension deals with the creation and division of wealth, which can be conceived in classical political economy terms as production, distribution and redistribution. The second deals with the more secondary, indirect and aggregated factors influencing the first, which can be divided into supply-side factors, demand-side factors and terms of trade or wages. These interacting dimensions help to clarify how different approaches to conceptualising poverty and its reduction, as well as theoretical perspectives in economics and social sciences more generally, usually place selective emphasis on different combinations of elements across these two dimensions, even though all elements are needed to understand the evolution of social needs and the reproduction of poverty. More specifically, prevailing approaches to understanding poverty, which implicitly rely on neoclassical theoretical approaches, generally overlook several key dimensions.

The theme of social policy is then taken up in Chapter 7, the penultimate chapter, framed in terms of the fundamental tension in poverty studies and policy of identification versus segregation. The theme of social policy is given a selective focus because of its centrality to understanding processes of social integration and ordering, thereby carrying on with some of the themes raised in the previous chapters, in particular Chapter 5 on social exclusion, and also because it is the policy realm in which most direct action on poverty reduction is enacted.

More specifically, the focus of the chapter is on the key role of universalistic modes of social policy in both rich and poor countries as some of our most powerful policy tools to date for dealing simultaneously with poverty and inequality, especially in combination with broader developmentalist agendas, and that are crucial to bring about more egalitarian and equitable processes of social integration and citizenship. However, the meaning of universalism has been watered down and coopted within current global development agendas. The chapter therefore proposes an antidote, with an attempt to conceptualise universalism in social policy as an umbrella term reflecting a set of guiding principles along three dimensions: provisioning modalities, which includes issues of access and coverage; costing and pricing, which relate to commodification; and financing, which involves the principle of (social) insurance. This proposed approach bears more general and practical applicability beyond ideal type northern welfare states and it clarifies much of the conceptual confusion surrounding the term, particularly with respect to its application to developing countries or development goals.

However, such issues are fundamentally political, not merely technical. Hence, they require a politicised engagement within current development agendas in order to create the space for serious deliberation of the possibilities for universalism, rather than relying on the apparently apolitical moral ground of goals and indicators. The risk of not explicitly anchoring future development agendas within politicised policy debates is that these agendas can be (and are being) subverted towards policy agendas that possibly undermine inequality reduction and/or fragment citizenship rights in many contexts. The conclusion offers some reflections on the necessity of politicising the policy debates along these lines.

The final conclusion of the book then wraps up with a discussion on the de-politicisation wrought by these statistical projects transposed from global development agendas and how this interacts with and reinforces the prevailing neoliberal ideology as well as rising conservative impulses in the current context. This is followed with reflections on the rise of segregationism as an increasingly normalised principle within social provisioning and of the need to move beyond restrictive notions of poverty in order to have a better appreciation of these dynamics of social integration. It ends with an argument for the need to politicise poverty studies. Poverty measurement needs to be understood fundamentally as part of a political project of building state capacity in social provisioning and policy-making, as well as strengthening processes of local accountability with citizens on these matters.

Appendix: Note on the use of the terms 'neoliberal' and 'globalisation' in this book

My use of the term 'neoliberal' refers specifically to the ideological creed that, because neoclassical economic theory refers to the axiomatic principle of the pure, perfectly competitive market as the first-best outcome in terms of efficiency and pareto optimality, policy should therefore strive towards creating or imitating perfectly competitive markets as much as possible, including the engineering of what Foucauldian scholars refer to as 'neoliberal subjectivities' where necessary. Practically, this roughly refers to a combination of monetarist, purportedly neutral but often pro-cyclical macroeconomic policy, the trio of privatisation, liberalisation and deregulation, as well as attempts to introduce market-type or market-mimicking mechanisms into spaces that operate according to different logics, particularly in the public sector, such as with New Public Management. (See Peck 2010 and Kiely 2018 for two excellent expositions on neoliberalism.)

Neoliberalism is differentiated from neoclassical economic theory insofar as the latter generally recognises that the axiomatic pure market has never really ever existed in reality and thus should not necessarily be the object of policy-making, at least not without recognition of various market imperfections, whether transitory or intrinsic, that prevent first-best market outcomes from occurring. It is in this sense that many economists who adopt a neoclassical theoretical framework (e.g., Dani Rodrik, Amartya Sen, Joseph Stiglitz, etc.) are social democrats or even socialists who argue vigorously against neoliberalism. See Fischer (2014b) for a detailed discussion of this point, which is generally not well understood in the non-economics literature on neoliberalism that tends to lump together and conflate the two.

Instead, neoliberalism can be described as a form of axiomatic faith bordering on fundamentalism, in the sense that the axiomatic principle by which policies are advocated can never be proven or falsified because it is something that has never existed or that cannot be identified empirically, particularly in the realm of more macro, societal markets. As a result, the neoliberal defence for failed market liberalisations and deregulations is often made along the lines that the problems were not with the policies, but instead with the fact that they were not implemented far enough. The introduction to Karl Polanyi's *The Great Transformation* by Block (2001), and Polanyi himself (on the liberal utopia of self-regulating markets, not neoliberalism *per se*), provides an excellent discussion of this circular logic – that the impossibility of ever being able to implement a fully self-regulating market system due to its social and political destructiveness provided the liberal defence of such a system by virtue of the fact that it was never fully implemented (in the nineteenth century). The impulse from all sectors of society to protect the social fabric, so to speak, through attempts to regulate processes of commodification and liberalisation, is what Polanyi referred to as the 'double movement'.

The term 'globalisation' itself has been related to a variety of narrative struggles closely related to the dominance of neoliberalism from the 1990s onwards (which is one of the reasons why I avoid it in this book, except as a representation of such narratives). For one, it is not clear when globalisation actually started and what it precisely entails. Processes of what could be referred to as the second wave of globalisation have been occurring throughout the post-Second World War era or even before, although the term is specifically used to refer to the post-1980 or post-1990 phase of this era. In this sense, it is effectively used as a signifier for neoliberalism, in particular, post-Cold War neoliberalism. As such, the use of the term effectively serves as a depoliticising device in the discussion of policy (similar to the role of development goals, as argued in this book), given that it makes the neoliberal paradigm appear as an inherent and natural aspect of globalisation, or an imperative determined by globalisation. According to this logic, rejecting neoliberalism implies rejecting the good aspects of globalisation. For instance, if one accepts the 'good' of globalisation, such as increased human mobility, improved global communications and the dissemination of medical technologies, it must necessarily follow that one accepts a neoliberal ideological and policy position. It is in this sense that the anti-globalisation movement arguably succumbed to forfeiting the narrative battle given that what has really been at stake is the nature of policy, not whether globalisation is inherently a good or bad thing.

2 | UNPEELING THE POLITICS OF POVERTY MEASURES

As a means to preface the deconstructive endeavour of the rest of the book, it is useful to elaborate on the aspects of politicisation and ideology discussed in the Introduction, in order to make clearer what, precisely, is at issue. These aspects can be elaborated along three main themes, from the more explicit to the more implicit and nuanced. The first is the politics of representation, in terms of how the recent past is interpreted, portrayed and remembered. The second is the politics of prioritisation, with respect to the consequences of placing poverty reduction as the central goal of development strategies. The third is the politics of conception and production, in terms of the inherent ideological biases that permeate the conception and production of social statistics, especially with respect to 'absolute' conceptions of poverty. This third point reinforces the two previous points and it comprises the focus of the core of the book.

The politics of representation

As mentioned in the introduction, past politics of representation with regard to poverty measures often played out over interpretations of colonialism or occupation. More recently, the politics of representation have been mainly concerned with struggles over controlling the narrative about the most recent phase of global capitalism, variously referred to as 'neoliberal' or euphemistically as 'globalisation'. How are we to interpret and remember the legacy of this phase? Has it been progressive or regressive?

These politics of representation need to be foregrounded by the historical context of recent debates about poverty. Much of the contemporary focus on poverty was spurred by concerns over the development collapses of the 1980s and 1990s – the so-called 'lost decade' of Latin America and the two 'lost decades' of sub-Saharan Africa. These concerns obviously built on their antecedents in the

1960s and 1970s, such as the increasing critiques of 'growth without development' or 'growth without equity,' and the increasing emphasis of basic needs and redistribution in the global development agendas of that earlier period. These critiques emerged in tandem with more radical approaches to understand the persistence of poverty and marginalisation despite growth, such as by Latin American scholars of dependency.

The severity of the international debt crisis in the early 1980s and the radical rightward shift in economic ideology that informed crisis responses nonetheless made the previous contentions appear as a golden age in retrospect. Various international organisations tried to raise mainstream awareness about the enormous social costs of the stabilisation and adjustment programmes that followed in the wake of debt crises in the early 1980s throughout most of Latin America, Africa and much of the Middle East. The emphasis shifted from 'development with equity' to 'adjustment with equity', or as coined by UNICEF at the time, 'adjustment with a human face' (Cornia et al. 1987). This momentum was carried into the first Human Development Reports (HDRs) of the UNDP in the early 1990s, which gave a more human counterweight to the World Development Reports (WDRs) by the World Bank that were pushing the structural adjustment agenda. As noted by Saith (2006), the first HDRs were much more at odds with the World Bank than later in the decade, when their positions became more aligned (with the UNDP moving more towards the World Bank than the Bank moved towards the UNDP).

As neoliberalism became triumphant in the early 1990s with the end of the Cold War and then morphed into various post-versions later in the 1990s when things became somewhat less triumphant, debate settled around the question of whether or not neoliberal reforms were making poor people better or worse off – 'neoliberal' in this sense referring specifically to policies of liberalisation, deregulation and privatisation (see the note at the end of Chapter 2). This was stoked by the fact that the case for these reforms was often framed in terms of the interests of the poor (e.g., WB 1990). This was also characteristic of the rise of New Labour in the UK or the New Democrats in the US, exemplified by Tony Blair. He was often known to speak in the name of the poor, arguing that inequality is not a problem so long as poverty is falling (which of course is a tricky position to take when poverty is measured relatively, as it is in Europe).[1] Similar arguments were made by the likes of Dollar and Kraay (2002) that growth is good for the poor, assuming of course that neoliberal policies are good for growth and constitute 'good policy', which is an ambiguity that these studies generally take for granted. This was also the period when the World Bank was going through its image reform under the presidency of James Wolfensohn, especially following the East Asian crisis of 1997–1998 and the anti-globalisation protest movements, such as in Seattle in 1999, which gave prominence to the politics of representation. Control over the narrative of poverty and its reduction was tightened following the kerfuffle around the resignation of Joseph Stiglitz as Chief Economist of the Bank in 2000, and then the debacle of the 2000/2001 WDR on 'attacking poverty', which saw the resignation of Ravi Kanbur as director and lead author of the WDR.

These struggles spilled over into the erstwhile Millennium Development Goals (MDGs). The quandary of these goals was that no formal clarification had been articulated about the policy means that should be used to achieve the targets of multidimensional poverty reduction despite the ample indicators provided to identify when these targets would be achieved.[2] Many obviously came to fill the void of policy guidelines, more or less reproducing the political and ideological spectrum of policy positions that pre-dated the MDGs. However, the MDGs arguably facilitated a de-politicisation of these policy debates and thereby gave the upper hand to the more orthodox positions within the spectrum.

Predisposing the narrative towards revisionism

The crudest way of gaining the upper hand was in the millennial goal-setting itself, which was predisposed towards a revisionist reading of the recent past. For one, the starting benchmarks were set at the (estimated) poverty levels prevailing in 1990, even though the goals were determined following the Millennium Declaration in 2000. For Latin America and sub-Saharan Africa, the two world regions that were most subjected to international debt crisis, austerity and structural adjustment programmes in the 1980s and 1990s, the year 1990 represented about the worst point in a disastrous and highly contentious period, from which things could have presumably only gotten better (although they generally did not for a while longer).

Poverty rates started to rise in these two regions from the late 1970s onwards and in many cases reached their apex around 1990. For instance, according to CEPAL estimates (if we are to believe these data),[3] poverty rates in Latin America and the Caribbean rose from 40.5 per cent in 1980 to 48.4 per cent in 1990, and extreme poverty rates from 18.6 per cent to 22.6 per cent. The poverty rate only fell back to below its 1980 level by 2005, and then sharply fell down to the trough of 28.1 per cent in 2013. The latter reduction was a particularly exceptional episode of recent Latin American history. It has been contentious in its combination of new left governments, commodity booms, 'neo-extractivism', and a strong presence of China squeezing the 'Washington Consensus' in its traditional seat of dominance in the continent. This exceptional conjuncture appears to be unwinding and reversing in any case. However, the fact remains that close to half of the improvement in these poverty rates since 1990 effectively represents the recuperation of lost ground from previous development gains, following the debilitating assaults during the 1980s on the means that were used to achieve these previous gains.

The choice of 1990 as a start date for the MDGs in this sense is predisposed towards revisionist narratives bent on erasing the memory of these previous gains and the damage that was done to development in the 1980s. Instead, it lends itself to interpreting any recovery from deep economic depression as a vindication of the prevailing international economic and political system that in part caused the depression in the first place. This includes the role of leading international financial institutions (IFIs) in engineering the severe austerities imposed on the debtor countries. There was internal questioning in the ranks when times were still dire up in the early 2000s (e.g., Easterly 2000 or Prasad et al. 2003), although never as a matter of official policy and these were mostly admissions that they had been too fervent, not that the direction taken was wrong. Besides a few more recent *mea culpas* of a similar nature (e.g., Ostry et al. 2016), structural adjustment has nonetheless been retrospectively self-celebrated by these institutions as providing the foundation for growth recoveries through their imposition of sensible discipline and constraint on national governments (in contrast to the simultaneous deliria occurring in international finance, which seemingly faces no discipline or constraint). Mkandawire (2014) makes this point with regard to how quickly the admissions of guilt were forgotten once Africa started growing rapidly from the late 2000s onwards. The possibility that growth recovered simply as a result of relaxing the shackles, allowing countries to start breathing financially again and to return to their interrupted development endeavours, is rarely considered within such self-congratulatory narratives.

It is similarly circumspect that many of the well-known millennial books on global poverty and development, such as Sachs (2005), Easterly (2006a), Collier (2007) or Moyo (2009), almost all start their statistical trend analyses from 1984 or even later. This start date coincides with the depths of the international debt crisis at the time. In contrast, discussion of previous periods is usually relegated to anecdotal and at times almost mythical narrations of development failures by myopic, corrupt and ineptly interventionist governments. This is reflective of the paradigmatic shift in an age of neoliberalism, in which the state has been reframed as oppositional to markets, and state intervention in markets or in production as inherently bad policy. Nonetheless, the sheer lack of analysis of the pre-1980 period is notable. In his critical review of Sachs (2005), Easterly (2006b, p. 100) does point out that Sachs' evidence of an African poverty trap is only from the period since 1980, whereas the poorest countries did experience significant positive growth from 1950–1980, but he himself more or less ignores the implications of this insight in his own work. Rather, in setting out his case against bad government, he admits on the same page that the earliest data we have on corruption is from 1984. That his arguments, like those of Sachs, rely exclusively on evidence from an age of post-crisis austerity and structural adjustment when the fiscal and operational capacity of the effected states were under a sustained assault does not seem to perturb his convictions. The unaddressed causal question is whether bad governance was one of many symptoms exacerbated by austerity and IFI-preferred forms of adjustment, instead of somehow being the cause of development failures in the first place.[4]

Collier (2007) also seems to go out of his way to avoid mentioning the elephant in the room, that is, the debt crisis that ushered in structural adjustment to Africa in the 1980s. For instance, in recounting how international banks were no longer willing to lend to Nigeria in the mid-1980s (p. 41), he does not explain the international circumstances that led to this situation, implying instead that it was due domestic causes. Notably, Nigeria was one of the few sub-Saharan African countries that had good access to international commercial bank lending in the 1970s given its oil wealth. It was therefore severely hit, like Latin American countries, when US nominal interest rates suddenly more than doubled in 1979 and were sustained in real terms at a historically unprecedented level through to 1982, causing a quadruple blow of sharply increased interest payments, drying up of new loans, stagnant demand for commodity exports and capital flight.

Ignoring this global context, Collier instead asserts that '[since] 1980 world poverty has been falling for the first time in history' (p. x). This perplexing statement might refer to the fact that internationally comparative data produced by the World Bank only starts around 1980, implying that something only exists once a World Bank economist creates a standardised data set for it.[5] Or, the statement might be understood as a feigned reference to the beginning of opening and reform in China. This presumes, of course, that poverty was increasing in China before 1980, enough to counteract the development gains elsewhere, and that poverty reduction in China in the 1980s was sufficient to counteract the development debacles in Latin America and Africa during the same decade. Yet neither of these presumptions are at all evident. Meanwhile, his narrative on China provides no insight into the very interventionist factors that brought about sharp reductions of income poverty in that country in the 1980s (if 'interventionist' is indeed the appropriate term to describe an economy that was still effectively mostly state-owned and -controlled). Nor does his narrative provide insight into the sharp improvements in human development prior to the 1980s, such as in health and education.

Similarly, his insulting characterisation of conditions in large parts of his bottom-billion countries as 'fourteenth-century' (p. 3) ignores important aspects of mortality decline well below historical levels in sub-Saharan Africa, hence resulting in rapid population growth even despite the HIV crisis (e.g., see Cleland and Sinding 2005). It also ignores their long histories of integration into capitalist centres and the resultant modernisation of consumption and the dependency that this generated. Indeed, how can one conceive of conditions in twentieth- or twenty-first-century Afghanistan or the Democratic Republic of Congo in the absence of modern weaponry? It was precisely such aspects of modernisation that put poor countries in the very vulnerable financial positions they were in as global instability intensified in the 1970s.[6]

Of course, Collier might not be entirely to blame for his reading of at least China, to the extent that he was relying on World Bank data. The World Bank purchasing power parity (PPP) poverty rates would lead us to believe that almost the entirety of China's population was undernourished or even on the verge of starvation in 1981. As explained by Chen and Ravallion (2008), according to the 2008 revision based on 2005 prices for an international poverty line set at $1.25 PPP, consumption poverty rates in China in 1981 were 87.4 per cent without adjustment for lower rural prices and 83.8 per cent with this adjustment. Such statistics must be taken with a grain of salt, insofar as the $1.25 PPP poverty line appears to approximate (if it approximates anything) a very minimal food-based definition of basic needs, e.g., a diet of 2100 calories of mostly cheap cereals.[7] As discussed in the next two chapters, this is only marginally above the basal metabolic rate for a person engaged in a moderate level of physical exertion, i.e., much less than a farmer typically exerts, at a time when about three-quarters of the Chinese workforce was employed in rural areas, mostly in farming. Even though the country was very austere at the time, it is highly unlikely that more than eight out of ten people were living in a state that is best described as one of hunger or starvation. Instead, as discussed in the Introduction and further in the next chapter, it is more likely that these poverty measures are very poorly adapted to reflect the profound structural and institutional transformations occurring since the early 1980s in China. Through these transformations, the nature and experience of poverty has profoundly transformed, particularly with respect to the commodification of health care, education or housing, as well as the breakdown of various provisioning systems that, despite the evident austerity of the late-Maoist economy, would have nonetheless permitted a decent level of health and other basic needs. In this manner, the linear transposition of current metrics into the past obfuscates the important development improvements that were key preconditions to China's emergence in the 1980s, particularly in areas of human development, such as the huge improvements in health and education in the 1960s and 1970s. Instead, the linear transposition reinforces narratives, as popularised by the likes of Collier or

Easterly, that China was essentially a basket case until it liberalised and privatised.

As the noughties became the teens and millennial goals were transitioning to sustainable goals, similar often bellicose attempts to determine the narrative and the terms of debate continued, even as the integration of inequality goals became increasingly accepted. As I argued in Fischer (2012), the consensus that emerged among mainstream international institutions on the need to address inequality, alongside closely related and hitherto-sidelined distributive issues such as work and employment, risked similar problems of masking a de-politicisation of policy debates about how to actually address inequality. The politicised contention surrounding the issue of inequality in this sense is again not about the end of reducing inequality but about the policy means of doing so. As noted above, rising inequality and polarisation were long recognised in earlier development economics in the 1960s and 1970s and were central to the criticisms of structural adjustment and Washington Consensus-style reforms in the 1980s and 1990s by a whole slew of less-than-orthodox economists and other social scientists. Simply naming the problem now does not solve these intractable policy debates of the past. Rather, the pressure to conform to consensus within multilateral processes arguably induces a tendency to censor more radical positions within these debates, despite the fact that these positions have led the criticism of worsening inequality under the mainstream policy paradigm over the last 30 or more years.

Hence, as with the MDGs, the emerging consensus about inequality also allowed the discussion to be usurped by orthodox policy agendas that have arguably been at the heart of rising inequalities over the last 30 years in the first place. A good example of this predicament can be found in an issue of *The Economist* (2012) published at the time of the UN-led initiative in 2012 to engage with issues of inequality in the planning of the post-MDG development agenda. While recognising the dangers of inequality, albeit with some reservation, *The Economist* essentially turned the problem into one of labour unions and government welfare policy in rich countries, and state-owned enterprises in middle-income countries, rather than Wall Street financiers. The editorial asserted with a gall that would seem to belong to a bygone era, when labour unions actually held of modicum of power in the US, that 'no Wall Street financier has done as much damage to American social mobility as the teachers' unions have', and goes on to advise targeted government spending on the poor, curtailing universalism in health and education, and pension reform. The implications of such policy positions are discussed further in Chapter 7; it suffices to note here that the diagnosis and the cure proposed by *The Economist* were essentially the same as the orthodox policy package that has been on the mainstream policy agenda since the 1980s and 1990s, which many would argue is at the root of increasing inequalities over this period.

Similar narratives have abounded in the mainstream literature with varying hues of nuance, if not rebounded with increasing vigour in the aftermath of the recent financial crisis. *The Economist* simply provides – as it usually does on most current issues – one representative and particularly seductive narrative for relatively easy erudite public consumption. Nonetheless, the ideational undertones pervade even relatively more moderate positions, such as those found in the recent World Development Reports of the World Bank.[8]

Even the recent idea that the geography of poverty has changed and that the majority of the world's poor people now live in middle-income countries has also been susceptible to these politics of representation. This idea was first innovatively unearthed and explored by Sumner (2010), who has been hugely successful in entering this idea into the upper echelons of policy consciousness and discourse, perhaps partly through co-authoring with Ravi Kanbur (Kanbur and Sumner 2012) and more importantly through the publicising of the idea by the Centre for Global Development in Washington, DC. While Sumner then went on to do further innovative work on the 'Palma Ratio' (Cobham and Sumner 2013, 2014; Cobham et al. 2016), the momentum of the idea has now reached the status of an accepted stylised fact, to the extent that it is often repeated, usually with an air of revelation, although often without attribution to the original source.

It must be noted, of course, that there has been little or no change in the geography of poverty. Instead, what is really at stake is a threshold effect. In other words, a number of large countries passed from lower-income-country status to lower-middle-income-country status (according to the World Bank Atlas method of calculating per-capita gross national income). For instance, India passed from 1000 US dollars in 2000 to 1110 US dollars in 2009, thereby passing the threshold of lower-middle-income-country status (which was set at 1026 US dollars as of 2017). Indeed, Sumner acknowledges this and probes it in detail in his work, and also stopped referring to geography after his first several papers (e.g., see Sumner 2016), but the point has been largely ignored in the popular uptake of the idea.

Sumner (2016) nonetheless suggests that this change in status fundamentally changes the distributive logic facing such countries, in terms of the amount of domestic resources (per capita) that are now available to address poverty in these countries. This contrasts with lower-income countries that lack such domestic resources and therefore must rely on aid (or at least, that more readily lend credibility to the case for aid). Hoy and Sumner (2016) further developed this to show that most countries actually have the resources to eliminate a large part of at least extreme poverty, through reallocating public spending or potential tax revenues, or dipping into foreign exchange reserves, etc. The aim of their argument has been to try to revive attention to the importance of redistribution, particularly in the face of ongoing mainstream resistance to go down that road.[9]

We might nonetheless question the significance of the threshold in driving such a fundamental qualitative shift. For instance, it is clear that the Indian economy has been growing relatively rapidly since around 2002, particularly since 2009, and per-capita GNI reached 1,820 US dollars in 2017 according to the same World Bank data. However, this increase in per-capita GNI by 820 US dollars since 2000 is arguably not significant enough to have fundamentally altered the distributive and redistributive options facing the country, particularly in light of all of the possible measurement and calibration issues involved in these estimates.

The importance of redistribution that always was

While the threshold is arguably not that significant, the more important point is that the essence of postwar development debates was *always* about national distribution and redistribution. Indeed, despite the talk of the emergence of billionaires from the Global South as if this is a new phenomenon, among the richest people in the world in the nineteenth century were Indian and other national elites in colonised countries. National liberation leaders and movements were intensely aware of the need to redistribute highly concentrated wealth inherited from the colonial era in support of decolonisation, which was encouraged by the socialist proclivities of many of these movements. The failures to do so in most cases must be understood in terms of complex political economy conjunctures facing various countries rather than in terms of simplistic narratives of either populist politics or bad economic policies, or both.

Redistribution was also one of the main messages of the Latin American structuralists in the 1950s. This was a logical corollary to the proposition of Raùl Prebisch (UN 1950), among others, that peripheral economies possess an underlying structural tendency towards domestic polarisation. This message also became stronger as they became more and more critical of import substitution industrialisation policies that were being usurped by strategic doses of transnational corporate investment and ownership. The argument that radical redistribution was required to set even poor countries on a healthier development trajectory was always on their table.

Redistribution was also a big lesson from South Korea and Taiwan. Extensive state-led land reform was implemented in these countries at the beginning of their postwar development trajectories, while they were still very poor, not once they had attained middle-income-country status (e.g., see Putzel 2000; Kay 2002). The reasons why some African countries that attempted similar strategies (e.g., Tanzania) and apparently failed remains contested in interpretation (e.g., see Gray 2018), although the principle of strong asset redistribution remains a powerful lesson from the few obvious cases of postwar development success.

One vital reason for this is because the domestic resource mobilisation strategies that were common among poor countries in that era, such as policies to extract surplus from rural populations in order to subsidise and finance industrialisation, were possible only in the absence of high levels of rural inequality. Otherwise, in the context of high inequality, as was typical in Latin America, policies of rural surplus extraction would tend to drive the rural poor into even further crippling poverty, as evidenced, for instance, by the way that colonial strategies of rural surplus extraction caused widespread and intense famines in India (e.g., Mukherjee 1974; Davis 2001; Mukerjee 2010). Indeed, this point is raised in the seminal classic by Simon Kuznets (1955), regarding the sharper impacts of rising inequality that can be expected in very poor and unequal settings.

In any case, such strategies never stood a chance in high-inequality countries given that they were blocked by powerful wealthy constituencies of landowners and associated elite factions, which is precisely a political economy characteristic of high-inequality settings. Or, when all else failed, the US helped to arrange coup d'états (e.g., Guatemala 1956, Chile 1973, etc.) or provided massive support to right-wing military regimes opposing surprisingly successful revolutionary movements (e.g., El Salvador and Guatemala from the 1970s to the 1990s). These events made clear that domestic inequality and its political repercussions were definitely on everyone's radar then, even if suppressing the latter was the preferred option of so-called liberal capitalist axis of the Cold War.

The calculus of rural asset redistribution arguably also applied to China. Collectivisation in the Maoist period followed by de-collectivisation in the immediate post-Maoist period established a very strong equalisation in the individuated use of land assets among the rural population. The strategies pursued up to and including the 1980s, such as the implicit subsidisation of urban industrialisation by rural areas through a variety of price and financial mechanisms, arguably could not have been pursued if the starting point in late 1970s had already been at a high level of inequality, as it had been under the Nationalists (Ch. *Guomintang*) prior to their defeat in 1949.

The point here is that the role of redistribution in setting the stage for domestic resource mobilisation strategies has always been relevant for very poor countries; it has not required their emergence into middle-income status in order to make it so. Indeed, this point is generally ignored in the contemporary revival of attention to domestic resource mobilisation, such as in the current financing for development agenda, particularly as donors retreat from a variety of aid-dependent countries in Africa. In the lacuna, the main default strategy for domestic resource mobilisation is through value-added taxes – which are generally considered regressive – in the absence of any ambitious transformative agendas and lacking vision or programmes of radical redistribution that could render their suggested strategies socially and politically sustainable or legitimate.

Rather, the discussion over income status thresholds encourages a framing of the debate in terms of the commonly presumed tension between growth and redistribution. Indeed, the primacy of growth over redistribution is regularly evoked for poor countries given that poor countries lack sufficient wealth to redistribute and hence should focus primarily on creating wealth (e.g., productivity). This encourages a more implicit framing in terms of (absolute) poverty reduction versus inequality (or relative poverty) reduction. Moreover, productivity is generally conceived in mainstream (neoclassical) economics as a form of efficiency (even though productivity and efficiency are subtly but fundamentally different).[10] As a result, poverty reduction via productivity increase is generally framed in terms of (market) efficiency, rather than, say, through government interventions in production. The latter are deemed as obstructing efficiency, even though they have been crucial to supporting increases in productivity in successful cases (again, such as with industrial policy and also agricultural extension programmes in South Korea and Taiwan). The mainstream logic thus forces the debate into questions about what degree of intervention is a necessary ill to correct for unrestrained inequality or market failures. This leads to an in-built tendency for the case of state intervention or regulation to be on the defensive, in tension with and morally trumped by freedom, rather than as an enabler of freedom within complex modern market societies.

In this sense, the focus on thresholds as signifying some sort of fundamental change distracts us from the vital synergies that have been historically observed in successful cases of development between simultaneous or closely sequenced public interventions in both domestic redistribution and production. As I have discussed in Fischer (2014b, 2016a), the dichotomy that is conventionally presumed to exist between redistribution and production (and between states and markets more generally) has limited a more holistic consideration of the role of redistribution in development. To a certain extent, this view has even pervaded the discourse of the Left in development studies, in part due to a decades-long struggle to defend productionist development strategies such as industrial policy from neoliberal ideological attack, together with the presumed primacy of production over redistribution in the exceptional growth of China. As a consequence, the idea of redistribution has been sidelined and to a certain extent even coopted by more conservative agendas, such as with the rise of the residualist social protection agenda among major international donors. Even the intergovernmental agencies that once championed more radical approaches to redistribution in the face of structural adjustment and austerity have now largely neglected the topic beyond a restrictive focus, although there has been some tempered re-engagement with notions of universalism among some UN agencies. Indeed, *The Economist* has again also jumped on that bandwagon (*The Economist* 2018), albeit with a discrete defence of private health insurers and an implicit disguised critique of formal social security regimes. Without diminishing the importance of recent social protection and related initiatives, this narrow framing of redistribution limits our understanding of the possibilities of inequality reduction and of modern economic development more generally.

The politics of prioritisation

Leading on from this last point, some critical authors have argued that the emphasis of poverty in various global development agendas has also shifted our conception of the broader development project towards one that is much narrower and less transformative in scope. Barbara Harriss-White (2005) referred to this as an impoverishment of the concept of development, from an understanding of social and economic transformation in the context of capitalism, to one of poverty reduction in abstraction of this context. Enriched conceptualisations of poverty therefore essentially abide in a theoretical vacuum. In other words, poverty reduction is generally discussed in the absence of a broader consideration of the social and economic transformations that have traditionally been considered as constitutive of development and as instrumental in actually reducing poverty. Instead, poverty reduction itself is considered to be development. In the process, the role of governments in guiding such broader transformations is also sidelined, in deference to an understanding of developmental governance as one that primarily provides welfare and safety nets for the poor, while letting markets take care of the rest.

In this regard, there is much truth to the claim that the MDG agenda was embedded within the Washington Consensus (including its various 'post-' reiterations and derivations). It is important to recall that focusing on poverty is not particularly antithetical to this consensus and its associated ideologies. Indeed, the World Bank dedicated its *World Development Report* specifically to the theme of poverty for the first time in 1990, at a time when neoliberalism was triumphant, as noted above. (Interestingly, this WDR emphasised the multidimensionality of poverty, despite more recent insistence that income poverty was the singular focus during those years and that the multidimensional turn is something new – this point is further discussed in Chapter 5.) Lipton et al. (1992) famously called this the 'New Poverty Agenda'.

Accordingly, poverty is quite comfortably explained within this theoretical prism by way of market imperfections. Poverty persists precisely because markets – whether labour, product or credit markets – do not function efficiently, causing market failures, meaning involuntary unemployment or underemployment, or incomes below potential. Whether the original dysfunction is due to lack of modernisation or inept government interventions, the latter invariably compound the difficulties and tensions associated with development, resulting in numerous economic distortions in need of structural adjusting. Until such adjustments are completed, targeted safety nets should be provided for those who fall through the cracks, provided they are deemed as deserving (meaning that they actually have fallen through the cracks and are not just pretending when they could actually work instead, or work harder, or pay for health and education privately, etc). This logic also leads to a view that such safety nets are essentially temporary measures to mediate the transition, rather than as more permanent or regularised forms of extending social security and income or wage support to the informal and poor.

The Post-Washington Consensus, with its intellectual support of New Institutional Economics and the Good Governance Agenda as policy derivative, essentially added the weakness of market-supporting institutions to the list of reasons why markets fail, without challenging the underlying logic – hence the reason that the various tangents of New Institutional Economics remain fundamentally neoclassical, despite claims to the contrary by some of its proponents, such as North (1995). These institutional weaknesses include insecure property rights or poor enforcement of contracts, as well as bad governance, such as clientelism and corruption (e.g., see Besley and Burgess 2003 for a good example of this position). Indeed, these factors are often blamed for the failure of structural adjustment programmes (SAPs) rather than SAPs having been disastrous policy in the first place (as we have seen more recently, for instance, in Greece).

Within this logical stream, accurate targeting then necessitates accurate poverty measurement. Precise identification of the poor becomes particularly vital when broader systems of social protection, including more traditional systems, have been stripped back, uprooted, reformed or phased out, or when broader social services such as health and education have been privatised or forced to implement cost recovery measures such as out of pocket payments, user fees, co-payments and so forth. The imperative for refining tools of means testing, identification and measurement also becomes accentuated when attempts are made to streamline social protection systems, through the increasing emphasis of providing only one system for all of the poor, reinforced through the increasing use of single registries. In contrast, more fragmented and duplicating protection systems offer poor people more chance to be caught by one system or another in the event that targeting precision turns out to be imprecise, as it invariably does, especially when state capacity is under strain or even attack (see Chapter 7 for further discussion on targeting precision). The mission to refine targeting evidently becomes a heyday for economists, as witnessed by the boom in poverty studies since the early days of adjustment policies in the 1980s.

A discursive emphasis of poverty therefore does not necessarily signal a shift away from this paradigm. Rather, it is often symptomatic of the paradigm. As noted by Marc Wuyts (2002), in the past it was indicative of more conservative agendas that emphasised charity and paternalism, such as Victorian social policy in England. In contrast, more progressive and redistributive agendas have typically emphasised equality, rights and employment, rather than poverty. The transition in OECD countries from Keynesian welfarism to neoliberalism has similarly involved shifts in discourse from full employment to flexible labour markets; from social security/insurance to social safety nets; from welfare to workfare; from a basic standard of living as a right to the 'deserving poor' and conditioned incentives. As such, the discourse of poverty can serve as an interpretive lens to understand the political climate over last century; the more the climate was Left and pro-poor, the less discourse itself was about poverty; the more the political Right was ascendant, the more discourse referred to poverty and charity, as well as making poor people responsible for their poverty. In the latter, narratives about perverse incentives become accepted wisdom, how helping the poor can actually hurt them (à la Malthus), as in recurrent debates about unemployment insurance or minimum wages in the US or elsewhere. Flexible labour markets are thus deemed as optimal for poverty reduction (although this argument is ironically never applied to tenured economists and other forms of protected labour at the upper end of the labour hierarchy).

We have nonetheless been witnessing a break in recent decades of this pendular discursive tendency that characterised twentieth-century politics, in that the rise of the so-called New Left across the world has, in many cases, adopted the narratives typically associated with the more conservative Right. Perhaps this is a reflection of the deep dissemination of neoliberal ideology over several decades, or simply an adventitious strategy to actually win power in contexts where the traditional support base for the Left has eroded. Regardless, Margaret Thatcher's famous statement that her greatest success was Tony Blair might be also applied to the subject of poverty, insofar that more conservative notions of targeting, self-responsibility, efficiency and the segmentation of social provisioning have come to be internalised by much of the political Left around the world, to the extent that these are not even seen as problematic by many so-called New Left governments.

Moreover, the earlier phase of poverty studies from the 1980s onwards was largely focused on measurement, whereas recent studies have increasingly focused on incentives and behavioural approaches. This is epitomised by the idea of 'low-hanging fruit' by Banerjee and Duflo (2011), meaning small nudges to change the behavior of the poor so that public interventions to eradicate poverty could be made more efficient in health, education and agricultural markets (admittedly, much of the attention on their work has focused on this point, rather than their parallel consideration of structural issues, expressed as the economic environment of the poor). Popular liberal microentrepreneurial models of poverty alleviation, as typified by microfinance (which Banerjee and Duflo actually criticise), also fit into a logic of self-help rather than redistributions of wealth and power. These aim at understanding how to influence poor people to act in ways that we think are good for them, or that make them deserving, and are clearly rooted in the more conservative conceptions described above, such that the causes of poverty are primarily located in the behaviour of the poor themselves. (Again, this is how Banerjee and Duflo are often interpreted, although in their defence their argument was more precisely that all people, rich and poor, make good and bad decisions, but the consequences of making bad decisions for the poor is much more severe.) Or, at the very least, that regardless of the broader political economy and structural forces that constrain such poor people, their route out of poverty should be one of self-discipline and self-improvement, if only because of the ineptitudes of the state in being able to do anything better, or more likely making things much worse.

Of course, this does not mean that all poverty studies are complicit with such conservative or neoliberal impulses. As noted above, much of the push to invest more into studies of poverty in the 1980s came from those who were deeply critical and concerned with the social devastation caused by stabilisation and adjustment programmes in that decade, followed by structural adjustment policies into the 1990s. An early example is the series of studies commissioned by UNRISD, such as Ghai and Hewitt de Alcántara (1990). Many studies on poverty in those years were aimed at refuting the argument that such devastation was an exaggeration or even a myth, and that SAPs were in fact having a beneficial effect, or at the very least were a necessary short-term pain to lead countries to subsequent growth recoveries and beyond.[11] Along these lines, many important criticisms about poverty measurements have also been made by critics of neoliberalism and globalisation in its current form, such as the seminal criticism of the World Bank PPP poverty lines and rates by Pogge and Reddy (2002a, 2002b), followed up by Wade (2004). Of course, many of these debates were then eclipsed by the uptick in growth in the 2000s and 2010s, which allowed the World Bank and other institutions to overlook the fact that poverty had been performing so dismally under their watch for an extended period of several decades.

Orthodoxy redux

Despite these critiques, the tendencies towards orthodoxy persist in the more recent iterations of the poverty agenda, although perhaps with less introspection and self-awareness. For example, multidimensional conceptions of poverty (which, as noted above, are not at all new, although they have come to be presented as such) can be easily coopted into a supply-side human-capital policy approach, more or less Washington Consensus in nature. As argued in Chapter 4, even the shift from Amartya Sen's original entitlement approach to the more recent capability approach reflects this subtle shift from a demand-side to a supply-side logic. In other words, in emphasising the importance of education and health for poverty reduction and development, there is a tendency to treat these as a matter of supply-side factors (i.e., increases in the supply of more educated or healthier workers), as if prior levels of education or health were the principle causes of poverty or development debacles. The demand side is similarly avoided, such as the fiscal and monetary prioritisation of employment or wider development strategies of industrialisation and wealth redistribution that are central to employment generation, particularly in the context of transitions out of agriculture.

Instead, the focus tends to be on increasing the supply of these outputs, through whatever mechanisms (public, private, etc.), and then allowing supply to create its own demand, ideally through the operation of efficient markets. As such, these approaches are easily fashioned into the position that supply creates its own demand, classically known as 'Say's Law', and that public policy in this sense should be focused on enhancing supply, not on demand-side interventions, such as in the labour market or through Keynesian-style counter-cyclical macroeconomic policy.[12] In other words, increasing supplies of goods and services will find buyers, and increasing supplies of labour will find gainful employment, as long as the government does not interfere with the market system that allows the economy to manifest demand for its own output or factor inputs.

Supply-side economics is usually associated with neoliberalism because of the premise that the process is best mediated by free markets and private actors, or what Friedrich Hayek referred to as the market process of price discovery. Another reason is its association with the Reagan presidency in the 1980s. Reagan used it to justify what was effectively a regressive redistribution to the wealthy through tax cuts, with the view that free markets would assure the trickle-down to the general population more effectively than government spending. As is well-known due to the work of Galbraith (1998, 2012), Piketty (2014) and many others, this initiated a sharp rise in inequality, to its high level since the 1920s. Of course, in order to secure all bets, the Reagan presidency also ramped up government spending from 1983 onwards, through military spending in particular, in what some have referred to as military Keynesianism (cf. Brenner 1998; Arrighi 2003). So, the true neoliberal supply-side experiment never truly came to pass, or at least only long enough to break the backbone of labour resistance, which was arguably its main purpose in any case.

The current popularity of cash transfers – particularly conditional cash transfers – also generally falls into this logic. As a social protection policy instrument, it is usually conceived as demand-side from a service user perspective (e.g., the user uses the cash to 'demand' services) and also from a partial macroeconomic perspective (it augments the aggregate demand of the poor). However, the human capital justification for the policy – which finds its zenith in the promotion of conditionalities or 'co-responsibilities' – is better described as deriving from a supply-side logic, with respect to the employment and poverty reduction dynamics beyond the one-off transfer of cash. The cash provided is often seen as just the carrot to induce people to make 'good' choices about 'investing' in such human capital (that is, school attendance and health checks), rather than as income support or as simply providing social security to the poor and informal. As with human capital theory more generally, the argument is that long-term poverty reduction, beyond the immediate and negligible impact of the cash transferred, is driven by such increases in human capital. The assumption in this 'theory of change' (as has become popular to say) is that the increased supply of human capital, or the increased number of people with augmented human capital, creates its own demand, presumably in the form of more employment that corresponds to the increased embodied capital, with higher wages and non-wages conditions, etc.

Indeed, the analogy to capital is also generally taken literally, to the extent that providing meagre cash transfers with schooling conditionalities is presented as 'investing' in education. It is not. Investing in education should mean improving the physical and human resources of the education system, whereas conditional cash transfers are merely providing social assistance with conditions. The emphasis on human capital is also sometimes referred to as 'productionist', although this is also a misnomer because there is nothing particularly production-oriented with the conditionalities, besides the theoretical imagination that somehow poor women will be nudged into becoming mini-industrialists. Rather, such jargon distracts from the classic understanding of productionist social policy, meaning social policy that supports industrialisation, as it was practised in Bismarck Germany, for instance. Moreover, the emphasis of human capital as the primary guiding principle behind such social protection policies also undermines their case for expansion, regularisation and eventual institutionalisation into a broader social security system, insofar as the human capital argument for cash transfers becomes redundant once full enrolment is achieved. In other words, the discursive framing of cash transfers as human capital investments undermines their more transformative potential to serve as a basis for extending social security systems to the poor and/or informal.

The point is not that conditionality is inherently wrong or that cash transfers should not be an important part of wider social protection systems. Rather, it is that their adoption within the current paradigm has tended to reinforce a perspective that seeks the causes of poverty in the behaviour of poor people themselves or else in the failings of state intervention beyond a restricted scope of targeted measures focused mainly on activating the poor to help themselves (or at least to get them off welfare, now popularly referred to as 'graduation'). Hence current 'best practice' tends to focus excessively on school enrolments or financial inclusion, while neglecting serious consideration of the social stratification that occurs through the education system, or of employment generation to support 'inclusion', particularly employment with decent wages and with terms negotiated by strong labour organisations. Rather, as noted above, employment generation is vaguely evoked by way of 'flexible labour markets', despite the excessive degrees of labour market insecurity that already exist across wide swaths of employment in poorer countries (e.g., how much more flexible can informal labour markets become?).

While human rights-based approaches are less obviously associated with such orthodox policy tendencies, they can also carry a similar propensity to be coopted due to their ambiguity on a variety of policy fronts. Human rights-based approaches are arguably founded on a universalistic agenda of social provisioning and social security, as pointed out by Langford (2009). Accordingly, many advocates of rights-based approaches implicitly (and sometimes explicitly) evoke a universalistic approach to social policy through their discourse of rights. Indeed, the attractiveness of human rights, like the MDGs, is in the impression they confer of transcending messy ideological disputes by imposing ethical standards to which all policy paradigms must conform. However, in the quest to operationalise these approaches, a degree of ambiguity enters into the translation from ethics to practice. For instance, does the principle of non-discrimination imply universalism (i.e., the same treatment for all) or targeting? As pointed out by Mkandawire (2005, p. 5), postmodern and/or feminist scholars have criticised universalism in that purportedly universalistic policies have often reflected fundamental underlying societal biases, such as racial or gender biases. In turn, this implies that a degree of selectivity is required in order to allow for the practice of affirmative/positive action and other forms of preferentiality for disadvantaged or discriminated groups.[13]

Similarly, in the good programming practices specified in the UN Common Understanding (see UNDG 2003), the principle that programmes should focus on marginalised, disadvantaged and excluded groups can be easily construed as a rationale for targeting, particularly when asserted in absence of any substantive discussion of policy. This emphasis on reducing disparity does not, in itself, resolve debates between targeting and universalism, particularly that targeting has been posed by its proponents as more equalising than universalism. The principle that people should be recognised as key actors in their own development, rather than passive recipients of commodities and services, can also be attributed as a rational for using conditionalities in cash transfers, for labour market activation policies or for other means of restricting welfare more generally. This logic – that welfare renders people 'passive recipients' – has been typical in right-wing political attacks against universalism over the past decades.

The point is that all of these policy options are fundamentally political in the choices that they elicit. Ethical principles do not necessarily resolve these politicised choices along any predictable path, whereas an emphasis on targeting the poor, while often appearing to be progressive in its evocation, often alludes to quite regressive approaches to social provisioning and integration. These points will be taken up further in Chapter 7.

The politics of conception and production

From the perspective of these previous points, it is evident that the political and moral dilemmas involved in the exercise of making choices about poverty concepts and measures are crucial because they bias the ways that poverty is perceived and represented, and the ways that policies are formulated in order to address such perceptions and representations. Moreover, these biases are implicit within all poverty approaches given the degree to which all approaches involve large ranges of choice, most of which are effectively arbitrary, and usually identify different groups of people depending on the range of choices taken. Choice is also inherent to social and economic measurement more generally, although poverty approaches compound this aspect through the use of thresholds for the purpose of identification. The fact that identification is usually tied to actual policy and social provisioning means that this aspect of arbitrary choice inherently falls into the moral realms of political economy.

The problem is not, as is commonly stated, that there is no agreed definition of poverty. It has become common to preface any discussion of poverty with the trope that there is no agreement on how to define poverty, or that poverty is not clearly understood. This is then commonly followed up by deferential reference to the paradigmatic breakthroughs wrought by the work by Amartya Sen on the capability approach as a huge advance in understanding poverty.

With all due respect, this trope derives from a confusion between the definition of poverty and the concepts and methods that we choose to measure or evaluate it. The definition of poverty is actually quite straightforward and non-controversial, especially to those experiencing it. It is essentially the study of human need, understood in terms of a lack of means or outcomes relative to some minimum social or subsistence standard or norm deemed necessary for human survival or functioning. If the focus is on a lack of means, this is generally understood to result in a substandard outcome.

The more precise problem is operational rather than definitional. For instance, it is often said that a recent innovation in poverty studies has been the multidimensional approach, although as noted above, there is nothing new about multidimensional understandings of poverty. As discussed in greater detail in Chapter 4, poverty has always been understood as multidimensional, even if measurement has tended to be unidimensional, usually out of practical necessity (something that so-called multidimensional poverty measures do not actually escape). It is an idea that can be found in the earliest modern studies of poverty from the late nineteenth century, if not earlier, such as in the work of classical political economists such as Smith, Malthus, Marx and others. It is also found in the work on poverty in the first postwar decades. Hence, the recent emphasis of multidimensionality does not change or challenge pre-existing definitions as such, but simply proposes new or revised ways of operationalising measurement, often with the aim of also establishing a self-acclaimed genesis of concept or agenda. The originality is more about branding rather than substance.

However, if we take a generic definition of poverty as a lack of means or outcomes relative to a social or subsistence standard or norm, this immediately raises a variety of tricky questions about how minimum standards should be set. They could be set in terms of outcomes, regardless of individual means. However, this would only be realistic in situations where fairly blunt outcomes can be managed within certain attainable standards, such school enrolments (although even this can be notoriously difficult to control in contexts of weak state capacity). As the World Bank has been lamenting since at least its World Development Report for 2004 (WB 2003), more qualitative issues such as quality of schooling are far more difficult to control. Outcomes such as nutrition are also much more difficult to control given that they are determined by means as well as a variety of other individual or contextual/environment factors. Hence, the usual default position is to set standards with regard to means, such as income. In a nutshell, even though the principle of insufficiency underlying the notion of poverty is straightforward, the specification of standards is not.

The proliferation of 'definitions' in the poverty studies literature is mostly about proposing such specifications, or about describing various attributes of poverty, rather than about defining poverty *per se*. Much of the debate is essentially about claiming that 'my standard is better than yours'. However, the specification of standards is fundamentally a political exercise. Scholarship can inform the exercise, but it cannot not determine it due to the inherent relativity implied by the principle of insufficiency. In other words, insufficiency of what and according to who?

In this respect, any attempt to specify a generic definition into more precise operational terms inherently raises a variety of conceptual, methodological, political and moral dilemmas related to how we conceive and then measure the means or outcomes, and the standards or norms against which these means or outcomes are evaluated. This is particularly complex given that the criteria are deeply relative, in terms of understanding the nature of needs and norms in specific contexts and historical periods, and how these change over time, especially alongside modern development, as discussed in the Introduction.

These dilemmas are doubled given that most poverty measures require choices about both the means or outcomes (e.g., income), and the standard by which these should be judged (e.g., income poverty lines). While the former are elements of social scientific measurement, the latter is related to the idea of a threshold that is common to most measures of poverty, below which one is considered poor (or vulnerable, or however the threshold is meant to be conceived). An important and unresolved (or unresolvable) debate within poverty studies is the degree to which the idea of a threshold is arbitrary or scientific. For instance, how do thresholds relate to either subsistence and/or social norms? Even if this could be determined scientifically at an individual level, could it ever be measured in any standardised way that would allow for population-based measures of poverty, given that standards invariably vary depending on the person, time and place and so on?

Absolutism versus relativism

Such questions further relate to issues of absolute versus relative poverty. The absolute refers to the idea that there is some identifiable objective threshold below which things essentially start to fall apart, such as starvation, sickness and/or death. Amartya Sen (1983) refers to this, for instance, as the 'absolutist core' of poverty. 'Relative' refers to the idea that poverty thresholds are inherently relative to social or other norms. Peter Townsend, a seminal scholar on relative poverty or deprivation, defined it as lacking 'the resources to obtain the type of diet, participate in the activities and have the living conditions and the amenities which are customary, or at least widely encouraged or approved in the societies to which they belong' (1979, p. 31). As he points out in Townsend (2006), 'relative' in this sense is still grounded with reference to some objective standard of deprivation, rather than simply being relative to a norm or average and hence disconnected to minimum standards. The EU poverty line is an example of the latter, in that it is set at 60 per cent of national mean income and hence is more a measure of inequality rather than poverty given that it can change without reference to minimum standards. Rather, he contends that the criterion of such relative deprivation 'lends itself to scientific observation of deprivation, measurement and analysis' (Townsend 2006, p. 21).

Despite the imprecision by which such relative criteria should be determined, Townsend's position is ironically more positivist than that of Amartya Sen, despite Sen's own defence of absolutist conceptions of poverty in his famous debate with Townsend in the mid-1980s (Sen 1983, 1985; Townsend 1985, 1993). In other words, Sen insisted in this debate on the relevance of absolute minimum standards, such as with respect to hunger and starvation, and yet he has argued elsewhere in relation to his capability approach that the identification of essential functionings should be determined through democratic processes within communities (see Chapter 4 for further discussion). Sen (1985) nonetheless concluded his debate with Townsend that they were both making essentially the same or a similar point, which is on the social nature of needs, which in turn must be determined (objectively or subjectively) relative to context.

Townsend's more fundamental challenge, however, was with reference to the idea that it is difficult if not impossible to identify a hard objective threshold, independent of social norms. Even extreme conditions such as hunger and starvation have large ranges of gradation within which the cut-off points for thresholds are not at all obvious. Choices are as much about practical expediency as they are about science, such as for the purposes of triage in famine situations, in which limited resources require the identification of the neediest and where thresholds are therefore set by the exhaustion of resources rather than by the exhaustion of need. Outside of such extreme humanitarian settings, establishing an absolutist core of poverty becomes even less obvious and more arbitrary.

Regardless, the common argument is that absolute poverty measures are more appropriate for poor countries, where the bulk of people face basic constraints in terms of food scarcity and hunger, whereas relative poverty measures are more appropriate for richer countries where very few people are absolutely poor in this sense. However, such distinctions carry tendencies to homogenise the poor in poor countries, or else divert attention away from problems of inequality and social differentiation in poor countries, despite the importance of such issues in these countries, as noted in the previous chapter.

The plentiful pathways of poverty analysis

From these broader conceptual issues, the study of poverty then breaks off into a variety of different approaches that grapple with precise conceptualisation and operationalisation. As extensively discussed in the poverty studies literature and further in this book, the main approaches include: income/expenditure approaches (or what I prefer to call money-metric approaches); basic needs approaches; entitlement, capability and multidimensional approaches; asset, livelihood and participatory approaches; social exclusion approaches; gender approaches; and wellbeing approaches, among others.

Underlying and overlapping these approaches are the methodologies of direct versus indirect measures. Direct refers to the measurement of actual outcomes, such as undernutrition, which is something that we can presumably measure or observe. Indirect refers to the measurement of proxies for these outcomes or else of the means that are used to acquire outcomes, such as income or expenditure, with the assumption that sufficiency of income will result in sufficiency of nutrition (hence, it is an indirect approach to reflecting nutrition, or other aspects of wellbeing). An emphasis on means usually alludes to indirect approaches in this sense.

Conversely, it is assumed that insufficient means will result in some form of deprivation below minimum living standards. For instance, insufficient income will likely lead to hunger or malnutrition, or to a substandard consumption of essential goods and services deemed necessary for survival and functioning in society. The distinction is important given that insufficient means might not necessarily result in substandard outcomes. For instance, poor children might perform well in school under the right circumstances. Or else substandard outcomes might occur even when means are sufficient, such as ill health, which occurs across all social classes and is intrinsic to the human condition. It is for this reason that Gordon (2006), for instance, distinguishes between means (e.g., income) and outcomes (e.g., standard of living) in the conception of poverty – we assume that they are tightly correlated and thus the former is a good predictor for the latter, but there is always some deviation around the average.

Amartya Sen's intervention – first with the entitlement approach and then the capability approach – was essentially to shed light on this space between such means and ends. In particular with the capability approach, he brought attention to situations where sufficiency in the former does not convert into the latter. Examples include when sufficient income does not convert into sufficient outcomes (such as nutrition), or also when sufficient basic direct outcomes do not result in sufficiency in more complex social functioning (e.g., sufficient nutrition leading to an ability to function more broadly in society). These points will be discussed further in Chapter 4.

Similarly, objective versus subjective measures of poverty have been amply explored. Objective measures refer again to outcomes (including indirect outcomes such as income) that can be measured and confirmed independently by a researcher regardless of the perception of the person being evaluated. As noted by Gordon (2006), this includes relative poverty in the way it was proposed by Peter Townsend, as discussed above. Hence relativity is not necessarily the same as subjectivity, even though relative comparisons are very central to subjective perceptions. Subjective measures refer to people's own perception about their state of poverty. Subjective approaches have also been closely associated with the use of participatory methods, which involve greater degrees of external mediation in the revelation of subjectivities, or else anthropological approaches, which purportedly involve less mediation, although with proportionately greater degrees of reliance on the subjectivity of the researcher.

Within these myriad concepts and measures, even if we choose one set of concepts and determine the related measures, other methodological or epistemological issues related to social and economic measurement bring in many layers of complication. For instance, even if we accept the 'commodity space' (even though criticised by Sen, perhaps unfairly), it is extremely difficult to maintain comparable standards over time within this space given changing relative prices, consumption patterns and product cycles, particularly within rapidly transforming contexts that generally wreak havoc on relative price structures and consumption profiles.

These issues are compounded by the completely different economic and social realities observed in cross-country or even cross-regional comparisons. Indeed, social realities can vary enormously even across neighbourhoods of a city, particularly in highly unequal settings, let alone across rural and urban areas. A common stylised fact is that ordinary consumer goods are relatively cheap but services relatively expensive in rich countries, although the opposite prevails in poor countries (and in the past in now-rich countries). Indeed, this has been a common critique, such as by Pogge and Reddy (2002a), of the World Bank purchasing-power-parity poverty lines.

The relation of poverty to employment is similarly difficult to translate. Unemployment is associated with poverty in rich countries or some highly polarised middle-income countries, such as South Africa. However, most poor people in poor countries are better conceived as working poor, or as disguised unemployment, as once coined by Joan Robinson (1936) to describe conditions in the UK during the depression of the 1930s, or as disguised unemployment and underemployment, as adapted by Rosenstein-Rodan (1956–1957) for application to developing countries. However conceived, in the absence of any significant social security, poor people in poor countries must accept work in whatever jobs and for whatever wages are available, whereas unemployment tends to be a relatively privileged status in such contexts, reserved for those who have the resources to be able to sustain bouts of not working. That being said, the category of the working poor has been an increasingly emerging phenomenon in many rich countries, in particular in the US and the UK. The point is that comparisons of unemployment statistics across contexts and across time need to be questioned given that the data are highly relative to institutional specifications and structural settings.

Even if we move away from the commodity space (meaning measures of wellbeing in terms of commodities consumed) and into the now-preferred multidimensional measures, similar problems arise and are amplified by the dilemmas of aggregation. What dimensions of poverty do we measure and how do we decide what poverty threshold to apply in each dimension, especially over time? This is a notorious problem of so-called proxy measures of poverty, which have become popular targeting devices related to the distribution of benefits to selected poor households. These are based on correlations observed at particular moments in time, in certain contexts and by certain studies, between the consumption of certain easy-to-observe goods (e.g., mobile phones, TVs, electric light bulbs or quality of flooring or roofing) and the likelihood of being in poverty. However, even strong correlations can easily break down over time, when the consumption of such goods becomes popularised over time, even among poor households, such as with mobile phones. Even if we realise this, how long does this realisation take to become translated into the institutionalised practices of surveying and then into public policy? And how then do we weight each dimension and aggregate them with others? And should improvement in one dimension offset deteriorations in other dimensions (if this is the result of aggregation)? For instance, does improving health obviate concerns over income poverty or income inequality? Or inversely, in lower-middle-income countries such as India or even middle-income countries such as Ecuador, income poverty is apparently falling even though undernutrition has remained stubbornly high.

The fundamental intractable problem is that different choices and approaches generally identify different groups of populations. Many of these groups overlap but many do not (e.g., see good studies on this methodological point by Laderchi et al. 2003; Lu 2010; Roelen 2017). The choice of approach and its application are therefore crucial in determining who gets identified (or, vice versa, the choice of target group might also have huge implications on the type of targeting measure that gets used). This is not only an intellectual problem but also has huge implications for policy, particularly when identification becomes tied to the delivery of benefits (or inversely when not being identified leaves one without benefits).

Conclusion: The moral politics of poverty studies

The implications and consequences of the discretionary exercises involved in conceiving and measuring poverty involve a wide variety of political and moral dilemmas, particularly once applied to policy and social provisioning. There are essentially three facets at play. One is the role that concepts and measures play within policy paradigms and ideologies, and within representations of their outcomes, as discussed in first section on the politics of representation. Inversely, the second is how ideologies and politics inform concepts and measures, as was addressed in the second section on the politics of prioritisation and also partly in the third on the politics of conception and production. The third facet is the question of what happens when abstract concepts and measures are applied in social and political realities. No matter how well refined a concept or measure of poverty, it can run seriously afoul once applied in such realities.

In this sense, we need to differentiate poverty analysis as an evaluative device versus a tool of policy implementation. Some of the criticisms regarding poverty measures are inherent to the difficulties of social and economic measurement more generally and thus must be taken in step, dealt with as an inevitable and even enriching element in the intellectual exercise of interpretation. However, other criticisms are related to the use of poverty measurements in the allocation of benefits. As soon as any poverty identification exercise is tied to the allocation of money, goods or services, fiscal decisions, the organisation of social provisioning and benefits, the definition of rights and entitlements or even the representation of highly contested experiences, it inherently falls into the moral realms of political economy.

This is an issue related to broader modes of policy and cannot be resolved within the conceptualisation or measurement of poverty itself. Conceptualisation and measurement are important, however, given that all poverty lines are, to various extents, constantly shifting targets, which makes them especially susceptible to manipulation in application. Choices must inevitably be made. The point is not that there is one choice to fix them all, but that the inherent political subjectivities involved in the act of choosing must be recognised, along with the inevitable limitations and implications of every choice. Humility in this regard is especially important in poverty studies given that hubris can be dire for those who bear the brunt of its consequences. Transparency is also important to dispel any false sense of confidence and air of authority that might otherwise be conveyed to a wider lay, somewhat beguiled, public.

The arbitrariness of choice also raises a variety of questions around the agency and de-politicisation of choice. Why should we be forced to make choices? The calculus of choice itself is often driven by factors other than social-scientific concerns, such as tightening budgetary constraints, refinement of targeting practices or the desire to demonstrate improvement in poverty rates. Who should be making the choices? The field of poverty studies has become increasingly professionalised, in particular within the discipline of economics. This includes an increasing array of sophisticated statistical tools that few but the inducted can hope to comprehend, even though those few are usually not required to spend extended (or any) periods of time living with poor people as part of their training. Professionalisation in this sense disempowers the lay person and especially the poor from understanding and negotiating or contesting the discourses that address their poverty. This concern is often raised by advocates of participatory approaches, but such approaches also often fall into similar traps of professionalization.

As noted by Laderchi et al. (2003), even though the concept of poverty easily lends itself to be dominated by economic approaches and measures, it is fundamentally a social and political issue. The question then is whether technocratic approaches developed in the field of poverty studies, or in allegiance with it, distract from or even disguise such social politics. We will continue to explore this question through the next three chapters, each on one of the dominant poverty approaches within current global development agendas.

3 | MONEY-METRIC MEASURES OF POVERTY

This chapter presents an overview of the most conventional poverty measures: indirect measures based on income or expenditure, measured in units of money, here referred to as money-metric measures. The purpose is to highlight the degree of arbitrary and subjective discretion and choice that is involved in even these most restrictive forms of poverty measurement, which many consider the most scientific or objective, at least in principle, if exercised carefully. This arbitrariness is inherent in many of the steps of conceptualisation and measurement, implying that these poverty measures can easily be tweaked and adapted to support broader narratives and agendas, as discussed in the previous chapters. Political and ideological biases can also enter at each of these steps, even before these measures are applied to social and political economy realities, which invariably distort the measures even further.

The emphasis of the chapter is on the key axes of discretion that allow for the entry of politics and ideology into the calculus of these measures, to the extent that even carefully managed measures provide little reliable scientific indication of whether basic needs are actually being met and, especially, how this might be changing over time. In other words, given the wide variety of fairly arbitrary assumptions and choices that are required in order to first choose a line and then to apply this line to presumably accurate survey data in ways that are broadly consistent, accurate and comparable across time and regions, it is no exaggeration that poverty estimates – even estimates based on national lines – are quite arbitrary, even before considering the technical complexities of second-order measurement issues such as the World Bank purchasing-power-parity (PPP) conversions.

This point is acknowledged in some of the seminal texts by the doyens of poverty studies, such as Ravallion (1992). However, his response to this quandary is that we must ultimately chose a line, whatever the line, and stick with it in order to allow for comparison and evaluation, so long as the line and the income it is judged against are accurately adjusted over time. But this just simply kicks the problem forward, given that adjustments to the line over time, in addition to evaluations of the nature and structure of incomes, are even more complex, involving yet further arbitrary choices and biases.

This leads to the classic quandary of whether poverty trends over time reflect actual changes or else errors of adjustment and conception. For the sake of being provocative, even the income of a beggar will rise with rising prices. If the poverty line is set too low or adjustments to the line are insufficient, his or her situation could appear to be moving out of poverty even in the absence of any substantive change, besides receiving dimes instead of pennies. Moreover, this is with respect to national poverty lines. The international estimates provided by the World Bank involve even greater degrees of arbitrariness and, as such, are highly contestable even though they are the main data relied upon by the leading international organisations spearheading the promotion of various development goals. The evaluative emphasis also sidesteps the dilemma that, once applied to the social and political economy realities of policy-making and actual distributions of benefits and poverty relief, the problems of these poverty measures become compounded by social and power relations.

The last point on actual application to social political realities of course applies to all poverty measures and will be addressed further in the conclusion of the book. However, one additional particularity of absolute money-metric measures that is broached in the last part of this chapter is that these measures are prone to a secular tendency to gradually underestimate absolute poverty over time in the context of structural and institutional changes associated with development. This is due to three fundamental sources of bias in such absolute measures. One is based on declining terms of trade for food, which gives greater relative prominence to non-food essential needs over time. This is not reflected in poverty lines that continue to be anchored by reference to minimal food requirements and that more or less treat non-food needs as a constant share of food needs, as is standard. The second is more fundamental, in terms of the shift from self-provisioning to commodified consumption, which in many respects overestimates the value of the latter relative to the functional value of subsistence of the former. The last is more proximate to the neoliberal era of commoditised social provisioning, in particular the substantial commoditisation and privatisation of health and education. A fundamental problem with money-metric measures of poverty is that they are biased by design against universalistic and decommodified forms of social provisioning, such that a move towards greater commodification can actually be reflected as an improvement in poverty, all else held constant.

These points are discussed in the following three sections. The first clarifies my use of the term 'money-metric' and also discusses the notions of dimensionality and indirect measures, as represented by such approaches. The second presents an overview of such poverty measures in order to clearly highlight the degree of arbitrary and subjective choices that are involved in the successive steps of measurement and the huge difficulties in setting any measure that can be considered rigorously reliable as an evaluative standard over time. The third section elaborates the three institutional and structural sources of bias that have led to a secular underestimation of money-metric poverty rates over time.

Clarifications on the metric of money and unidimensionality

As a starting point, my use of the term 'money-metric' should be clarified. Income and expenditure measures are often referred to as 'monetary' measures (e.g., see Laderchi et al. 2003). This label gives the impression, however, that their primary concern is with income or expenditure that occurs in monetary form, which is a common but misconstrued criticism often levelled against these measures. Indeed, there is an increasing reaction against such measures along such lines, usually conjoined with an advocacy of multidimensional measures. Similar to criticisms of GDP, the focus on monetary measures of wellbeing is often purported to cause or reflect an obsession with money and economic growth as development goals.

While there are plenty of problems with such money-metric measures, as explored in this chapter, the common perception that they are primarily concerned with monetised incomes is misconceived. Conventional income or expenditure surveys – especially rural surveys – are usually designed to record all sources of livelihoods, including monetised sources (e.g., selling crops for cash or wage labour) as well as non-monetised sources. The latter are referred to as 'income in kind' or 'own consumption'. They are also often conceived as 'subsistence production', meaning that the household directly consumes much of what it produces and supplements this consumption with lesser or greater degrees of commodity consumption, financed through the sale of the non-consumed surplus or through other sources of income. This is in contrast to so-called 'commercial farmers', who sell most of their produce and then use the proceeds to purchase most of what they consume, as is more typical in richer countries or among large-scale farms everywhere. The value of 'own consumption' is usually approximated in surveys by using market prices, as if it would have been sold, and then this value is included within the measure of incomes.

Obviously, many things might be missed by such attempts to calculate the volume and/or value of non-monetised income or consumption (calculating the value of owner-occupied housing faces comparable problems). In many cases people might also forget or not know the exact amounts they consumed. However, similar problems also face the reporting of monetary incomes, especially given the tendency of people to under-report these incomes.

There is also much debate, such as in the feminist and gender studies literature, about what gets included or excluded in the calculation of non-monetary incomes, particularly with respect to unpaid domestic work. The inclusion of own-consumption of food follows a traditional logic of production, in that something tangible is produced and consumed, even if it is not sold. However, this distinction is less credible when located within the increasing prominence of service-sector work in poor countries. The distinction in such cases would therefore seem to rest on whether an activity contributes income (monetary or non-monetary) that can be used to provide for basic needs, or else enhances consumption. The question then, from this narrow poverty perspective, is the degree to which unpaid work offsets some of these needs or enhances consumption through some other means. Simply calculating the hours worked and then multiplying these by a reference wage, as is a common way of estimating the value of domestic work, is not necessarily appropriate given that it does not necessarily give a sense of how such work contributes to achieving a minimum standard of consumption.

Similarly, much of unpaid domestic work is directly related to production, such as in farming households or in many urban households engaged in informal activities such as hawking or catering, and as such is essential to survival. However, the question from a poverty evaluation perspective is whether such work should be calculated as an income that augments consumption versus an input that is required to realise income. The latter accentuates the problem faced by the poor of 'low labour productivity' or, more appropriately, of low value-added earned for their labour time. In other words, just because something can be ascribed a monetary value does not necessarily mean that it will have a substantive effect on poverty and/or its reduction. Slave labour can be ascribed a monetary value, but this does not mean that the slave will be any better off as a result.

For the purpose of the present discussion, all of these points of contention highlight that conventional measures of income are not restricted to only monetised incomes. Due to the confusion, I prefer to use the term 'money-metric' versus 'monetary' measures because, in effect, the issue is more precisely about the choice of a metric for the purposes of aggregation rather than the valuing of money. Poverty evaluation invariably requires adding up various measures through a common unit that can be compared to a threshold measured in the same unit, e.g., dollars and dollars, calories and calories, kilograms and kilograms, etc. The use of a unidimensional metric in this sense does not necessarily mean that only one dimension is being measured, but that various dimensions must be converted into a common unit for the purposes of evaluation. The same is ironically required in so-called multidimensional measures, which ultimately must also convert multiple dimensions into a single metre in order to make poverty evaluations, as discussed in the next chapter.

With money-metric measures, the choice of this common unit is money, with the logic that income remains a primary concern and a strong indirect indicator of poverty, regardless of other legitimate concerns raised by other dimensions such as health and education. Using money as a unit obviously restricts measurement to only those things that can be logically converted into money units and excludes those things that cannot be converted (such as health, education, etc.), hence the criticism that it is only concerned with the commodity space (as per Amartya Sen) or with private versus public goods (e.g., see this point in Laderchi et al. 2003, p. 249). However, as discussed in the following chapter, the alternatives also present their own sets of problems.

For instance, the commonly used alternative to money-metric evaluations of income or wealth is based on using proxies, referred to as proxy means testing (e.g., Grosh and Baker 1995; Brown et al. 2016).

In practice, this is often referred to as a consumption measure. The proxies are things that are easy for a surveyor to observe during a visit to a household, thereby circumventing the problems of people recalling and self-reporting their incomes or consumption, or otherwise measuring incomes or consumption in the absence of formal data or even numeracy of the surveyed respondents. Proxies also generally reflect the results of consumption, especially of durable items. Examples include the state of flooring and ceilings in a house, the number of light bulbs, existence of piped water, ownership of assets such as cattle, bicycles or cars or the ownership of durable goods such as televisions or mobile phones. The choice of proxies is supposed to be based on studies that find a strong degree of positive association in certain contexts at certain periods of time between the possession of these proxies and the likelihood of not being in income poverty. In other words, the proxies (or lack of them) are argued to be strong predictors of whether or not a household is poor (although Brown et al. (2016) critically assess proxy means testing in nine African countries and conclude that, while generally effective in filtering out the non-poor, proxy means testing usually also excludes many poor people and is particularly deficient in reaching the poorest). However, it is important to point out that unidimensionality is not avoided in the case of these proxy measures. Rather, the proxies are converted and aggregated into a common unit, hence they are equally as unidimensional as money-metric measures.

In this respect, there are advantages and disadvantages to all approaches. The enduring quality of money-metric approaches is that they are intuitive (besides the one-or-more-dollar-a-day purchasing-power-parity poverty line of the World Bank, which seems intuitive but actually is not, as discussed below). National poverty lines expressed in national currencies are intuitive for residents of those countries. The rough significance of a poverty line of 1000 pesos a month is clear to someone living in a country that uses this currency and understands the relative value of the amount. However, in the case of proxy 'consumption' measures, a poverty line is usually expressed as simply a number, such as 35, which has no meaning whatsoever for anyone outside of the circle of experts who devised the measure or who are trained to comprehend it.

The tangibility of a money-metric line can provide the basis of contestation by the poor or those representing the poor, whereas the opacity and obscurity of proxy measures would have a tendency to disempower such contestation if only through the force of sheer incomprehension. Indeed, it might even be argued that a certain degree of deception is involved in surveying for such proxies, to the extent that a surveyed person might not understand that their poverty is being judged when a surveyor asks them whether or not they own cattle or counts the number of lightbulbs that they might have in their home.

The relevance of the proxies might also change over time and, given their focus on durable goods, they are not helpful for understanding short-term fluctuations in incomes (hence one reason why they miss out a lot of poor people). For example, the ownership of a mobile phone might have been a relevant indicator of not being in poverty in 2005 but much less so in 2015, when mobile phone ownership became much more affordable and pervasive among the poor. Similarly, past purchases of assets or durable goods might not reflect current conditions. The fact that proxies might reveal poverty only once assets are eroded or sold off is, itself, a major fault of such measures. Even if proxy means surveys are conducted regularly enough to provide insight into short-term fluctuations, which generally they are not,[1] these deficiencies should be important considerations for social protection programmes that aim to provide short-term income support to households in the event of economic shocks and downturns.

Hence, while much ado can be made about the use of money as a metric, the approach remains one means to aggregate within one important dimension of poverty, among a range of other imperfect options, and aggregation is also a problem with other approaches. In this sense, it is important to avoid building straw men. Money-metric poverty measures do have biases and it is essential to understand these biases in order to compensate for them, but the use of a money-metric does not necessarily imply a belief that money or income are primary overriding goals and priorities. Rather, they reveal very important information, even though they do not reveal all of the information that is relevant to understand poverty, nor were they necessarily conceived to do so.

Indeed, a similar case can also be made for national accounting (i.e., GDP) statistics. These have also been criticised as instilling a fetishism for growth and as being inappropriate for measuring the wellbeing of a society, even though they were not conceived for this purpose. Rather, national accounting data are conceived for measuring the creation and circulation of monetary value added in an economy and, as such, are very important for understanding how value added is distributed, across sectors and in particular between profits and wages. They are important as such in their ability to provide information to governments about where profits are being made in an economy and hence where they might be taxed, among other information that is necessarily expressed in monetary terms because economic actors effectively operate with money and are motivated by monetary value. The danger of efforts to transform national accounting into something that might, according to various propositions, better reflect wellbeing, sustainability or other objectives is that this original information then becomes obscured or even lost, particularly if efforts to reform result in more abstract metrics given the inclusion of many non-monetary variables. Indeed, this obscurity might even advantage powerful economic interests, who otherwise would continue to track the circulation of value in the economy as a means to profit from it, increasingly through their own private means. In other words, the risk of obfuscation is that, despite the progressive intentions, it dilutes our ability to understand and contest the core dynamics of power and wealth in modern economies.

Indirect measures

As briefly presented in the previous chapter, money-metric measures of poverty are also the epitome of indirect measures. Money is not happiness (or welfare) and it does not even have a direct relationship to standards of living (e.g., see Gordon 2006 for a discussion of this). However, it is nonetheless a crucial dimension in the economics of human existence, for survival, basic needs, functioning and beyond. This is especially the case in societies that are immersed in monetised forms of commodity consumption and where poor people are acutely aware of their relative insufficiency of income even if they have access to acceptable levels of education and health care. The same consideration even applies to non-monetary forms of income or consumption in less-commoditised economies, insofar as the amount of consumption permitted by so-called subsistence production is generally understood within such societies as an indicator of wealth (e.g., see Fischer 2006, 2008b, 2014 for a discussion of this). Hence, while income (in both monetary or non-monetary forms) is not necessarily a cause of wellbeing in a positive sense, a lack of it below certain survival needs is definitely a source of illbeing, for all but the enlightened perhaps. In this restrictive sense, it can be considered an appropriate indirect reflection of poverty at the lower bound, in that it identifies situations where we can expect standards of living to be deficient, with the likelihood that this also has a negative impact on wellbeing.

There are, of course, a multitude of debates about whether income or consumption reflect welfare, and even different understandings about what constitutes welfare. In his seminal text on poverty measurement, Ravallion (1992) discusses the relation between income and welfare in some detail, although he uses the term 'welfare' in reference to the idea of 'utility' in modern welfare economics, which is not exactly how welfare might be popularly understood by the layperson as referring to actual objective needs. Rather, his discussion relates to the standard utilitarian welfare economics presumption that utility is imputed by the market value of consumption, as 'revealed preferences'. This presumption, however, is very difficult to prove and also results in a circular, if not tautological, reasoning. It is particularly problematic in real-world contexts where poor people might not have enough income to reveal all of their preferences, where their choices are constrained through various economic and social forces, and/or where they are not necessarily free to make certain choices or to withdraw from hypothesised market bargaining processes, whether due to poverty, coercion or else by more nuanced processes of social conditioning. Hence, despite Ravallion's digression and much theoretical musings on this in economics more generally (and occasional attempts to measure 'utility'), the discussion does not have much practical relevance within poverty studies and income is typically understood as an indirect measure of poverty rather than a direct measure of utility. Direct measures of poverty are instead mostly focused on 'objective' measures of wellbeing, such as nutrition, education and health, as discussed in the next chapter.

The arbitrariness of money-metric poverty measurement

Whereas the fetishism of money is not necessarily a valid criticism of money-metric poverty measures, they nonetheless succumb to several fundamental problems. One concerns the arbitrariness of choice in such measures, such that evaluation is in effect very difficult to do in practice, particularly once social scientific pursuits are applied to the social and political economy realities of policy practice. This is important because it provides the ease with which such measures can be manipulated for political purposes. Another problem concerns certain fundamental biases against more universalistic forms of social provisioning that are built into such measures, as an artefact of how these measures are constructed. For the purpose of highlighting and clarifying these problems, it is useful to first briefly examine the standard methods in the study of money-metric poverty in order to reveal the arbitrariness of choice involved.

As noted in the previous chapter, there are essentially two sides involved in poverty measures. In the case of money-metric measures, one is the measurement of income, expenditure or wealth, and the other is the calculation of the poverty line, that is, the threshold under which one is considered to have deficient income, expenditure or wealth. The former is used for measuring other things than simply poverty, such as household inequality (except when surveys are conducted solely for the purpose of measuring poverty, such as when samples are drawn from social registers that only cover parts of the population where poverty is expected to be most concentrated, in which case, other surveys need to be relied on to measure inequality). The key difference between inequality and poverty measures in this respect is that inequality measures do not generally rely on the idea of a threshold (although, as highlighted in debates over various inequality indices and their interpretation, they also have their share of problems). In this respect, the poverty line is the particular source of contention.

Surveying

The first step in the measurement of income involves the fundamentals of surveying, as examined in great detail, for instance, in the formative work of Angus Deaton (1997). Surveys typically use clustered stratified random samples in order to guarantee some degree of representativity of the larger population, to the extent that relatively accurate social or civil registers of the entire population exist, which is a problem in many countries. As commonly noted, this leads to problems of excluding those populations that are hard to reach, such as homeless or temporary residents, particularly in cases where such populations are not sufficiently recorded in various civil registries that are used as the basis for random sampling. This is a problem in China, for instance, where household income and expenditure surveys are generally drawn from households registered as permanent residents in that locality, meaning that they omit migrants or even long-term residents who are still formally registered as temporary residents (see Hussain 2003; Fischer 2005). Different methods are also used to record incomes or expenditures, from one-off interviews relying on on-the-spot recall by interviewees, to keeping log books in households, which are filled by household members, presuming of course that they are literate, numerate and also able to conduct basic accountancy tasks.

The choice between measuring expenditures versus incomes has received much attention in the literature. Expenditure is conventionally said to be better because it is more regularised due to consumption smoothing, whereas incomes are more volatile. This would be especially common in agricultural areas; incomes are concentrated around harvest time and are otherwise sparse, and people borrow or use savings in periods when incomes are not sufficient in order to maintain consistent consumption, of food in particular. Financial intermediation is common in poor rural communities precisely for this reason, as classically noted by Hill (1966),[2] even though this basic insight ironically runs contrary to the assumption in the microfinance literature that poor people need to learn the savings habit. Expenditure reporting is also said to be less subject to the tendency of people to under-report their incomes. Moreover, it is said to be better because it is often easier for people to recall what they consumed rather than what they earned, especially in rural economies with diversified livelihoods, many of which might not be monetised, and in which much income might be shared across households in extended family or community networks. Indeed, many people consume even if they do not earn income, through pooling and sharing within such networks. The standard way of dealing with this in income or expenditure surveys is to deal with households rather than individuals as the basic accounting unit in order to deal with the income and resource pooling and sharing that typically takes place within a household. However, household boundaries can be tricky and sharing does not necessarily happen within them, in terms of how they might be identified by a surveyor (e.g., see Randall and Coast 2015; Palacio 2017).[3]

Despite these contentions, the case for expenditure or consumption has been arguably oversold and there is a growing scholarly reaction against it, as synthesised by Jolliffe and Serajuddin (2018). The reaction includes doyens in the consumer behaviour of the poor, such as Banerjee and Duflo (2007) and Banerjee (2016). The main point, as noted by Parker (2015), is that poor households (in income or in liquid wealth) typically do not smooth consumption, partly because they are not able. As would be obvious for anyone with experience living in rural agrarian settings, consumption and expenditure actually do vary substantially throughout the year, particularly between lean and harvest seasons, and they tend to spike in the latter, similar to the case of income. Volatility is also exacerbated by expenditures during festivals (e.g., Christmas or Diwali), or lifecycle events such as weddings or funerals, all of which can amount to major sources of variation depending on the timing of a survey (this point is made by Banerjee and Duflo 2007, although it has been well established in anthropological literature since the origin of the discipline). Consumption also includes consumer durables, especially when economies of scale are sought at the household level, which can also lead to lumpy expenses over time. Hence, while ordinary recurrent expenditures might be smoothed over a year, such as on food (but not necessarily, as noted above), overall consumption typically is not. To reinforce these points, Jolliffe and Serajuddin (2018) note that while most poverty estimates are based on enumerations taken at a single point in time, poverty estimates can vary substantially if households are interviewed at multiple times throughout the year. Using an example from Jordan, they illustrate that repeat visits result in a poverty rate that is 26 per cent higher than the estimate based on a single-visit interview. The fact that it has taken so long for the consumption smoothing proposition to be challenged (even though it continues to be reiterated) is a case in point about how these 'truths' are established through the force of uncritical repetition rather than being based on grounded experience.

In addition to these critiques, expenditure measures do not indicate how expenditure is financed, that is, whether it is paid for through earnings, savings or debt. They might therefore miss out important information about the sustainability of consumption, which incomes can reveal, such as whether consumption is eroding savings and assets, or if households are borrowing in order to sustain consumption. Income is arguably preferable to consumption measures precisely for this reason.

In any case, many surveys include both income and expenditure and, on average, expenditure amounts to a fairly regular fraction of incomes. As noted by Hussain (2003) in the case of household surveys in China, which measure both, the use of expenditure rather than income effectively operates as the equivalent of a higher poverty line (because the same line is used against expenditure data that are, on average, a fraction of the income data). He recommends using both in order to have a better understanding of the gradation of poverty as well as the sensitivity of poverty rates to changes in such measures or the poverty line.

Without even advancing to the subsequent step of determining a poverty line, much information can be derived from this initial step of measuring income, expenditure or wealth. Indeed, the most useful information is arguably attained at this stage and the poverty line itself is a fairly arbitrary exercise, although one that receives most of the attention, as described further below. For instance, as noted above, information about inequality can be derived from these data. The structure of income distribution can also be observed through frequency distributions, which show how many people or what proportion of people are at each level of income. Such frequency distributions are much more informative than poverty rates given that they show the clustering of populations at various income levels as well as the polarisation of income distributions, among other information, such as in the excellent studies of both population and consumption density distributions based on World Bank PPP data by Edward and Sumner (2013, 2014, 2015, 2016). Useful information can be similarly gleaned through analysing representative households, such as at the 10th, 25th, median, 75th and 90th percentiles of a sample (presuming that the sample includes a representative range from poorest to richest households, which is often not the case), or else by analysing the average characteristics of each decile or quintile of the population sampled. The use of representative households or deciles must be interpreted with caution because they do not represent a consistent household or group over time due to churning in the population from survey to survey, whereby households change positions, some rising and others falling, with the net effect often being cancelled out. Moreover, these latter methods are not able to tell us what proportion of the population falls beneath a fixed poverty line (unless the poverty line is set relatively at a particular percentile, as discussed below).

Varieties of poverty lines

In terms of setting poverty lines, the key question as discussed in the previous chapter is whether or not there is some scientific or conceptual rationale for establishing a threshold, in this case, an income or expenditure threshold. In other words, is there some point that can be identified below which things start to fall apart, or people experience a reality flip in terms of their ability to maintain nutrition, health and other functions?

There are a variety of different approaches to conceptualise or operationalise such a threshold. As discussed further below, the dominant 'absolute' approach is in terms of basic food and non-food needs. Food (or physiological) needs are expressed in terms of calories needed per person per day, supplemented with an allowance for a minimum of non-food essentials (e.g., at the very least, the poor need to be able to cook their food). Other approaches, as reviewed by Saith (2005), include the so-called inductive empiricist approach, such as using consumer behaviour studies to determine a consumption basket, and self-defined approaches. However, these are not as common, especially for large-scale surveys designed to evaluate poverty at regional or national scales.

On the other hand, political-administrative methods are abundantly used, although these are associated more with policy interventions rather than with accurate evaluations of poverty. They are often referred to as 'benefit lines', in the sense that they are used for means-testing whether or not people qualify for poverty relief or benefits of various kinds. Precisely for this reason, the level at which such lines are set is usually driven by political and budgetary considerations and they often change due to political or economic circumstances. Indeed, benefit lines are often not indexed to inflation (in contrast to social security, which generally is), which becomes an important means of depreciating these lines over time. Lack of indexing also requires (often politicised) discretionary government interventions to raise these benefit lines, which does not particularly inspire confidence as to their accuracy or comparability over time. In this sense, such lines usually cannot be used for any credible evaluation of poverty, especially over time, even though they are often miscon-struedas such.

For instance, in the late 1990s, the National Bureau of Statistics of China estimated the absolute rural poverty line, based on 2100 calories a day, at around 865 yuan a year, whereas the official (or benefit) line was only 635 yuan (Hussain 2002). Despite this dis-crepancy, it was the latter official line that was commonly referred to at the time in official pronouncements on poverty by the government or by international organisations such as the World Bank, which cited that the rural poverty rate in China had dropped to 3.5 per cent by 2000, or about 32 million people (ibid., p. 3). In addition, there might be many benefit lines for different purposes, such as in China where the official 'benefit' line in the late 1990s was again different from the lines that were used to determine whether particular coun-ties were to be considered 'poverty-stricken' and hence eligible for poverty relief funding. Notably, all of these administrative lines that are used for the allocation of resources and benefits become con-tested in the political economy struggles over budgetary allocations, citizen entitlements and so forth. Even the absolute line in China in the late 1990s was contested, including by the then-Premier Wen Jiabao in 2003, given that many people deemed it far too low (see Fischer 2005, pp. 96–99). It has since been revaluated upwards sev-eral times, up to 2300 yuan in 2015, which represents an adjustment that is far beyond the rate of price inflation over these years.

More relative approaches to setting the line emphasise the idea of social norms or socially acceptable minimums, as discussed in the pre-vious chapter. The common relative approach, such as that used in Europe, is to define the poverty line as 60 per cent of average incomes. However, this is more of an inequality rather than poverty measure, insofar as such a threshold offers no indication of whether those below the threshold are meeting basic needs (although the European Union tries to compensate for this by also measuring 'severe material depri-vation' alongside 'monetary poverty'). It is also unreliable as constant standard because the line changes with changes in the average. Indeed, the line would fall in times of recession, when average incomes fall, contradicting the fact that more people would logically be poor under such conditions. As noted above, using representative households is a similar relative measure, whereby one observes the characteristics of households at fixed percentiles within the income distribution. In order for relative measures to go beyond such inequality-type measures, they arguably need to be grounded in some conception of minimum needs or standards, except through a relative rather than absolute conception of need, as discussed in the previous chapter.

This relates to the debates about absolute versus relative poverty lines, exemplified by the classic duel between Amartya Sen (1983, 1985) and Peter Townsend (1985, 1993). The absolute archetype is starvation, but as noted by Townsend, even starvation is a gradual process with many gradations, such that it is difficult to determine a precise cut-off point whereby a deficient income becomes hunger and hunger becomes starvation. Townsend argued instead that minimum standards for subsistence are relative to societies, groups and contexts, including the basket itself, the pricing of the basket and the entitlements needed to access the basket or other essential needs. But this raises the perennial question of how to measure such standards, especially if one's motivation is to devise standardised and comparable measures for an entire national population or even across countries. This latter point is perhaps part of the reasoning for Sen's critique of Townsend, in terms of cutting through the semantics and arguing for a decisive absolute minimum standard applied to all. The irony is that Sen himself has similarly argued elsewhere that such absolute minimum standards should be the construct of local democratic deliberative processes, which more or less ends up agreeing with Townsend's position.

Interestingly, Ravallion (1992) himself has argued that the notion of absolute poverty should not be about mere survival, such as with food poverty lines based only on calorie minimums. But in recognising the difficulty of being able to objectively determine such a line, he has argued instead that what is more important (for comparison purposes) is that the line, whatever line, however chosen, should remain fixed and constant across space and over time. This is probably why his subsequent work became so focused on measuring purchasing power parities across countries and across time – the only justification for such measurement projects are for global comparisons and evaluations.

World Bank purchasing-power-parity poverty lines

Amidst these various approaches that are grounded on at least some attempt to provide a rationale for basic needs, the line that currently dominates attention is the one-dollar-(or-more)-a-day purchasing-power-parity (PPP) poverty line of the World Bank. More precisely, this started as $1.08 a day, then was increased to $1.25 in 2008 based on 2005 data, and was further revised to $1.90 in 2015 based on 2011 data. In non-technical public presentations (e.g., WB 2015), the claim is that the revisions represent changes in the cost of living. In practice, however, they represent both cost-of-living adjustments as well as the inclusion of new information derived from the newer surveys. As a result, it is not actually clear whether the $1.90 line in 2011 is actually the equivalent of the $1.25 line in 2005, as is often implied by the Bank. Indeed, this was a major focus of a high-level Commission on Global Poverty that the Bank convened in 2015 (see WB 2017a).

Even more fundamentally, the line is not clearly grounded on any social-scientific approach to measuring basic needs. Rather, the Bank defers to and relies on national poverty lines for performing such assessments, as it specifies in its response to the recommendations of the high-level Commission in WB (2017b). This refers to the original determination of the line at $1.08 (once converted into PPP terms), which was based on averaging the national poverty lines of six poor countries that had reasonably sufficient data. The revision in 2008 extended this to the national poverty lines of 15 countries.

To be clear, 'national poverty lines' in this sense refers to the politico-administrative lines – or benefit lines – mentioned above. The problem, as noted above in the case of China, is that these official poverty lines in poor countries are usually notoriously deficient, often because of resource constraints given that higher lines might oblige governments to spend more than they are able. Angus Deaton has noted this problem in the case of India (Deaton 2010). Statistical systems in many of these countries are also seriously deficient, particularly after years of structural adjustment programmes that crippled state statistical capacity (e.g., see Jerven 2013). Indeed, statistical capacity was highlighted by the Commission as a major point of concern in global poverty evaluations (WB 2017a). Moreover, even where such statistical systems are sufficient, such as in India or China, official poverty lines are a subject of constant political contestation and are regularly revised (or not) in function of these contestations between various contending power factions. For instance, as previously mentioned, the 'absolute' line in China was revised from 865 yuan per person per year in the late 1990s to 2300 yuan by 2015. Meanwhile, poverty lines in India were modestly revised upwards after the Tendulkar Committee recommended this in 2011, up to roughly 27 rupees per person per day in rural areas and 33 rupees in urban areas. However, subsequent revisions have not been made despite similar recommendations from the follow-up Rangarajan Committee in 2014, which recommended that the line be raised to 32 and 47 rupees, respectively. Since that time, the 'Great Poverty Debates' in India seem to have been eclipsed by other issues.[4]

As a result of relying on such official lines, the very birth of the dollar-a-day concept was arguably underestimated as an effective measure of even absolute poverty and it lacked any rigorous or reliable grounding in notions of basic needs. Instead, it was an artefact of the very politicised exercises of minimal poverty line setting in very poor countries with very weak social assistance systems and very constrained fiscal resources. Indeed, this is one reason that is given for the regular revisions that have been made to the line since that time, with the inclusion of new information that might better reflect absolute or basic needs. However, any serious revision according to these considerations has been resisted because it would undermine the legitimacy of the line as a gold standard of international poverty comparisons over time. For this and other reasons, the World Bank has defended its choice to remain with the original logic of using national official lines as the basis for calculating the international PPP line. It argues this case in WB (2017b, pp. 6–7), claiming 'that it would be paternalistic and disrespectful to question the choices of the world's poorest countries in terms of what constitutes poverty for them' (even though, on other matters, the World Bank has shown no proclivity to avoid paternalism in its dealings with such poor countries). As such, the precise meaning of the line is unclear, even though the idea behind it seems intuitive: a universal measure that everyone can relate to, especially people living in the United States (although perhaps less so for poor people in other countries who have never had any contact with dollars).

An additional layer of obscurity is caused by the PPP conversions used, whereby a dollar does not really mean a dollar. This is a confusion that is so rampant in the general public understanding of the line, despite World Bank attempts at public education on the matter, that it even enters in places that are purported to clarify such matters.

For instance, the Wikipedia page on 'Poverty in India'[5] states that the Indian poverty line of 26 rupees a day, or 43 USD cents, is 'lower than the World Bank's $1.25 per day *income*-based definition', emphasising 'income' as if to suggest that this partly explains the difference, which it does not. Rather, a dollar is converted to local currencies based on the estimated relative purchasing powers operating in each location (hence the PPP line of India is substantially lower than one dollar's worth of rupees at market exchange rates, whereas the PPP line of Japan is higher than one dollar's worth of yen, and so on). The World Bank Commission recommended reporting the lines in national currencies to avoid the common confusions created when journalists and others simply convert $1.90 into local currencies at market exchange rates (WB 2017a and 2017b). However, this simply resolves the public relations issue, not the meaningfulness of the lines reported in whichever currency units. The more fundamental problem is that the project of setting a universal line to which all are evaluated in a standardised manner effectively obscures the meaning of that line in any particular context.

Much of the controversy has been focused on the question of how to make a comparable basket that is relevant for poor people. This was highlighted in the debates in the early 2000s between Ravallion (2002), from the side of the World Bank, and Pogge and Reddy (2002a, 2002b), who launched the original critique. This debate was also summarised by Wade (2004) and was implicitly alluded to in WB (2017a). The problem is not just with evaluating different purchasing powers for the same goods, but that the goods consumed by the poor in each context are different, relative to both other countries but also with respect to the local setting. Poor people typically consume different types and qualities of goods than wealthier people consume. The poor also typically pay different prices than wealthier people do. Indeed, one of the largest components of the general consumer price index (CPI) of Brazil is the cost of domestic servants, which poor Brazilians obviously do not employ, and a different CPI calculation is made for the poor that excludes these types of costs.[6] The logic works in both directions; whereas it is commonly noted that poor people pay more per unit of various goods than wealthier people do (because the latter can purchase in bulk amounts, etc.), wealthier people often pay more for their goods because they shop in wealthier areas, especially in highly segregated societies (such as Brazil).

All of these considerations can have huge effects on the calculation of the basket consumed by the poor, and hence on the poverty line and the resulting poverty measures, requiring careful and meticulous study of their consumption patterns (to the extent that these can reveal basic needs rather than substandard consumption due to deficient means). However, as noted above, the PPP conversions are not based on baskets consumed by the poor but on more general standardised baskets.

In this respect, the initial idea of PPP conversions was oriented towards making comparable assessments of the domestic purchasing power of national economies, that is, GDP.[7] Because whole economies consume a much wider range of goods than poor people, it made sense to include luxury items that the poor would never consume, or else things like the cost of housing in, say, Tokyo. However, as the idea became applied to measuring poverty, the problem is that many of these items remained, despite having no relevance to the consumption of the poor, especially in poor countries. Pogge and Reddy (2002a) pointed out, for instance, that an increase in the cost of housing in Tokyo, all else held constant, would have the effect of lowering the PPP poverty line for everyone else, thereby lowering poverty rates in poor countries even though nothing would have effectively changed for the poor.

A comparable problem is evident, for example, in the well-known 'Big Mac index' produced by *The Economist*. In this index, the cost of a McDonald's Big Mac in various countries around the world is used as the basis for comparing purchasing power and whether exchange rates are over- or undervalued. The fundamental problem with this idea is that a Big Mac is a poor person's food in the US or in Europe, while it is considered to be a relatively wealthy person's meal in poor countries such as India. A better comparison, for the sake of comparing purchasing power, would be to compare the cost of a Big Mac in the US with the cost of a dal bhat typically consumed by poor people in India, which would lead to very different results. In particular, it would raise the estimate of purchasing power of ordinary Indian incomes (although the Big Mac index is not used for this purpose).

Similarly, as I have analysed with regard to debates about whether China's currency is undervalued (Fischer 2010c), an important point that is generally not considered in these debates is that a currency can be both over- and undervalued depending on whose consumption or production is referred to. While it can be debated whether China's currency was undervalued relative to its manufacturing exports in the 2000s on the basis of its increasing trade surpluses in those years, it could equally be argued that its currency was overvalued for its farmers, given that the liberalisation of international trade in agricultural goods since the 1990s had been putting downward pressure on domestic agricultural prices and, hence, on rural incomes in China.

For these types of reasons, the international comparison lines based on the PPP conversions used by the World Bank are, to a certain extent, meaningless for the purpose of actually understanding local realities facing poor people in any particular context. At the very least, they muddy the water much more than they clarify, especially for the ordinary person's comprehension. It is for this reason that many have come to increasingly argue for a return to the use of national poverty lines based on national data, that is, national lines based on credible or at least transparent and verifiable evaluations of basic needs or 'absolute' thresholds, rather than simply expressing the World Bank PPP lines in local currencies as recommended (WB 2017a) and accepted (WB 2017b) by the World Bank. By keeping things national, the basis for determining such lines becomes more tangible and accessible for public debate and contestation, and such deliberation remains within the national sphere rather than being relegated to supranational international agencies. Of course, this would not resolve the fundamental arbitrariness of such poverty lines, but at least it would make this arbitrariness more apparent and accessible for public debate.

Standard absolute approaches

As noted above, the World Bank (2017b) excuses itself from the task of evaluating the basic needs of poor people in specific contexts because it argues that basic needs or 'absolute' approaches to poverty measurement are already widely employed in the derivation of national poverty lines. Those national lines to which they respectfully defer, however, are generally administrative lines rather than 'absolute' basic needs lines determined in an independent social-scientific manner. It is nonetheless worthwhile to make a brief overview of the standard methods of the absolute approaches as this helps to highlight how even the best-case scenarios are so arbitrary and prone to subjective and often politicised judgements.

Absolute or basic needs poverty lines use a mix of both minimum calorie requirements (often known as the food poverty line) as well as an allowance for non-food items. The calorie component is in reference to physiological needs, framed in terms of the most basic level of nutrition deemed necessary for human survival. While this is attractive for giving the appearance of a hard objective standard, physiological needs are nonetheless heatedly debated in the literature and there is no consensus on what should be an appropriate number of calories to define a poverty line. Part of the problem is that there are huge individual and regional variations, such as with respect to height, climate, types of work, age, specific lifecycle needs such as those related to pregnant and lactating mothers and children, and so on. As a result, any standard will be inevitably wrong for a wide range of individuals that fall outside the standard.

In this sense, food poverty lines must be understood as reflecting population averages, for the purpose of making population-scale evaluations. However, this point itself runs counter to the logic of using of such poverty lines to target individuals for poverty relief and other benefits on the basis of individual need. That would arguably require taking into consideration individual differences in evaluations of need. While the latter option is generally seen by economists working on poverty as ideal but wildly unattainable, it also suggests that these practices of poverty measurement and targeting are not the best suited institutionally for identifying needs.

Common calorie standards typically work with 2100 calories per person per day, as is recommended by the World Bank (e.g., see Haughton and Khandker 2009). For instance, the food poverty line in China is defined according to 2100 calories (recall, this is not the official line, but the absolute line estimated by the National Bureau of Statistics, as discussed above). Sometimes 2400 calories or higher standards are used, and/or different amounts are differentiated for men and women, or for rural and urban areas (with the assumption that women need fewer calories on average than men, or that work in urban areas typically requires fewer calories than in the rural areas). India, for example, uses a standard of 2400 calories for rural areas and 2100 calories for urban areas.

As extensively documented by Sathyamala (2016), these calorie standards were whittled down over the course of the twentieth century. The Food and Agriculture Organisation of the UN (FAO) recommended 2830 calories for 'moderate activity' in 1957, whereas the Indian Council of Medical Research (ICMR) recommended 2700 calories in 1982. Lipton (1983) then recommended taking 80 per cent of the ICMR amount (2160 calories) to reflect the 'ultra-poor'. Even lower levels were then recommended to reflect sheer physiological survival, based on a fraction added to the basal metabolic rate (BMR), which, it should be recalled, is the number of calories required for the basic functioning of a body at rest, engaged in no activity, variously estimated to be in an average range of around 1200 calories. For instance, in 1985, the FAO recommended an amount of 1550 calories based on 1.27 times the BMR (Payne 1990, p. 15, cited in Sathyamala 2016, pp. 106–107). In the FAO update on minimum dietary energy requirements in 2008 (FAO 2008), a hypothetical example resulted in an overall minimum daily per person energy requirement of 1680 calories per day, which appears to be consistent with the previous reductions in standards.

These reductions in standards were not necessarily for well-established empirical or scientific reasons (even though every standard is at least justified on the basis of some studies). Rather, as noted by Sathyamala (2016), they represented a reduction of norms from optimal to minimal levels of calories (let alone nutrition, which is generally not addressed, although it is notable that the FAO has more recently started to integrate nutrition into its conception and presentation of food security).[8] Within the minimal, choices are taken on the degree to which the minimum should represent mere survival at fractions above the BMR or degrees of activity above the BMR. Indeed, given that human bodies are known to adapt to lower calorie intakes, as famously argued by Sukhatme and Margen (1978, 1982),[9] choices even involve judgements about whether poverty should be evaluated relative to such adaptive survival abilities of the poor.

The standardisation of the 2100-calorie norm therefore needs to be put into perspective because it represents a lower range of minimal norms in sedentary work (whereas most poor people are not employed in sedentary work), rather than a level that could be considered optimal for healthy functioning (especially in non-sedentary work). Even higher calorie measures, such as 2800 calories, could be considered insufficient for the needs of adults working in heavy forms of manual labour, such as rural poor people engaged in agriculture (who dominate measures of poverty), or women involved in extensive domestic work, or even the urban poor, who are generally engaged in manual labour (e.g., porters, street vendors, rickshaw drivers, domestic labourers, etc.). In particular, poor people typically work harder and longer than wealthy people in poor countries, given that poverty is not typically associated with unemployment but rather with poorly valued albeit often quite intense forms of manual labour. For instance, Sathyamala (2016, p. 118) notes that, around the same time that the Tendulkar Committee in India utilised the FAO's revised calorie norm of 1770 per person per day in its calculations in 2009, for no reason other than that it was closer to the actually observed intake of 1776 calories, the Indian Council of Medical Research recommended in 2010, based on studies of Indian populations, 2560 calories for a male of 55kg engaged in moderately heavy work and 2050 calories for a 50kg female engaged in the same (Indian Council of Medical Research 2010, p. 50). Meanwhile, the National Institute of Nutrition in India recommended 2730 calories for a 60kg man engaged in moderate work, and 3490 calories for the same man engaged in heavy work. The standardisation of the lower norms therefore already represents the institutionalisation of certain normative choices about what should constitute poverty, ultra-poverty or extreme poverty, by relegating them to the space of hunger and starvation.

The question, then, is whether one should be considered poor if one's consumption (or ability to consume based on income) falls below the recommended optimal norm, or whether the poverty line should be set at a level that is much lower than the recommended norm, and by how much and for which people. As noted above, the argument that food poverty lines should be set lower that the optimal norm is often driven by budgetary resource constraints, issues of triage in emergency situations or even Victorian-type conservative arguments against any overly generous allowances for poor people, lest this creates dependency and lessens their will to work. The argument that bodies adapt to lower calories and that Indian bodies, for instance, are smaller and more efficient (e.g., Sukhatme and Margen 1978, 1982; see Sathyamala 2016 for a critique) is also problematic because some bodies are able to adapt while others are not. More direct testing would be required to differentiate between the two, although of course we need to ask the prior question of why we should expect such poor people to adapt, especially in the knowledge that adaptation to lower calories is associated with higher morbidity and lower longevity.

Again, the arbitrariness of choice quickly becomes political and moral in terms of the standards that are applied to the poor. Indeed, as analysed by Sathyamala (2016), contestations over nutritional norms and requirements can be traced back to the mid-nineteenth century in relation to the practice of the setting of different, inferior standards for the working classes and the poor. The fact that current standards are essentially only applied to poor people in developing countries, through the deliberation of non-poor professionals, suggests that the same biases persist today, including across classes within these countries.

The choice of calorie threshold is just the starting point in food poverty measures. Subsequent steps involve decisions about what should be included in the food basket in order to constitute the required calories, and then how to price such a basket, with prices that are relevant for the poor. In terms of the basket, the standard approach is to use local consumption patterns at local prices, although this itself involves a huge latitude of subjective choice about what patterns and what prices. In particular, if the understanding of such patterns is derived from studies of the consumption of the poor or near-poor, these might themselves already represent deficient or repressed consumption.

An important factor concerns the balance between cheaper and more expensive foods. Should the diet be balanced, including vegetables and other more expensive calories, or should it be largely made up of the cheapest calories, such as grains? To give an example, the absolute rural poverty line in China in the late 1990s was based on a diet that was 90-per cent grain (Hussain 2002). A large part of the revision to the line since then (e.g., from 865 to 2300 yuan) has not been based on cost-of-living increases (which account for a fraction of the revision) but on more realistic evaluations of appropriate diets that include other, more expensive calories, even while maintaining the 2100-calorie standard.

Another fundamental question in such calculations is whether diets should be based on what people want to eat, or what is made available to them through subsidised provisioning systems – or even whether subsidised provisioning systems should provide better quality foods, for that matter, or what quality of food would remain accessible to the poor if such systems were eliminated. Any variety of foods can be compiled to make up 2100 calories, from very poor quality foods that anyone in their right mind would avoid if given the choice, to varied diets of good-quality foods aimed at attracting people to enhance their nutritional intake. Similarly, as noted by Saith (2005), should allowances be made for discretionary foods, such as sweets, alcohol or even cigarettes? And of course, who should be making these choices?

The common approach, as expressed, for instance, by Ravallion (1992), is to calculate for enough money to afford a relatively balanced diet and then to leave it to the poor to spend it wisely. If they do not, then it is their fault for having made the wrong choices. The same thinking was reflected in the early work by Seebohm Rowntree (1901), who defined poverty in terms of primary and secondary poverty, the first representing a lack of income for basic necessities and the second representing situations where income was sufficient but not actual consumption because some of the money was being spent on other things, some justified and others not, such as 'wasteful' spending on alcohol. This view represents a mix of liberal and Victorian mindsets that were typical in thinking about poverty in the nineteenth century. It finds a contemporary re-expression in the behavioural work of Banerjee and Duflo (2011), for instance, who also emphasise how poor people often make consumption choices that do not seem aligned with how we might think poor people should be making good choices (such as buying a TV). Notably, this is a vision that reduces 'good' consumption to its purely utilitarian value of supporting workers to maintain their most basic functions.

The next step is in the pricing of food. Ideally, these should be the prices faced by the poor, but as noted above, for what food? What if prices are used for food we think the poor should eat, even though they eat other food? The standard approach is to use consumption surveys of the poor or near-poor and to base consumption profiles and prices on this information, but again there is the question of whether such surveys are able to acquire the appropriate information, or whether the information acquired reflects repressed consumption. Such surveys might hide prices that the poor are occasionally forced to face, particularly in the case of repressed consumption, or situations where the poor might face exploitation in pricing, which surveyors might have difficulty in detecting.

Regional price differences can also wreak havoc on the accuracy of estimates, particularly if national lines are used for evaluation purposes (such as with PPP poverty lines). A single national line carries the bias that poverty tends to be overestimated in cheaper rural locations and underestimated in more expensive locations, such as in large cities. An excellent example of this can found in the work of Hussain (2003) on urban poverty in China. Up to the time of his work, the conventional wisdom based on national poverty lines was that poverty rates were higher in the western China and lower in eastern China. For instance, Khan and Riskin (2001, p. 67) concluded from their regression analysis on a large national survey in 1995 that 'the incidence of broad poverty is, by and large, lower for the provinces with higher per capita income. Spearman's rank correlation coefficient between the provincial rank in head count rural poverty and the provincial rank in per capita rural income is highly significant at –0.69.' Hussain (2003) demonstrates that the correlation – at least with respect to urban poverty – is to a large extent an artefact of differences in price levels, not poverty rates. With access to urban income and price data of sufficient disaggregation for 1998, he was able to construct an urban 'absolute' poverty line for each province individually. On the basis of this, he found that urban poverty rates in the southwest were in fact lower than the national average, very close to those of the southeast, and considerably lower than those of the north and northeast (Hussain 2003, p. 18). He was not able to conduct the same revision for rural areas because of lack of disaggregated price data but, based on experience in rural China, it is clear that a similar corrective would have applied.

Such a radical revision of the received wisdom reinforces the point that poverty rates measured by a single national line are not comparable across provinces or regions with different price levels, even though they might reflect at least some notion of poverty within each province or region, as measured by an arbitrary line. However, for purposes of evaluation, even an arbitrary line should be indexed to local inflation rates rather than national inflation rates, given that the latter again introduces a bias over time. These are fundamental problems with poverty mapping using national lines, especially between rural and urban areas, given that such maps reveal as much price differences as poverty differences across regions. Many national poverty measurement systems do use regional lines, or differentiate between rural and urban areas, such as in India, where each state sets its own line, in addition to the national line that is used for evaluation and budgetary allocations from the centre to the states. However, again, such systems are usually tied to the allocation of benefits in the population and for determining eligibility for poverty relief, and hence political-administrative and budgetary issues usually overwhelm any of the more social-scientific concerns of poverty measurement.

Beyond the determination of the food poverty line, even greater methodological problems and arbitrariness enter with the determination of non-food basic needs, such as fuel, housing, clothing, transport, etc. While food arguably has at least some underlying scientific basis to guide the debate, the determination of non-food items is far more arbitrary. As described by Saith (2005), there are a variety of methods, such as: simply adding 50 per cent extra to the food poverty line; using Engels curves to determine a more precise proportion; or observing the non-food consumption of those whose food expenditure or even total income is on the food line, with the assumption that if something is an absolute non-food basic need, then those people will forego food in order to consume it (such as fuel to cook food). Again, in all these methods, we are not even asking the equivalent of the food question, which is what should non-food needs be and whether they are being met. The risk again is that we are simply basing our poverty lines on compounded measures of repressed consumption.

As a last step to poverty measurement, the line is combined with the survey data to compute a measure of poverty. Much of the focus in the poverty studies literature is on these measures, such as the straightforward headcount ratio, the Foster-Greer-Thorbecke Index for depth and severity of poverty, or the competing Sen poverty index (e.g., see Shorrocks 1995) and so on. The increasing complexity of these measures – to capture issues such as depth of poverty or inequality among the poor – often come, however, with a loss of tangible meaning. Moreover, while the technicality of these various measures receives much of the attention in scholarship, this is the stage that is actually most removed from the political and moral choices involved in poverty measurement, given that the arbitrariness of choice primarily enters through previous stages of determining the line. This allows statisticians and technocratic practitioners to feel that they are removed from such politics, particularly if they are simply using national survey data and poverty lines rather than collecting and calculating these themselves, as noted above with respect to the World Bank's position in its 'Monitoring Global Poverty' report for 2016 (WB 2017b). However, through the process, they place formal technocratic legitimacy onto processes that, in their essence, are fundamentally political. This puts the relevance of these measurement issues in perspective, especially the very precise ones, which run the danger of methodological fetishism over the creation of useful and reliable analysis.

Sensitivity and evaluation over time

To wrap up, even the most restrictive form of basic-needs poverty line is arbitrary, given that it is unable to provide any reliable indication of whether basic needs are being met. Depending on the range of assumptions that are made at a variety of different points in determining the poverty line, a large range of poverty rates can be estimated on the same data. The quandary is all the more problematic given that the incomes of populations in poor countries tend to be densely clustered around a typical poverty line, resulting in an extreme sensitivity of poverty estimates to small adjustments to the line, whether or not these are accurate.

Examples are replete in the scholarship. Székely et al. (2000) applied sensitivity analysis to household survey data from 17 Latin American countries in the 1990s. By varying the poverty line parameters within 'reasonable boundaries',[10] they estimated poverty rates as lying anywhere from 12.7 per cent to 65.8 per cent of the total population. The ranking of countries with respect to poverty rates was also highly sensitive to their exercise. Hussain (2003) demonstrates a similar point with respect to urban poverty in China in terms of both sensitivity and rank orderings across Chinese provinces. Helwege and Birch (2007, p. 6) note that, ironically, 'the institutions that generate poverty data are well aware of how methodological choices affect poverty estimates. They simply have not established standardized approaches to measuring poverty.' Hence, in their assessment of alternative poverty estimates from the World Bank and the United Nations for Latin America, Helwege and Birch advise caution in interpreting trends from any of these data.

Practitioners of poverty measurement have acknowledged these pitfalls for decades. Indeed, in the opening pages of his seminal text

Poverty Comparisons, Ravallion (1992, p. 2–3) admits that poverty lines are arbitrary. He argues, however, that even arbitrarily chosen lines nonetheless allow for comparison and evaluation so long as they are accurately adjusted over time. The importance is in the evaluation, he maintains, not the precise poverty rate.

However, the possibility of adjusting poverty lines over time merely compounds these problems of poverty measurement. It does not absolve these measures of their original methodological precarity. In particular, the question of adjustment over time leads to the classic quandary of whether poverty trends reflect actual changes in poverty or else errors of adjustment to the poverty line or other elements of the calculus. This is particularly important in most poor countries where populations are generally clustered around the line, such that small changes in the line produce large changes in the poverty head count. Trends can also vary depending on the level of the line.

A good example of this can be drawn from rural poverty estimates in China in the late 1990s, as already discussed above. As shown in Table 4.1, rural poverty was decreasing in China from 1998 to 2000 according to the unreasonably low official ('benefit') poverty line of 635 yuan per person per year (i.e., the one usually cited in World Bank publications in the early 2000s), but it was rising according to the more credible absolute poverty line calculated by the China National Bureau of Statistics. The latter line was based on the estimated average minimum annual income required per person for the food and non-food items deemed essential to be able to subsist at approximately 2100 calories a day, at local prices and with local consumption patterns. The National Bureau of Statistics in China estimated this line to be 880 yuan per person in 1997 and 1998, and 865 yuan in 1999 to 2001, the adjustment reflecting deflation at the time.[11] As noted above, many in China argued that even this line was far too low, including Premier Wen Jiabao in 2003.

The difference between the two main national lines – 230/245 yuan per person per year (about 25 USD at the time) – was extremely significant due to the clustering of the rural population around and between the two lines. As shown in Table 3.1, the absolute line, which was about one-third higher than the benefit line, doubled the national poverty headcount in 1998 and almost tripled it in 2000. This sensitivity is the result of clustering, such that small changes in the line produce large changes in the poverty headcount. As a result,

TABLE 3.1 National rural poverty rates in China measured by different lines

	1998	1999	2000
Official line: 635 rmb (%)	4.8	3.7	3.6
Absolute line: 880/865 rmb (%)	9.5	9.8	10.1
Ratio absolute/official	1.98	2.65	2.81
Official line (millions of people)	42.1	34.0	32.1
Absolute line (millions of people)	86.6	90.0	93.2
Difference (millions of people)	44.5	56.0	61.1

Source: Hussain (2002, p. 6), cited in Fischer (2005, pp. 96–99).

different poverty rate trends can be observed at each line,[12] reflecting the degree to which the effects of rising inequality, for instance, were differentiated among various income strata within the poorest decile or quintile of the population. Over these years, during which China was growing rapidly at 6 to 9 per cent a year in real terms despite the East Asian crisis, the most extreme forms of poverty appeared to have fallen to a very small share (or else the official line had depreciated over the 1990s to an irrelevantly low level due to insufficient indexing). However, rates of absolute poverty were apparently on the rise, at least for a short time (the incongruence appears to have been ironed out as the economy started to surge from the early 2000s onwards). This case might be taken as one of the outliers in the matrices of Dollar and Kraay (2002) in their argument that growth is good for the poor. Given the size of the population involved, it is an important outlier.

Similar issues have led to fierce debates in India, the other country driving most of the commonly cited global poverty reduction since the 1980s (see Himanshu and Sen (2014) for a recent review of these debates). Based on their efforts to correct inconsistencies in Indian survey data from 1999–2000, Himanshu and Sen (2004) concluded that there had been little poverty reduction in India in the 1990s, contrary to the dominant consensus. Deaton and Kozel (2005, p. 117) contended that such claims are 'frankly political' and that there is good evidence that poverty fell. However, further findings presented by Himanshu (2007), based on new data from

2004–2005, confirmed his earlier results that most poverty reduction since the early 1990s was concentrated in the period from 1999 to 2005. While these findings continue to be met with a barrage of dismissal, they were broadly supported by the Tendulkar Committee, the expert group of the Planning Commission of the Government of India (GOI) that was set up to review these matters (GOI 2009; also see Himanshu 2010). They also corroborate much more coherently with the findings of other studies that calorie deprivation had actually increased in India in the 1990s (e.g., see Meenakshi and Vishwanathan 2003).[13]

While some might argue that the latter incongruence is due to consumer sovereignty (i.e., poor people choosing to spend their extra income on bidis rather than chapattis), the more plausible explanation is that some of the poverty calculations are quite simply inaccurate or that poverty lines are set too low and not sufficiently adjusted over time. The fact that measures of hunger and malnutrition remain stubbornly high in India (see the evidence reviewed by Sathyamala 2016), suggests that this continues to be the case up to the present. Indeed, similar incongruences of slow progress in hunger and malnutrition despite decent poverty reduction are observed in other countries (e.g., Ecuador) and globally (e.g., see FAO 2017 and WHO 2013). In addition, there have been increasing observations of widespread food insecurity in rich countries such as the US, among families that would technically be well above an 'absolute' poverty threshold in the way it is calculated for poor countries. These incongruences suggest that something has gone awry with our conventional practices of measuring absolute poverty.

Our ability to track poverty trends over time is critically based on our presumption that we can accurately measure all of the changing cost factors faced by poor households together with their changing patterns of livelihood and consumption. This is especially challenging in contexts of the often-rapid socio-economic structural changes associated with development, such as migration, urbanisation, monetisation, commoditisation or an increased reliance on wage labour. Notably, the World Bank revised its estimates for global PPP poverty rates upwards in 2008, including an upward adjustment of about 40 per cent for China. This was based on new and improved cost of living data from 2005, which revealed a substantially higher cost of living in developing countries than was previously estimated from older data.

However, Chen and Ravallion (2008) optimistically stressed that, although poorer than previously thought, the world was just as successful in poverty reduction at the revised estimates, which simply moved the rates upwards but not the trends. They nonetheless reached this conclusion simply by deflating the new PPP poverty lines by the official consumer price indices (CPI) of each country back to 1981 (ibid., pp. 14–15). In other words, the fact that the resultant trends were the same as before is in part an artefact of their assumption that the source of error was the same in 1981 as it was 2005, i.e., that the changing cost structures and levels faced by the poor are represented by the overall CPI indices of each country. The other possibility that they sidestep is that the poor might have faced higher price inflation than that represented by the CPI, or that the older cost data might have been accurate for the earlier period and that cost levels did in fact increase accordingly.[14] That the poor might have faced greater cost-of-living increases than suggested by the general consumer prices indices is quite possible given the notable increases in inequality in many countries over the same period.[15] Thus, while Chen and Ravallion provided a politically convenient narrative, many intractable problems remained lost in past surveys. Similar problems plagued the revisions in 2015, based on new 2011 data, as discussed above.

Secular underestimations of absolute poverty

Several structural and institutional processes are arguably at the root of these incongruences of monotonically decreasing rates of absolute poverty across the world versus ongoing manifestations of distress and deprivations among the same poor populations. These processes have arguably resulted in a chronic secular (i.e., long-term) underestimation of money-metric poverty overtime over the course of the postwar period, or, more precisely, an overestimation of its reduction over time. There are at least three fundamental reasons for this. The first is more proximate and institutional, regarding the commodification of various services and/or the proliferation of private previsioning in social services over the course of the last 30 to 40 years, in what is often referred to as the neoliberal period (as discussed in the Introduction). The second and third are more structural, with reference to transitions away from 'subsistence'-based agrarian systems, and food and nutrition transitions.

The bias against universalistic social provisioning

With regard to the first institutional process of commodification and privatisation, the fundamental Achilles Heel of money-metric approaches to poverty measurement is that education and health costs are mostly not included in the calculation of poverty lines. Laderchi et al. (2003, p. 249) imply this problem by referring to an implicit bias in these approaches in favour of private income as against public goods provision given that they invariably include only private resources and omit social income, such as goods and services provided publicly (school, clinics, etc.). However, the problem is more specific than this.

The exclusion of health and education costs from money-metric poverty lines is for technical reasons, given that they constitute large and highly irregular expenditure items across households and across time. Hence, short of calculating individualised poverty lines for each household surveyed in each period, which is practically close to impossible in the absence of a functional and enforced government income-reporting system (as is the case in practically all developing countries), these costs are generally ignored with the assumption that they are randomly distributed across households and are generally proportionate across periods. Accordingly, they would not undermine the representativeness of the resultant poverty measures and trends. Notably, this solution does not address the issue of poverty targeting for actual social provisioning. It is only concerned with the social-scientific goal of performing accurate representative evaluations.

However, even with respect to representative surveying, the problem remains that education and health costs are included in the expenditures of surveyed households. This renders the comparison of poverty rates very difficult across households, let alone across regions with different provisioning systems or else across time when the costing and/or supply of education or health care changes. Increasing costs of education or health care, or else increasing school enrolments in schools that charge fees, would be invisible to most conventional poverty lines even though they effectively raise the poverty line for a large proportion of households. To the extent that large health costs are financed by incurring debt, they might even be reflected as increasing expenditures and falling expenditure poverty. These implications lead to an important source of underestimation of money-metric poverty rate trends in such contexts. This weakness is recognised in some of the literature, but it is also generally sidestepped in the same literature (e.g., see Ravallion, 1992, pp. 12, 28), for the simple reason that accounting for these factors – which is possible in theory – would render surveying unwieldy and extremely expensive in practice, and would also introduce ever more arbitrary assumptions and potential for measurement errors.

The innovative work by van Doorslaer et al. (2005) is one exception in this regard. Merely by deducting catastrophic out-of-pocket payments for health care from the expenditures of households surveyed in 11 low- and middle-income countries in Asia (most surveys taken around 2000), they show that poverty rates across Asia increased from 19.3 per cent to 22 per cent, or an increase of 14 per cent or 78 million people. The biggest increases were in Vietnam, where poverty rates increased by one-third, China (by 19 per cent), Bangladesh (by 17 per cent) and India (by 12 per cent). However, this does not take into account the repressed expenditure of poor people who would have otherwise spent more on necessary health care were it not for lack of resources, which is a major problem that the authors consider but cannot measure.[16]

As insightful as this work is, it is nonetheless based on insights from single surveys taken at particular points in time. The results offer no indication on how these considerations might alter our perception of trends over time, particularly in cases where education and health care costs have increased substantially. For example, falling income poverty rates in China since the early 1980s do not factor into consideration the parallel shift from very cheap to very expensive health care or post-primary education. More specifically, while the general consumer price index in China remained more or less unchanged between 1997 and 2003, prices for tuition and child care more than doubled over the same period, and prices for health care services almost doubled (see Figure 3.1).

Tuition and health care services were especially inflationary in some of the poorest western provinces (see Figures 3.2 to 3.4). In Qinghai, where prices for health care services increased by more than six times by 2008. In Xinjiang, they increased by more than four times by 2005. Both price categories almost doubled by 2003 in Gansu, the second-poorest province in China in terms of per-capita GDP. In these three western provincial cases, much of the divergence took place around

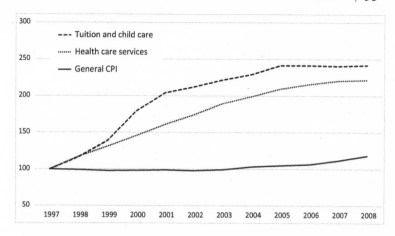

FIGURE 3.1 Selected prices indices for China, 1997–2008 (1997=100)

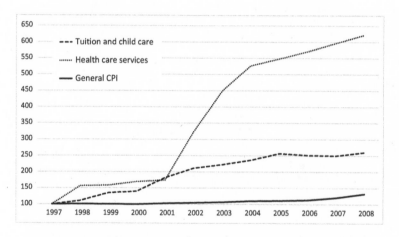

FIGURE 3.2 Selected prices indices for Qinghai Province, 1997–2008 (1997=100)

2000, reflecting a form of shock therapy with respect to the pricing of these social services under what was otherwise a reorientation of regional development policy towards this region. The sharp increases in tuition would have been particularly onerous for poor households given simultaneous efforts by the government to increase enrolment rates (see Fischer 2009a, 2014a; Fischer and Zenz 2018). By ignoring such dramatically changing price structures (as do Chen and Ravallion 2008), we cannot know to what degree the appearance of falling

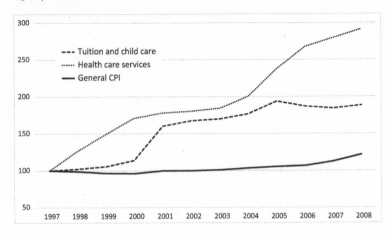

FIGURE 3.3 Selected prices indices for Gansu Province, 1997–2008 (1997=100)

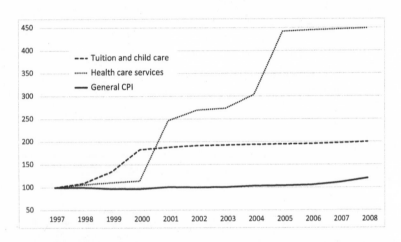

FIGURE 3.4 Selected prices indices for Xinjiang, 1997–2008 (1997=100)

Source for all figures: Fischer (2005, p. 48), based on data compiled from various China Statistical Yearbooks.

poverty rates merely represents increasing relative prices for these essential services that are not included in the poverty line.

It is in this sense that absolute money-metric poverty measures can be said to be biased against universalistic modes of social policy. A movement towards free education or health care financed through progressive taxation would not necessarily appear as decreasing poverty even though it would lower the effective poverty line for households previously paying fees. Similarly, it is difficult to calibrate poverty rates in any meaningful way across countries with very different provisioning systems, such as between Cuba, with its free health care and education, and Vietnam, which had the greatest reliance on out-of-pocket payments among the Asian cases studied by van Doorslaer et al. (2005). Indeed, a significant proportion of the appearance of falling poverty in the latter case or in China might actually signify the commodification of previously socialised health care and education.

The general trend across most countries since the early 1980s has been in the direction of commodification, increasing private provisioning, cost recovery and so forth. In many cases these changes have been impelled quite dramatically by the austerity imposed on government finances by recurrent financial crises. It is in this sense that these institutional changes would have in principle led to an increasing underestimation of poverty rates over these decades. The precise empirical effects are difficult to evaluate outside of specific contexts and cases, although the logic of this implication is quite clear given the way that poverty lines are constructed. Indeed, it is ironic that the poverty impact of quite marginal programmes such as cash transfers have been so widely and enthusiastically researched, with the endorsement and financing of major donors and international organisations, whereas these more systemic issues that are much more significant to poverty dynamics as well as to the dynamics of social integration and stratification have been largely neglected. That they are far more difficult to fit into convincing econometric techniques of analysis is a poor excuse for the neglect.

The erosion of subsistence capacity

The second two processes are more structural in nature and less specifically associated to the neoliberal era, even though they have been exacerbated by it. The first is related to the gradual transition of rural populations out of situations that might be described as subsistence-based over the course of the last century, as briefly discussed in the first chapter. Standard measures of income, consumption and poverty under-evaluate the implicit value of what I have called 'subsistence capacity' (Fischer 2006, 2008b, 2014a). Hence, they exaggerate the significance of an increase in explicit monetary incomes as rural livelihoods become increasingly commodified.

In deference to Polly Hill (1986), this term 'subsistence' needs to be used with caution. In her frontal critique of the conventional wisdom in much of development economics, she pointed out that the standard derogatory association of subsistence with poverty or traditional pre-market economic systems may actually be the inverse to how subsistence is subjectively experienced by rural communities (see pp. 18–20). Moreover, she argued that such associations ignore inequality in rural communities given that, within such communities, it is usually only rich households that can hope for attaining a degree of self-sufficiency and it is precisely these households that also enjoy the most lucrative non-farming occupations. On this basis, she criticises the common assumption that traditional agriculture is characterised by degrees of subsistence, which are inversely related to market integration.

Keeping these points in mind, subsistence can nonetheless be characterised in terms of households or communities that consume much of their own output and then trade the rest, if and when some is left over. This differs from commercial farming, in which farmers sell most of what they produce and derive most of their consumption through similarly purchasing commodities from others. The latter can be characterised as a commoditised form of production, exchange and consumption.[17]

Accordingly, 'subsistence capacity' can be conceived as an ability to subsist on one's own production. Absolute subsistence capacity refers to the ability of a household to produce a surplus above the subsistence needs required to reproduce itself economically. At the most basic level, this can be understood in terms of food. This meaning is essentially synonymous with food security at a household, family or community level and, in this sense, also complies with Hill's contention.[18]

As I have argued in Fischer (2006, 2008b, 2014a) based on my fieldwork in western China, maintaining an asset base at a level sufficient to meet absolute subsistence capacity allows people to maintain autonomy from labour market dependence (or labour commodification). This in turn represents a fundamental source of economic opportunity given that it provides an ability to act strategically, primarily by avoiding dependence on subordinated forms of employment and/or by being able to wait for more lucrative or strategic opportunities, such as with respect to selling surplus production when prices are higher rather than lower. Hence, rural dwellers naturally seek autonomy from such dependence. One way is to re-embed themselves in an asset base, such as by investing in land and livestock, as a means to buffer themselves against the potential disadvantages of labour commodification in the short term, even though social and economic structural changes might simultaneously undermine the sustainability of these subsistence-based livelihood strategies in the medium to long term.

Subsistence in this sense serves both instrumental as well as symbolic (or cultural) wealth functions within rural communities. Contrary to arguments that such valuation of subsistence is only a characteristic of those living close to destitution, this idea that subsistence is an instrument for wealth is comparable to the way that monetary wealth provides freedom within a fully commoditised non-rural setting. Few would contest that the rich can do what they like with their disposable wealth regardless of whether their actions are deemed rational or otherwise; this is the privilege of wealth. Similarly, the ability to be unemployed in most poor countries is actually an attribute of middle- or upper-class status; the truly poor have no capacity to be unemployed. They must work, whatever the work, and whatever the remuneration. Indeed, even the ability to survive an unpaid internship, as is one of the pathways into eventually getting paid work in the UN system, in many NGOs, and increasingly in the private sector, generally depends on having some reserve of wealth, which thereby becomes a class- and/ or wealth-based screening mechanism within such forms of employment. In other words, this suggests a more generalised experience of 'subsistence' as wealth. This understanding of what it means to attain subsistence (and thus, in principle, to be a 'subsistence farmer') may not accord to the ways that non-rural academics or policy-makers expect 'disciplined' or 'deserving' poor people to behave, but this is more likely due to a misreading of the clues rather than any developmental deficiency on the part of rural-dwellers.

Along similar lines, an extension of the 'commodity' or cash economy is not necessarily antithetical to these subsistence strategies. Contemporary rural-dwellers across developing countries are invariably involved with the commodity cash economy in various ways, some due to choice and others necessity, and thus they cannot base their livelihoods solely on subsistence household production, if ever they did, as noted by Hill (1986). This is partly because they purchase, consume or invest in modern goods, be they mobile phones, motorcycles or fertilizers, among many others. Perhaps more importantly, rapidly increasing fees for education and health care in many contexts also act as strong compelling forces for rural-dwellers to move into cash-earning activities, particularly in light of livelihood strategies that target post-primary schooling for at least one child. Scarcity of rural cash-earning opportunities in turn drives rural-to-urban migration.

However, the cash imperative is often overemphasized as a driver of labour commodification, given that it can easily co-exist with subsistence-based livelihood strategies. In fact, the combination can be ideal. If subsistence capacity is sufficient, it offers a choice as to how and when to engage in cash-earning activities and these in turn can be used to bolster subsistence capacity. It offers autonomy from a dependence on regular low-wage employment, or from the forced selling of produce at inopportune moments, both of which can have impoverishing implications. The ability to wait thereby confers an ability to access better opportunities if and when they arise.

In this sense, the subjective proclivity for subsistence within rural communities is not merely cultural or symbolic. It also carries important instrumental wealth functions, not only in terms of the risk-averse insurance principle as argued by authors such as James Scott (1976), but also in terms of providing a position from which market and other forms of economic opportunity can be engaged advantageously. In other words, reinforcing subsistence capacity can serve as an important wealth-supporting strategy within rural transitions into more marketized forms of production, exchange and employment.

The problem, however, is that standard measures of income or consumption are poorly adapted to reflect such wealth-supporting functions, in the sense that a dollar of subsistence production and consumption is valued the same as any other dollar earned and spent. Hence, transition away from subsistence forms of production, such as when subsistence capacity becomes eroded and households are increasingly forced into labour market dependence, remains mostly invisible to household income or expenditure surveys, even though it can have a massive effect on the subjective and objective wellbeing of people undergoing such transitions.

I detected this in my own research in the Tibetan areas of western China through the observation that, although rural Tibetans were among the poorest in rural China in terms of incomes and consumption, they were among the richest in terms of asset ownership. The incongruence is partly due to the fact that rural household surveys are designed with farming communities in mind and are poorly adapted to pastoralist communities. More precisely, pastoral savings (i.e., an increase in herd size) are recorded as increases in productive fixed assets and are thereby not reflected in the data on pastoral household incomes, whereas savings of grain output are calculated as part of farming household incomes. However, it is also a reflection of relatively strong subsistence capacity, which is not mirrored in the income or consumption data but definitely in the wage expectations common among such Tibetans, as well as in their non-wage expectations regarding such things as daily hours of work, discipline, intensity of work, or tolerance of absenteeism. According to my observations, these tended to be higher than those of Chinese migrants coming from otherwise more affluent regions (in rural income or consumption terms).

Moreover, in certain cases there might even be an inverse relationship between income and assets. A remote pastoral household might appear poor in terms of income (and in terms of education and health) yet possess substantial livestock assets, enough to offer considerable subsistence consumption and even bouts of conspicuous consumption. In contrast, a pastoral household located closer to a populated area might have much more circulating income, due to its integration into the 'commodity economy', even while its asset base is depleted due to shortage of quality pastures or stronger state enforcement of livestock limits. Asset depletion might even be reflected as increasing income for short periods of time, such as when a herder is hard-pressed for cash in one year and sells off a larger part of their herd than they normally would. In these cases, an increase in income wealth may in fact represent considerable subsistence impoverishment.

All of these considerations suggest that there is considerable wealth generated and stored in subsistence-based rural economies that is often poorly captured by conventional household income and expenditure surveys, and that people living within such economies may be considerably wealthier than the income or expenditure data suggest. Moreover, these conventional measures may be poorly conceived for capturing the wealth dimensions of transition from more subsistence to more monetised or commoditised livelihoods. Smooth monotonic increases in income may not necessarily reflect actual changes in overall wealth and might hide the erosion of asset-based subsistence through population and economic pressures, or through government policies that undermine this asset base, such as resettlement or land reforestation programmes, or the imposition of livestock limits.

The decline in food relative to other needs

The second structural process that arguably leads to a secular overestimation of absolute poverty reduction is related to food or nutritional transitions, from insecure and perhaps austere, but more diverse, higher-quality and nutritionally rich foods, to ample supplies of cheap and highly processed, calorie-rich but nutritionally deficient foods. The best examples of the latter include sugars and oils, which used to be relatively luxurious items in the pre-industrial past but have now become so cheap that they have become part of the staple of the diets of even poor people. Indeed, this helps to explain the rise of obesity among the relatively poor in middle-income countries (e.g., see Kobiyama 2013).[19]

However, because poverty lines are focused on crude calories and on actual consumption patterns among the poor, they overlook these shifts in the quality of diet. Over time, this effectively amounts to comparing goods of different quality in the basket of the poverty line. The shift towards an increasing cheapness of calories therefore has an effect of reducing the poverty line to a declining lowest common denominator.

The falling terms of trade of such calories in particular means that calorie-based poverty lines are anchored on a foundation that is being compressed over time relative to other expenditures and consumption needs, especially in the context of urbanisation whereby the latter become more prominent.[19] This thereby introduces a further subtle but powerful source of underestimation in measures of 'absolute' near-starvation deprivation over time. In other words, productivity in the contemporary production of food, for instance, has increased to such an extent over the last century that substantial surpluses have been achieved even in the face of rising population. As a result, real food prices – or the terms of trade of food relative to other goods – are at close to an all-time low in historical terms, even despite the recent spike in food prices. For instance, Fuglie and Wang (2013) estimate that, on average, real food prices have fallen by 1 per cent a year between 1900 and 2010. Given rising productivity and the mass processing of cheap (and cheap-quality) foods, combined with increasingly integrated international markets, it is understandable how the condition of poverty has gradually changed over the last century from one of food scarcity and starvation to one in which calorie sufficiency is relatively easier to secure (although not necessarily nutrition sufficiency), while other compelling social needs take over in precedence, as discussed in the previous chapter.

Insofar as absolute poverty is restrictively designed to measure a minimal ability to procure food (not necessarily an ability or decision to procure food in light of other social needs or desires), it is understandable that this transformation in the condition of modern poverty would introduce a gradual underestimation of such poverty lines over time. Insofar as the ratio of food to non-food needs is not substantially revised to reflect the changing balance of relative costs, at least part of the long-term secular decline in such poverty rates would be reflective of this underestimation.

Conclusion

This rather extensive chapter provided an overview of money-metric approaches to measuring poverty, which are considered the most precise and restrictive, and serve as the cornerstone of various development goals by most international organisations. The aim was to demonstrate how even these approaches are inherently arbitrary, to the extent that they are unable to provide any reliable indication of whether basic needs are being met and how this might be changing over time. This is before consideration of all of the problems associated with international poverty comparisons, with reference to the ever-altering, one-dollar-or-whatever-a-day purchasing-power-parity poverty lines of the World Bank. Even if we accept the arbitrariness of a line but then adopt this as a means of evaluation, this merely kicks the problem forward into the classic quandary of whether poverty trends over time reflect actual changes or else errors of adjustment and even of conception.

This intrinsic arbitrariness is ideological given the fundamentally normative and political character of the wide range of choices that are involved in producing data sets, and in setting lines and adjusting them over time. The fact that they are so arbitrary also renders them prone to political manipulations in application. The evaluative emphasis of these approaches essentially sidesteps the problem that, once applied to the social and political economy realities of policy-making and actual distributions of benefits and poverty relief, the problems of these poverty measures become compounded by social and power relations. Indeed, in this respect, official poverty lines need to be understood first and foremost as the outcome of complex processes of political contestation and the balance of power between various contending power factions that find an interest in weighing in on these measures.

Money-metric poverty measures nonetheless remain attractive because they yield exact, seemingly objective and scientific statistics, in a technical manner that can be compared and analysed with an ever-expanding battery of increasingly sophisticated statistical techniques. Yet, we must ask what we are buying into when we adopt these approaches. At the very least, we must engage in them with awareness of their fundamentally ideological and political nature, as well as with transparency, honesty and humility as to their limitations.

This is all the more important because these measures do remain as one valuable means to aggregate within one important dimension of poverty, among a range of other imperfect options, and aggregation is also a problem with other approaches. They do have biases and it is essential to understand these biases in order to compensate for them, but they reveal very important information, even though they do not reveal all of the information that is relevant to understand poverty, nor were they necessarily conceived to do so. The danger of diluting this information with attempts to add in different dimensions and elements intended to better reflect wellbeing or other objectives is that this original information then becomes obscured or even lost. Indeed, this obscurity might even advantage powerful economic interests and, despite the progressive intentions, dilute our ability to understand and contest certain core aspects of power and wealth in modern economies as they manifest for poor people.

In the third section of this chapter, an elaboration was given on how the standard absolute money-metric poverty measures are arguably prone to a secular tendency to gradually underestimate absolute poverty over time in the context of structural and institutional changes associated with development and in particular during the recent neoliberal phase of change. One fundamental source of bias is based on declining terms of trade for food, which gives greater relative prominence to non-food essential needs over time. The second is in terms of the shift from self-provisioning to commoditised consumption, which in many respects overestimates the value of the latter relative to the functional value of previous subsistence modes of livelihood. The last is more proximate to the neoliberal era of commoditised social provisioning, in particular the substantial commoditisation and privatisation of health and education. A fundamental problem with money-metric measures of poverty is that they are biased by design against universalistic and decommoditised forms of social provisioning, such that a move towards greater commoditisation can actually be reflected as an improvement in poverty, all else held constant.

Indeed, in the face of global productive capacity, if anything it is surprising that so much of the world's population still subsists under or just above such minimally defined food-based poverty lines. Part of this is undoubtedly related to agrarian conditions in much of the Global South, where peasant farmers struggle to get by on the low food prices received for their output on shrinking per-person plots of land (if they produce a surplus), relative to rising prices in the range of other social needs (such as in health care and schooling, or else in inputs to production). However, much is not agrarian, particularly as poor people increasingly move out of such conditions, albeit bringing their poverty with them. Rather, as discussed in Chapter 6, much of it is related to the valuing of labour more generally, even as it is integrated into value chains that generate enormous value for those who control them. In this sense, workers integrated within such chains are still living under the predicament posited by classical economists such as Malthus, Ricardo and Marx, who assumed that workers' wages would always be squeezed down to a level of subsistence, that is, subsistence minimally defined by the price of food. Because absolute poverty lines continue to be established by the price of food, such tendencies could ironically be reflected as declining poverty rates correspondent to declining real prices for food.

This brings us back to the crucial question of social needs and how these are calculated by absolute lines. The mission is not impossible, but it is one that requires much more nuance and context specificity, as well as a much greater broadening of the scope of what we should include in the basket that is used to set the poverty line, all of which the World Bank has refused to do up to the present, despite some of the recommendations from its own high-level Commission (WB 2017a). As a result, we are left with poverty standards that are minimalist, whittled down to the necessities for mere food survival and that are arguably depreciating over time because of the logic of their construction, rather than anything that approaches a standard of decency or that can match the profound transformations that have been witnessed around the world over the past half-century.

However, even with the inclusion of a broader range of social needs, the fundamental weakness of these lines remains with the question of social goods such as health and education. Such goods render the comparability of absolute lines very questionable across contexts with very different welfare and social provisioning systems, in particular between those with more universalistic provisioning, free at the point of use and funded progressively through direct taxation, versus the less-universalistic systems, with user fees at the point of use and high degrees of stratified privatised provisioning. Ultimately, such differences cannot and should not be resolved through comparative poverty measures but instead need to be subjected to social and political debate regarding the types of societies we wish to inhabit together.

For these types of reasons, the international comparison line based on the PPP conversions used by the World Bank are to a large extent meaningless for the purpose of actually understanding local realities facing poor people in any particular context. At the very least, they muddy the water much more than they clarify, especially for the comprehension of ordinary people, and they render intangible and inaccessible a subject that should be a matter of national public debate and deliberation. In particular, making the arbitrariness of poverty lines more apparent would provide the basis for contestation by the poor or those representing the poor, whereas the opacity and obscurity of these measures has a tendency to disempower such contestation if only through the force of sheer incomprehension.

4 | MULTIDIMENSIONAL MEASURES OF POVERTY

As noted in the previous chapter, a fundamental problem with money-metric approaches to poverty measurement is the dilemma of how to deal with public goods such as health and education, or else how to evaluate actual outcomes in health and education that are difficult if not impossible to monetise. Both health and education expenses are not included in the calculation of money-metric poverty lines. They are reflected in expenditure surveys, although these only reflect what people spend and consume on such services, not necessarily what they would need to spend or consume, nor the quality of these services or their importance to wellbeing. As usual, revealed expenditures might in fact represent repressed expenditures relative to a reasonable assessment of need.

In response to these conundrums, many scholars opt to promote multidimensional measures of poverty, inspired in part by the capability approach promulgated by Amartya Sen (for instance, see Alkire 2002; Reddy et al. 2006). In particular, multidimensional measures are seen to address some of the incongruence between income poverty and wider human development outcomes, such as situations where falling money-metric poverty corresponds with stagnant or deteriorating health and education indicators, as noted previously with respect to nutrition in India, or else opposite situations where poor people have reasonable levels of health and education.

Although multidimensionality is often characterised as the new and improved cutting edge of poverty research, recognition and measurement of the multiple dimensions of poverty are far from novel. As discussed in Chapter 2, the measurement of non-economic dimensions of poverty draw in particular from the battery of direct measures of poverty and/or wellbeing that have long been a cornerstone of poverty studies, as well as in other fields such as epidemiology, nutrition or education. The use of such measures has evolved throughout the twentieth century along a variety of tangents. Earlier postwar versions were developed in the 1960s by Jan Tinbergen at the United Nations Research Institute for Social Development (UNRISD), which is rarely if ever acknowledged in the UN intellectual histories of human development. Tinbergen's work fed into the various quality-of-life measurement initiatives in the 1960s and 1970s, largely based on the use of direct measures of wellbeing, such as *On Measuring and Planning the Quality of Life* (Drewnowski 1974) or the seminal work on the Physical Quality of Life Index developed by Morris David Morris and colleagues (see Morris 1979). Again, these antecedents are rarely acknowledged by the UN intellectual histories.

Morris notably argued that the most essential, non-redundant direct measures of objective wellbeing could be distilled down to three: the infant mortality rate, life expectancy at the age of one, and the literacy rate. Income or wealth indicators were not considered essential, he argued, or were redundant to these measures in terms of revealing information on quality of life. While the institutional memory lapse of his work is sometimes explained as a function of its elementary nature (e.g., see Estes 2012), his approach was actually quite visionary from the perspective of contemporary demographic theory, insofar as it identified infant mortality as the fundamental remote causal factor driving much of what we have come to understand as human development, as explained further below.

Morris' radical position of excluding income or wealth measures was not carried through to the subsequent generation of multidimensional indices, which generally include some measure of income or wealth. The Human Development Index (HDI) of the UNDP, for instance, includes GDP per capita. The standard argument is that, despite other human dimensions, wealth remains an important dimension to peoples' wellbeing. Including it also originally served an important purpose of highlighting the discrepancy that often exists between income/wealth measures and human development measures (the latter essentialised as education and health). As noted in Chapter 2, the Human Development Reports (HDR) were also originally meant as a counterweight to the World Bank World Development Reports (WDR). In particular, they were a means to highlight the damage done by crises and crisis responses in the form of austerity and structural adjustment programmes. These crippled health and education systems despite claims from the international financial institutions spearheading the programmes that these systems were supposed to be protected from the otherwise-draconian treatments that the patient barely survived. What became a full-blown development crisis could have been a far more manageable economic malaise had the responses been more reasonable. In this respect, the HDI started with a simple good idea – to compare two non-economic indicators with an economic indicator. It was then criticised, tweaked, adjusted, modified and slowly became coopted. As noted by Saith (2006), the institutions and agendas essentially merged with the emergence of Millennial Development Goals in the late 1990s and early 2000s.

In the midst of the numerous upgrades to the HDI, the Multidimensional Poverty Index (MPI) emerged as an improved new generation of human development composite indicators, taking up the yoke of challenging the primacy of money-metric measures as the gold standard of global comparison projects. It was developed and promoted by Sabina Alkire (e.g., see Alkire and Santos 2010) and then adopted by the UNDP Human Development Reports. At the time of writing, even the World Bank appears to be showing an interest in it.

However, despite the promotion of the MPI and other multidimensional measures as improvements on money-metric approaches, these measures do not fundamentally resolve the problems associated with money-metric poverty lines because many of these problems are not inherently due to the use of a money metre. Rather, they are due to the use of thresholds, however conceived. Moreover, despite the rejection of the unidimensionality of the money-metre, the MPI, like the HDI before it, is effectively another composite indictor that is as equally unidimensional as a money-metre although far less intuitive. Hence, in adding more information and in requiring conversion of non-comparable units into a single metre, multidimensional poverty lines actually render the exercise of measuring poverty even more opaque, complex and arbitrary, thereby reinforcing the political implications discussed in the previous chapter.

The question also remains whether such measures really add any value, rather than adding more confusion, especially versus the alternative of using a range of disaggregated indicators, which would arguably be much more useful for policy-makers in actually trying to discern needs. The fact that such measures have been adopted as targeting mechanisms in many contexts and have already influenced the agendas of data collection in many state statistical agencies also reveals that they are as susceptible as money-metric measures to advancing particular policy agendas. The added obfuscation that renders them incomprehensible to the vast majority of people besides the inducted reinforces the deference to the experts producing such data or training others to produce them. It thereby continuously reproduces an institutional dependency on northern academic institutions and international agencies in the constant updating of poverty representations.

Even more fundamental, however, is the subtle supply-side bias that can be discerned within these multidimensional agendas, in particular as they have shifted from entitlement to capability approaches (both in reference to Amartya Sen). This refers to the underlying idea that supply creates its own demand, so long as markets are free to match suppliers and demanders. Indeed, the mainstream receptiveness to such approaches has arguably been encouraged by the fact that they essentially confirm and reinforce this underlying supply-side bias. The bias has also been associated with a general neglect for the precise mechanisms of delivering human development, in the sense that delivering these within highly segregated social provisioning systems could ultimately reproduce inequalities and social stratification as much anything else, as will be discussed further in Chapter 6.

This chapter presents these arguments in three sections. The first briefly presents a background of direct measures. The second elaborates further on the perils and pitfalls of composite indicators, particularly around issues of aggregation and thresholds, demonstrating that the many of the problems that plague money-metric measures also plague multidimensional measures, if not exponentially given the proliferation of dimensions, units and thresholds. Finally, the chapter engages with the contentious point regarding the slide into supply-side bias within current human development and multidimensional agendas. This is done through an analysis of the intellectual transition from entitlement to capability approaches within the work of Amartya Sen himself, which might be described as a subtle shift from a more Keynesian to a more neoclassical theoretical posture.

Direct approaches to poverty measurement

Part of the problem with indirect measures, as discussed in the previous chapter, is that they do not tell you if a person is able to convert income into actual outcomes of wellbeing, whether objective wellbeing such as health or education, or else subjective wellbeing such as happiness. For instance, someone might possess sufficient income but is unable to convert this into an appropriate education that would allow for social mobility, perhaps due to discrimination or other factors. Indeed, this is a key insight of Amartya Sen's work, in both his entitlement and capability approaches, and is also a major focus of the social exclusion literature, as discussed in the next chapter.

These problems have repeatedly led to advocacy of using direct approaches to verify achievements in at least objective states of wellbeing. These include, for instance, indicators dealing with nutrition, longevity, morbidity, education, shelter, water, etc. As mentioned above, for some such as Morris (1979), such measures might even do away with the need for money-metric measures altogether, to the extent that they are sufficient to assess the most essential needs or outcomes within a population. However, as noted in the previous chapter, income itself arguably remains an important dimension in its own right.

Some of the oldest and most common direct measures are related to nutrition, in the form of anthropometric measures. Measures of hunger, undernutrition and eventually starvation constitute the most restrictive cases of the direct measurement of poverty outcomes. As with absolute measures of food income poverty, they might be considered the most absolute direct indicators of illbeing, or what Amartya Sen calls the absolutist core of poverty (although with the rise of modern disorders such as anorexia and bulimia nervosa, even this direct connection between starvation and material poverty can at times be questioned). Common measures include the body-mass index (measured by weight in kilograms divided by height in metres squared), stunting (being shorter than what would be considered a normal variation within a comparison population) or wasting (having a lower weight for height than what would be considered a normal variation within a comparison population). In the two latter cases, both are measured by standard deviations – usually two – from the average of the comparison population, which is generally calculated from very large samples in order to allow for a degree of generalisability across population groups.

Even though such measures are considered to be the gold standard of absoluteness, they nonetheless succumb to problems of arbitrariness, as with calorie-based poverty lines. To start with, the choice of deviations from the mean is quite arbitrary, particularly in mixed populations with different genetics, in which some are shorter or lighter than the mean without necessarily indicating undernutrition. Indeed, working in the inverse direction of hunger, some studies have shown that health risks for diabetes and cardiovascular diseases increase for Asians below the cut-off point of BMI 25 that defines overweight by the standard of the WHO (Nishida and Mucavele 2005, p. 6). Suffice to say that given inter-group variations, any particular mean will be ill-suited for groups that do not conform to the norm. This often becomes a bone of contention in politicised representations of poverty. For instance, some members of the former Ecuadorian government of Rafael Correa apparently argued that persistent undernutrition measures in the Ecuadorian pop-ulation despite falling expenditure poverty rates under his tenure are due to genetic differences, particularly among the highland Sierra dwell-ers, rather than anything that would contradict the poverty measures. Similar arguments have also been made in India, with regard to the small but healthy and efficient hypothesis expounded by Sukhatme and Margen (1978, 1982), as discussed in the previous chapter.

Trying to infer current socio-economic status from such indica-tors is problematic for similar reasons. Age and height measures tell us about past health and nutrition, but not health and nutrition in the present. Someone who was poor in their childhood and stunted as a result could end up becoming rich later in their life, as was com-mon, for instance, among European immigrants who came to the US and Canada after the Second World War. Past childhood mal-nutrition might have adverse health consequences later in life and this information is important to inform health services, but whether it is a matter of current poverty evaluation of adults is questionable. Inversely, weight measures can quickly fluctuate in the short term, such as with sudden acute diseases related to the ingestion of food, resulting in rapid weight loss while infections persist or else during recovery. As with money-metric measures, these indicators are also plagued with numerous timing issues, such as the time of day when measures are taken, or else the season. The latter would be important in agrarian regions, particularly those still largely reliant on subsist-ence forms of production (as noted in the previous chapter).

Great care must therefore be taken in how these indicators are measured and used. Many were principally conceived and developed for use in emergency settings involving famine, particularly among children, who are most susceptible to infectious diseases and for whom short-term fluctuations in diet (or in the ability to absorb a diet) can have severe short- to medium-term consequences on their physical and cognitive development. The use of these measures in such settings is, in this sense, mainly oriented towards triage, that is, identifying the worst cases requiring the most urgent treatment or interventions, in contexts of limited short-term resources relative to need. Outside of these contexts, the logic of triage needs to be questioned if applied more generally as a matter of regularised social policy interventions. It is one thing if the measures remain at merely an evaluative level, as a means to keep track of developments in nutrition. However, when the measures become a logic guiding social policy interventions and welfare entitlements, in determining for instance who gets access to food stamps or food aid and who does not, this becomes more problematic given the arbitrariness that is necessarily involved in selecting thresholds and the relevance of many of these thresholds in evaluating short-term fluctuations of need.

Composite indicators and quandaries of aggregation

Beyond these specific 'absolutist' direct measures, a poverty measure that includes multiple social indicators, variables or dimensions (however one might wish to call them) is called a composite index (composite in the sense that the index is composed of these different indicators). The motive for doing so, as with money-metric measures, is for the purposes of evaluating who should be considered poor versus non-poor. The exercise invariably involves aggregation. Combining all of the indicators together in one unitary continuous index allows for a threshold to be drawn against this index, whereas such binary sorting would be far more difficult to do if we were to consider each indicator in isolation.

Much of the discussion of composite indices therefore revolves around the methodologies of making such aggregations given that each indicator is generally measured in different units, or, if measured in the same unit, the unit can have different meanings. For instance, different measures are used for mortality, with different scales of what would be a normal range of values. Crude death rates are measured in terms of the number of deaths per 1000 people in a general population, with contemporary rates ranging from below ten to over 30. Infant mortality is measured in terms of the number of deaths of infants under one year old in a given year per 1000 live births in that year (rather than population), with rates ranging from under five to over 100. The child death rate, however, is measured in terms of the number of deaths of children aged one to four in a given year per 1000 children in this age group. Maternal mortality is either measured in terms of deaths per 1000 women aged 14 to 49, or else in terms of deaths per 100,000 live births. Morbidity rates (occurrence of sickness in the population) are also reported according to similar frequency measures, but the scales depend on the nature of the illness. The fact that all of these are reported as rates makes for a relatively easy conversion into a common unit (such as a percentage), although questions nonetheless arise as to how to combine the different scales, as well as how the various measures of mortality should be weighted, given that each has different meanings and different implications, and refers to different sub-groupings of the population. Choices invariably need to be taken about how to combine scales and weights, and these are invariably arbitrary, depending on the priority that is given in each exercise of aggregation.

These questions are exacerbated when we move into other dimensions that use other units with completely different meanings. For instance, as mentioned above with respect to nutrition, BMI is measured in kilograms of weight per metre of height squared, stunting is measured in terms of metres (height-for-age relative to the median) and wasting in terms of kilograms over metres (weight-for-height relative to the median) and more precise biomedical measures of nutrition that rely on blood samples also use a variety of different units. In education, measures such as literacy, enrolment rates, completion and attrition rates mostly use percentage units, although the scales, meanings and implications of each are very different. Other measures such as levels of formal schooling attained use different units. Moreover, few of these percentage measures offer any indication of quality, which brings the temptation of using yet other measures, such as test scores, which are again recorded in different units and have also been subject to considerable contention.

The issues that arise in aggregating variables into a composite indicator involve not just differences in units, but also how to choose and prioritise indicators and then how to combine them, with what weights for each indicator. This invariably involves prioritisation of some indicators and exclusion of others. Depending on what one wishes to emphasise or prioritise, the weighting and results will vary considerably. Including too many indicators risks drowning out the weight of more crucial variables, whereas including too few risks missing important information.

As discussed in the previous chapter, weighting decisions are also faced in money-metric poverty lines, such as in questions of how much weight to give to food consumption in a basic needs basket and, within food, how much weight to give to basic coarse grains. However, at least the unit issue is straightforward in money-metric lines, insofar as everything can be converted into prices (although even this is rife with dispute and methodological quagmires). Within so-called multiple dimensions, the units are more complicated and the choice of indicators is much greater.

The potential for whimsicality is demonstrated by the constant proliferation of composite indices every time someone deems that the addition of a new dimension or indicator is important (perhaps even for their own career). This tendency is epitomised by the regular modifications to the initial HDI of the UNDP, which appear to be at least partly driven by the desire to do something new in each Human Development Report, or else by the variety of indices that have emerged to supplement or compete with the HDI. The latter have included the additions of variables for political freedom, human security, vulnerability and resilience, inequality and sustainability, as well as subjective perceptions such as happiness, violence and so forth.

Some of these things are difficult if not impossible to measure in an objective and comparable manner, such as happiness (despite a large scholarly field based on claims to the contrary). Others are hard to measure (such as rape or suicide, which are notoriously under-reported). And some are prone to reporting distortions, particularly when measures are connected to allocations of fiscal resources or to performance evaluations.

For instance, I observed in my own fieldwork in western China in the 2000s that communities would fill their schools even with non-students on days when it was known that education ministry officials would be visiting, given that enrolments were used to determine the core funding of schools. They did this as a collective effort in order to guarantee a minimal level of resources and staff positions for the school, which was driven by their concern about the chronic underfunding of such schools in the first place. Despite the noble intentions, it was nonetheless hard to take any of the enrolment figures seriously in such a context. Similarly, maternal mortality targets were used in performance evaluations of medical personnel (that is, medical doctors would receive fines if too many mortalities occurred under their care), with the result that maternal mortality was underreported, by reporting these deaths as due to other causes in order to avoid the fine.

In such types of cases, even though a particular variable might ostensibly be a good one, issues of data quality can or should disqualify its use. The response to this problem has been to conduct independent surveys to control the data collection and even the design of the data being collected, as advocated for instance by the MPI project. However, this in itself entails a whole range of other problems. In particular, it places considerable pressures on local statistical agencies that are already often overstretched and underresourced (particularly when their staff are being seconded to international research projects and consultancies), thereby further diverting their efforts away from the primary tasks of collecting accurate information for regular policy-making. That such independent surveys might be integrated into and even transform national statistical efforts is another concern, particularly when the information collected might not be the most appropriate or useful for regular policy-making.

Other issues relate to the comparability of certain indicators across time and space in terms of how they relate to poverty or wealth, particularly in contexts of structural transformation. For instance, literacy rates might be much lower among populations that are still rooted in subsistence forms of production, particularly in pastoral areas, even though pastoralists might be deemed as wealthier in certain respects than their better-schooled farming or wage-labouring neighbours (e.g., see Fischer 2006, 2008b and 2014a with respect to Tibetan areas in China). Literacy in this sense is at times an inept predictor of wealth or wellbeing in such contexts, or in contexts that are in rapid transition out of such subsistence modes, such as when educational norms change rapidly across generations.

Indicators also might or might not indicate poverty at an individual level, unless we deem them as a form of poverty. For instance, the richest man in a province of western China where I was conducting research in the early 2000s was apparently illiterate and had never been to school, but had built a manufacturing and construction conglomerate for himself. His children would have been schooled, and in this sense the household would not have been identified as poor by the MPI (unless one or more children would not have attended school). However, the point is that illiterate people can often be very entrepreneurial, whereas many poor people are able to read and write and have attended school, regardless of the quality of the schooling or whether it was of any benefit to their subsequent employment prospects or wellbeing. As noted above, this crude human development view stands in contrast to an understanding of schooling as an institutional vehicle of social stratification and segregation, of reproducing inequalities and class structures, or as signaling devices for social status. These aspects are analysed in the more critical sociological scholarship on education, which is generally ignored by the human development literature.

Problems of meaning

These points direct us towards several fundamental problems facing such composite indices. One is the loss of meaning. In other words, what does the resulting number of the composite indicator mean? Another is the question of why aggregate in the first place and the dangers of hiding trade-offs in the process. Are we in effect combining different things that would be better left disaggregated and distinguished, such as wealth versus health? A third is the deviation of purpose. The HDI, for instance, started out as a reaction to the severity of SAPs in the 1980s and the need to highlight and protect the space of health and education regardless of economic concerns or objectives. But as the UNDP merged closer to the World Bank as they approached the new millennium and its associated goals, the HDI and its younger sibling the MPI have been increasingly conceived and practised as targeting tools.

In the first case, the units that result from composite indicators are mostly intangible or unintelligible – besides perhaps for the expert who constructed the index – insofar as the units do not represent anything in particular besides a range in a numerical scale, typically from zero to one. A good example of this is the HDI, which in its origins combined three fairly crude components: health measured by life expectancy; education measured by a combination of literacy and enrolments; and per-capita gross domestic product or income, measured in purchasing-power-parity terms (drawing from the PPP measures of the World Bank). These components have essentially remained the same throughout the various modifications and updates to the HDI, although technical adaptations have been made along with the occasional inclusion of other variables, as detailed in the technical appendices of successive HDRs.

The exercise of constructing the HDI then involves two steps. The first involves scaling, meaning that each measure needs to be converted into the scale that is eventually adopted by the final index, which in the case of the HDI runs from zero to one. Hence, each measure needs to be given an upper and lower bound in which all countries can be placed along the scale. This can be done in a crude manner or with more sophistication. The more sophisticated includes things like imposing a marginally decreasing value as the indicator increases, such as income, with the logic that each additional unit of income past a certain point generates less and less additional wellbeing. The second step involves weighting, i.e., deciding whether each component is given the same weight (one-third each), or whether some components are given more weight. The result is an index ranging from more than zero to less than one, with most countries falling within a range of about 0.3 to 0.8. Notably, the index is relative, in the sense that a position within it depends on the upper and lower bounds, and hence an HDI of 0.67 in one year does not necessarily imply the same thing as 0.67 in another year. What 0.67 actually means in terms of outcomes is unclear, although we can presume that it is better than Somalia and worse than Norway.[1]

Of the many criticisms of the HDI, one of the most fundamental has been whether it actually provides any useful information as a composite measure, in comparison to the information already provided and more easily ascertainable across the three decomposed components. Besides the annual entertainment of seeing how countries rank against each other, particularly those that vie for top and bottom places, the information is not particularly useful for a policy-maker interested in more tangible information that could help inform how social needs manifest and where. The general argument is that it acts as an incentive for governments to perform. The exception, of course, is when the HDI is used for regional targeting for social policy programmes, as it has in several cases such as Brazil (e.g., see Souza 2006).

On this last point, the indicators used by the HDI are all population-based measures, meaning that they can only be measured with respect to a group of people. As a result, the index cannot be used for identifying poor people at individual or household levels. For example, the life expectancy of a person cannot be measured while they are still alive. It can only be determined once that person dies. Hence, life expectancy or mortality measures can only be measured with respect to a large enough group of people for the measure to be representative and meaningful. Similar considerations apply to illiteracy rates (although literacy can also be measured in a binary manner at an individual level, in terms of being literate or not). This is the reason why the HDI can only be used for regional targeting, not for individual or household targeting.

The Multidimensional Poverty Index

The Multidimensional Poverty Index (MPI) has tried to resolve this dilemma by rendering its measures appropriate for individual rather than group identification. For instance, in the method first developed by Alkire and Foster (2007) and subsequently adopted by the UNDP in 2010, ten indicators are proposed. Similar to proxy measures of consumption discussed in the previous chapter, these indicators are purported to have been carefully chosen on the basis of rigorous survey work (at the time) with the suggestion that these serve as the best proxies for poverty and are not redundant with each other (meaning that two of the indicators are not effectively giving the same type of information).

Under the dimension of education, the indicators include years of schooling and child school attendance. A household is considered to be deprived in these two dimensions if no household member aged ten years or older has completed at least five years of schooling, or whether any school-aged child is not attending school up to the age at which they would complete class eight. Extreme deprivation in this dimension reduces these thresholds to one year of schooling and the age related to class six.

Under the health dimension, child mortality is individualised by considering whether any child has died in the family in the five-year period preceding the survey, and nutrition in terms of whether any adult under 70 years of age is undernourished in terms of BMI, or any child for whom there is nutritional information is undernourished in terms of weight for age. Extreme deprivation raises the mortality threshold to two children and the undernourishment threshold to three instead of two standard deviations from the median of the reference population.

A proxy approach is adopted for living standards, including: whether the household has no electricity; whether the household's sanitation facility is not improved, or improved but shared with other households; whether the household does not have access to improved drinking water, or safe drinking water is at least a 30-minute-roundtrip walk from home; whether the household has a dirt, sand, dung or 'other' (unspecified) type of floor; whether the household cooks with dung, wood or charcoal; and whether the household owns fewer than one radio, TV, telephone, bike, motorbike or refrigerator, and does not own a car or truck. Extreme deprivation similarly raises these living standard thresholds, e.g., no electricity, no facility (open defecation), 45-minute walk, etc.

These solutions, however, are far from perfect, in part because the proxies are even more indirect measures of poverty than money-metric measures. In other words, as already mentioned above, the proxies do not necessarily represent poverty even though they might be associated with poverty. The association implies that, on average, they identify poverty, but many people fall outside of the average. Money-metric measures are also indirect, although their association is much more straightforward and direct. It is clear that someone with low income will have a limited ability to procure basic needs that require income.

The associations with the various indicators of the MPI are less straightforward. Mortality, for instance, obviously occurs across all social classes. While the rich can certainly avail of better health care than the poor and, on average, perform better than poor people in terms of life expectancy, they are certainly not impervious to mortality, particularly with respect to chronic diseases (as opposed to infectious and parasitic diseases). In many lower- and middle-income countries, one of the leading causes of death among adults is road accidents, and relatively wealthy middle and upper classes are particularly susceptible given that they own more cars and spend more time driving them.

In terms of child mortality, although the MPI indicator is individualised to the household level, the measure nonetheless arguably reflects the general mortality conditions of the community in which the household is located. Whether or not a child has died in the family might not necessarily have any relation to absolute or even relative poverty, unless of course the fact of living in a context of higher mortality is itself defined as poverty. However, this re-blurs the line between individualised versus population-based measures and also weakens the case for proxies as predictors of poverty rather than tautologically being defined as components of poverty.

Some of the indicators also do not appear to have been well chosen. For instance, the weight-for-age measure for nutrition in children is a problematic and odd choice given that small children can be healthy and that a position in a growth chart does not necessarily represent whether a child is over- or underweight. Rather, the more important medical concern is whether sudden changes in position occur. However, the choice in this case was probably determined by the ease of surveying for this particular indicator, which raises a different set of concerns, as discussed further below.

Nor does the MPI give any indication of quality. This is especially important with respect to schooling outcomes, whereby rapid increases in enrolments can be achieved within poor-quality schools and, when under-resourced, can also worsen quality in those schools due to the overloading of already strained and weak capacity. The choice of years or levels of schooling in the MPI is problematic in this respect, given that enrolment does not necessarily guarantee learning outcomes and even basic literacy might not be guaranteed after five or more years of primary schooling in many poor contexts. I have observed this, for instance, in many Tibetan rural areas of China (e.g., see Fischer 2014a), although the observation has also been made globally in several high-profile reports (e.g., WB 2011 and UNESCO 2015) and also by many prominent scholars in learning and development (e.g., see Wagner 2018).

Similarly, in many respects the living standard indicators are biased against rural areas and, in particular, against subsistence-oriented agrarian systems. Like with income measures, as discussed in the previous chapter, the indicators have a tendency to exaggerate the poverty of agrarian settings and thus exaggerate declines in multidimensional poverty as families transition out of such settings.

Open defecation, for instance, might be preferred in remote rural areas, particularly those with low population density and where sanitation facilities are not well maintained, whereas sanitation facilities become imperative in urban or more densely populated peri-urban areas. Similarly, it is notable that the MPI includes consumer durables (or 'assets') such as refrigerators and TVs, and yet it does not include any agrarian productive assets of substantial value such as cows, sheep, yaks, horses or camels, or anything in relation to land tenure for that matter. Urbanisation would also tend to be reflected as an improvement in the MPI by virtue of the fact that access to electricity, sanitation facilities, cement flooring, cooking fuel or possession of consumer durables become more accessible and normalised without necessarily indicating a change in wealth or socio-economic status (besides the fact that urbanisation itself is such a massive transition).

There is also a question of how improvements in these living standard indicators are achieved, similar to the point made above with respect to education. For instance, highly controversial resettlement policies, such as those implemented in some Tibetan areas of China, would be associated with strong improvements in most of these living standard indicators, even though they have simultaneously been associated with dispossession or depletion of land and livestock assets, high levels of unemployment and welfare dependence and a wide variety of problems stemming from social dislocation, exclusion and alienation (see Fischer 2008b, 2014a; Du 2012; Ptackova 2016; Sodnamkyi and Sulek 2017; Foggin 2018). The risk that the incentives provided by these measures encourage what James Scott (1998) has referred to as authoritarian high-modernist projects of failed social engineering is one that needs to be taken seriously.

Problems of obscuration by aggregation

The second problem of these composite indices relates to the aggregation of the identified dimensions or indicators. One issue is the danger of hiding trade-offs in the process of aggregation. This was discussed in the Introduction with respect to the aggregation of economic and human development dimensions, such as in the HDI. The original motivation for doing this in the HDI was to contrast how differently we might perceive 'development' once human development indicators are included, but this comes at the risk of masking different dynamics when one dimension cancels out the other.

For instance, the gradual improvements in mortality around the world over the course of the postwar period might have very little to do with economic developments, given that significant reductions in mortality can be achieved in quite poor settings, as has been well established in contemporary demography (also see Deaton 2013). This would lead to a gradual, secular improvement in the health indicators of the HDI or MPI (in the latter, this would be reflected by falling mortality at the household level as more children survive beyond five years of age). These improvements would occur regardless of whether or not this actually represents any broader improvements in wealth or even lifelong health. Similarly, poor countries around the world have been going through a veritable schooling revolution, with rapid improvements in enrolment rates over relatively short periods of time, although, again, whether or not this has had any effect on their economic prospects, living standards or well-being is debatable, particularly in situations where education leads to substantial debt or without any significant improvements in job prospects or upward mobility. Such improvements would nonetheless be reflected by a gradual secular improvement of the education indicators of the HDI or MPI.

By combining these various dimensions together, the question is whether we are compounding the problems already involved in trying to decipher what, exactly, is occurring in the economic dimension. Periods of economic downturn, for instance, would be compensated by these gradual secular improvements in the health and education dimensions, thereby attenuating the appearance of the impact of economic downturn on the poor, especially that most of the indicators are slow-moving outcomes of public or private investment and are definitely not cyclical. Hence, we must ask, if someone is formally schooled, should this lessen our concern for their income poverty if their schooling cancels out the effect of their income or wealth poverty in a human development type of measure? Or else, complex dynamics in both dimensions might become obscured, such in the 1980s in large parts of Africa, when economic crisis was compounded by health crises, such as the HIV crisis, even whilst not necessarily causing a reversal in the types of mortality measured by these indices (although there also appears to have been a stagnation in mortality declines in parts of Africa in the 1980s and 1990s, following the crippling of their public health and education systems by austerity and structural adjustment programmes). Are we confusing the issues if we merge them together? The alternative is to simply distinguish the human from the economic dimensions and analyse them separately.

The more sophisticated approach to aggregation is, again, proposed by Alkire and Foster (2007) with the MPI, or the so-called Alkire-Foster method, as coined by its authors. They propose two types of thresholds: one within a dimension, to determine whether a person is deprived within that dimension, and another across the ten dimensions that they propose, to identify whether someone is multidimensionally poor. The thresholds for determining deprivation and extreme deprivation have been discussed above. In the next step of aggregation, the two indicators under education and the two under health are each given a one-sixth weight, while the six under living standards are each given a one-eighteenth weight. A household is then considered multidimensionally poor if it is deprived in one-third of these weighted indicators (e.g., two in education and one in health; or one in education, one in health and three in living standards, etc.). On the basis of this exercise, the sophisticated battery of statistical techniques in poverty studies can then be brought to bear. These include calculations related to the incidence as well as the intensity of poverty, as mentioned in the previous chapter, as well as various measures of the composition of poverty across the ten dimensions or indicators.

While conceptually appealing, it is easy to see how the approach suggested by Alkire and Foster multiplies, perhaps exponentially, the issues related to determining thresholds and then using them to count the poor. In effect, they do not fundamentally resolve the problems associated with money-metric poverty lines because many of these problems are not inherently due to the use of a money metre. Rather, they are due to the use of thresholds, however conceived. Hence, even if we accept the dimensions proposed by the MPI, the method does not resolve the more fundamental issue of how weights and cut-offs should be chosen within these dimensions, even less so how an aggregated cut-off should be chosen, or what priority should be given to various dimensions. Rather, the complexity of the exercise renders the resulting index even more opaque and less intuitive than money-metric measures despite its apparent simplicity, as well as more prone to arbitrary choice. For instance, why should five years of schooling be deemed the cut-off for people aged older than ten years, or eighth grade for children, given the efforts of many countries to achieve nine years of compulsory schooling? Or why should the aggregated threshold be one-third, with no priority given to various dimensions? Moreover, should these thresholds be kept constant over time, despite contexts of often rapidly changing social norms, such as education campaigns that quickly raise enrolments among the poor, or in situations where norms of mortality fall over time, even among the poor? Similarly, merely between 2005 and 2015, the ownership of mobile phones became much more normalised, even among poor people, thus lessening its diagnostic value as a proxy for poverty over time. In such circumstances, should the minimum standard change over time? If so, or even if not, how then can the multidimensional threshold be considered comparable over time?

These questions make clear that the MPI does not necessarily address some of the more fundamental problems with poverty measures, even whilst it is a definite improvement to the HDI, at least in terms of an ability to identify households beneath the aggregate. For instance, as with the use of thresholds more generally, the MPI will not detect significant changes that happen above or below a threshold if the change does not cross the threshold. These could presumably be captured by measures of the intensity of poverty, as with money-metric measures (i.e., the distance that a poor household is located below the income poverty line), although the MPI measures this in terms of the average number of deprivations that poor people face at the same time, not necessarily the depth of deprivation within a single indicator. Moreover, intensity measures generally do not include changes that occur above the poverty line. On the other hand, as discussed in the second chapter with respect to the shift of countries into lower-middle-income status, threshold-based approaches such as the MPI amplify small movements that do cross the threshold. As a result, it is difficult to differentiate whether the resulting poverty trends are showing real effects or threshold effects.

Problems of priority

A third problematic aspect that is apparent in the project of these multidimensional indices is how they influence statistical and policy agendas, especially as they get taken up by influential international organisations, such as the UNDP and the World Bank. The MPI in particular has been increasingly operationalised as a targeting device rather than just an evaluative tool. Indeed, it was originally sold according to its amenability for targeting and this potential also probably explains much of the receptiveness of the approach for organisations that promote targeting (such as the World Bank). This is ironic because it claims intellectual inspiration and lineage from Amartya Sen, who himself has on many occasions been quite outspoken against targeting and, instead, has been a firm supporter of universalistic approaches of social policy. Nonetheless, the conception and design of the MPI as being amenable household targeting reveals a certain bias – perhaps implicit but sometimes explicit – of the policy priorities of its architects. Of course, this might not be perceived as a problem *per se*, depending on how one views targeting (see Chapter 6 for a discussion on targeting and universalism in social policy).

In turn, the uptake and increasing institutionalisation of the MPI, whether for purely evaluative purposes or also for policy application, have also had an influence on the development of state statistical systems by mobilising them towards the collection of MPI data. The problem is that much of the data actually required for the MPI does not necessarily exist in many country settings, given that they do not constitute the conventional measures collected by statistical agencies. Much of the data can be derived from conventional sources or demographic and health surveys (DHS), but much cannot, as noted by the authors of the MPI project. Moreover, where some of the official data is circumspect, the MPI authors have shown a preference for commissioning their own surveys in order to better control the data collection and quality. This has necessitated reorienting data collection efforts towards the requirements of the MPI, whether through conducting parallel surveys (the Multiple Indicator Cluster Surveys proposed by those advocating the MPI), or else even through changing the practices of data collection and survey methods in existing statistical agencies. The pressures to do this have been quite strong given the degree of relatively powerful institutional endorsement that the MPI has received, from the UNDP in particular (and now possibly the World Bank as well).[2]

This is problematic in contexts with weak statistical systems and limited capacity, as is common in many if not most poor countries (e.g., see Jerven 2013 in the case of Africa). The question is whether, under considerable resource and capacity constraints, these pressures to reorient data collection efforts are appropriate, or simply the latest tune to which government statistical agencies are expected to dance. This is important because the direction and choices are not necessarily the most important for these statistical agencies to be making and evolving their statistical systems towards. In a context of zero-sum choice given limited capacity, the distraction risks drawing effort and attention away from the more conventional tasks that are needed as basic functions of state capacity. These include continuing to develop capacity in more conventional education, demographic or epidemiological measures, or even the improvement of basic civil registries, in contexts where these are severely underdeveloped in many poor countries, thereby limiting the knowledge that a government needs to address basic needs among the populations that it governs.

Moreover, even where efforts are made to conduct surveys that are appropriate for measuring the MPI (or similar proxy-type measures of 'consumption', as discussed in the previous chapter), these are generally quite infrequent, typically conducted only once every five years at best, and not conducted as regularly as income/expenditure or employment surveys. If intended for actual targeting, the sample would need to be large enough to include all of those meant to be targeted (such as the two bottom quintiles of the population, if these can even be isolated). However, the surveying cannot piggyback with censuses given the strict privacy protocols involved in census-taking, whereas targeting requires identification. As a result, the survey data are partial at best, with huge potential for exclusion errors, and are often quickly out of date, even while they have been increasingly used as the basis for poverty targeting. When they are turned towards the actual distribution of resources and benefits, the purportedly scientific processes of selection invariably break down even further under the pressures of local power relations and the imperfections of actual administrative practices. This is shown, for instance, in the excellent study by Hirway (2003) on the application of a multidimensional (or proxy means-testing) approach in the identification and selection of 'below-poverty-line' households for poverty alleviation programmes in India. The alternative of simply using the MPI surveys as evaluative devices, drawing representative samples from the population as is currently practised, is probably the more modest and realistic ambition. However, the question then is whether this is the best or most effective project to put such energies and resources towards, as opposed to more conventional social-scientific surveying.

Subtle ideological shifts in Senology

Even more fundamental to these technical questions has been a subtle shift in the human development agenda over time towards a more supply-side approach in development policy. The concept of 'supply-side' will be elaborated further in Chapter 6, although suffice to say here that it refers to a focus on increasing the supply of human capital (through education, health, etc.), while leaving employment or productive accumulation to the vagaries of market forces. The assumption within supply-side theoretical and policy agendas is that supply will create its own demand (often referred to as 'Say's Law'). In other words, increased supply (in this case, of enhanced human capital) will create its own demand (that is, demand for the labour with the enhanced human capital), so long as markets are free to match suppliers and demanders (in this case, labour markets). The agenda has also been associated with a general neglect for the precise mechanisms of delivering human capital improvements, in the sense that delivering these within highly segregated social provisioning systems could ultimately reproduce inequalities and social stratification as much anything else, as will be discussed further in Chapter 6.

This shift towards a supply-side bias is even apparent within the theorisation of Amartya Sen. In order to clarify this point, it is useful to briefly recap the essential conceptual building blocks of his work. However, it is also worth foregrounding this discussion with a few points on the uptake of Sen's work by various measurement projects, given that he is the proclaimed inspiration of so many people behind the human development agenda and related efforts to convert his abstract capability approach into a valid poverty measure at the individual, household or societal level (despite Sen's own opposition to targeting, it might be added).

There are questions regarding whether the HDI or MPI are meaningful measures of capability, which, as conceived by Sen, refers to the ability to live one's life as one choses. The logic of Sen's capability approach is built upon a critique of utility notions of wellbeing rather than money-metric measures *per se*, given that Sen himself has maintained the importance of including income as one component of capability. Rather, the basic premise is that such components – which he refers to as functionings – cannot be assumed to simply convert into outcomes (of capability, freedom, development, wellbeing or otherwise). There are myriad processes of conversion from inputs to outcomes, and an outcome (such as poverty reduction) cannot necessarily be assumed to result from an increase of one of the inputs. In this sense, he expressed poverty as a capability failure, that is, a failure to convert functionings into capability, in addition to insufficient functionings (relative to the realm of possibilities that any particular society is able to offer). It is for similar reasons that he also criticised the basic needs approach as focusing on the commodity space of inputs, rather than on actual outcomes and on the intermediating space of conversion between inputs and outcomes.

Capability in this sense is a potential, which Sen presents as an essential but complex freedom that is instrumental to development while at the same time constitutes development (meaning that the essence of development is this expansion in the ability to live the life one wishes to live). This involves a degree of circular reasoning that, from the outset, does not predispose the approach to practical application, as it is never quite clear whether something, such as literacy, should be treated as an input or an outcome, or a functioning or a capability. Indeed, there seems to be much confusion on the precision and ordering of these terms in the broader scholarship. As such, his approach is as much as a philosophical statement from within the liberal tradition – as a critique and advance on Rawlsian theories of justice – as it is intended as a way of conceiving poverty.

His approach nonetheless presents a practical quagmire of how to measure such functionings and capability. To start with, Sen himself has refused to specify which functionings should be included in the 'basket', in part because he deems that this should emerge as part of a democratic process of decision-making at the community level. This idea in itself is idealistic, especially in an age of rising right-wing and authoritarian populism, and ignores the power relations that might influence such deliberative processes. It also removes the possibility that his approach could be used for cross-community or national comparative exercises, let alone international comparison projects.

The HDI and MPI remediate this dilemma by specifying what should be measured, thereby defying the otherwise reverential deference towards Sen. However, the subsequent problem is that essentially all of the measures boil down to functionings and do not represent the potential of capability. Moreover, these functionings end up being essentially the same as basic needs. Laderchi et al. (2003, p. 255) note that because capabilities represent potential outcomes and are therefore difficult to identify empirically, 'there is a strong tendency to measure functionings rather than capabilities (i.e., life expectancy, morbidity, literacy, nutrition levels) in both micro and macro assessments.' They argue that 'this risks losing the key insight of the capability approach, which is its emphasis on freedom', and 'makes the approach virtually identical with the [basic needs] approach in the measurement of poverty' (ibid). This tendency is demonstrated, for example, in Reddy et al. (2006), who claim to adopt a capability-inspired approach to calculating poverty lines, although their method is essentially a basic needs approach.

This point raises the question of whether all of the criticism of basic needs was deserved in the first place, by Sen and then by his followers. It possibly reflects the fact that the case for the basic needs approach is generally set up as a straw man within this scholarship. The approach is reduced down to a rudimentary caricature that is easy to refute, thereby allowing the protagonist to declare an easy but specious victory of originality and innovation, when really much less is actually contributed. Indeed, the basic needs literature of the 1970s was not originally conceived in terms of the 'commodity space' but instead dealt centrally with issues that could be considered as falling into the realm of potentials, rights and even freedoms. This is perhaps best represented by the work of Ul Haq himself, ironically the main author of the original HDI. In *The Poverty Curtain* (1976), he defended the basic needs approach against exactly this attack – that it went beyond commodity space and dealt with structure, institutions, processes, rights and so forth.

Hence, much ado might have been made about nothing in the reinventing of the wheel. The HDI, the MPI or any other measure purporting to operationalise the capability approach do not effectively offer a satisfactory measure of potentials or freedoms. Rather, they essentially offer ways of measuring whether various basic needs have been met, many of which in fact reflect the infamous 'commodity space'. They might be new and improved measures of this, but it is on these merits that they need to be judged.

Conversions from a demand- to a supply-side perspective on poverty

Beyond such operational problems, the transition from Sen's previous entitlement approach to the capability approach has involved what might be argued as a shift from a more demand-side to a more supply-side perspective on poverty. The latter has been particularly amenable to mainstream agendas, still largely influenced by a neoclassical supply-side perspective, as argued in Chapter 2 and further elaborated in Chapter 6. Sen's entitlement theory of famines, as the predecessor of his capability approach, similarly identified endowment sets, entitlement mapping and then entitlement sets. 'Entitlements' in this sense refers to command over resources, or the ability to convert endowments (i.e., land, labour, capital) into claims (on food). The conversion could occur through production, employment, trade, transfer, family, etc. Mapping refers to the various ways of converting endowments. For instance, one might think of an input-output system, with various means and methods of converting various inputs into various outputs. The importance of the insight that Sen was making was fairly straightforward: command over food depends not just on the supply of food (production), but also on prices and on wages to express demand; it depends not just on the supply of labour, but also on the demand for labour (which is crucial to allow labour to earn and thus command); it also depends on an ability for demand to be expressed through the various channels.

Hence, even in the presence of sufficient supplies of food, entitlements could break down (which he referred to as 'entitlement failure') and famine could occur. Sen contrasted this to the production failure approach of understanding famine, which was based on a crude understanding of food supply, or what he called 'food availability decline'. Rather, Sen pointed out that famine could occur in the presence of sufficient supplies of food through other forms of failure, such as exchange failure, transfer failure, endowment loss, etc. These latter types of failure break the ability to convert endowments into claims, or to be able express or actualise demand for available resources, and might occur just as people are most vulnerable. To generalise beyond famine, poverty can be seen as an entitlement failure.

Sen's empirics have been notably disputed, although this is rarely if ever acknowledged in the hagiographic renditions of his work. A debate recently broke out around the publication of Mukerjee (2011) between Tauger and Sen (2011) over claims by Tauger that Sen had treated forecasts as harvest data and ignored the scientific evidence of a catastrophic crop failure around the 1943 Bengal famine, on which he based his theorisation. Sen did not take this lightly and defended his position with the support of studies by other scholars, although of course he only picked those who supported him in his claims. He also pointed out that some famines are clearly the result of supply declines, just not the Bengal famine, and that 'good entitlement analysis must take note of both demand and supply conditions.' However, similar questions over the historical Bengal data have been made by other scholars such as Dyson (1996, p. 74), who revisited during fieldwork the data source that Sen used and came to conclusion that Sen essentially got the data wrong, or else got the wrong data. Instead, by triangulating with other sources of available evidence, Dyson points out that in all five of the famines that Sen considers in his *Poverty and Famines* research, there is actually very strong empirical evidence of food availability declines, opposite to the claims that Sen made in order to build his theoretical case.

Regardless, Sen was essentially articulating a theory of effective demand, or what might be referred to as a demand-side theory of how famine occurs. As noted by Wrigley (1999), he was thereby following in the tradition of both Thomas Malthus, whose demand-side understanding of famine and poverty differed from the supply-side understanding of David Ricardo, and of John Maynard Keynes, who similarly identified that unemployment could occur due to insufficient demand for labour despite the presence of sufficient productive capacity in a free-market economy. The central target of Keynes in this sense was Say's Law (or what Keynes referred to as the tail wagging the dog) – that supply creates its own demand (as mentioned above and discussed further in Chapter 6) – which he argued did not necessarily operate in the aggregate. Indeed, in comparison to these older theories, it could be argued that Sen was actually rendering a straightforward idea into something rather convoluted and obscure without necessarily adding much additional insight, although of course the mathematising of his theory won him accolades among the economics profession and eventually the Nobel Prize in Economics.

The capability approach then essentially involved changing the labels, while applying the lens more broadly to poverty and development. Endowments became functionings, meaning the things that one has or does. Entitlement became capability, and entitlement failure became a capability failure.

The relabelling has nonetheless involved a subtle shift in logic. The capability approach has arguably become more neoclassical, moving from a theory of effective demand (in famine theory) to something that is more akin to a Solow growth model. The implication is that the main way to develop is through the slow build-up of functionings among the poor. Freedom in a range of domains including markets allows for the expression of these functionings into capability sets, much like a production possibility frontier, rather than through demand-side or other state interventions such as fiscal transfers or industrial policy. This reading is not always explicit in the work of Sen and some would argue that he still uses the capability approach to explain demand-side failures of conversion between functionings and capability sets, particularly with respect to discrimination or other obstructions to expressions of demand (e.g., see the next chapter on social exclusion). However, the way that the capability approach has been generally taken up, particularly by economists, has been according to the more neoclassical reading, including in the tangents of capital or asset-based approaches to understanding poverty.

The neoclassical logic is also implicit in Sen's work. For instance, a capability failure that is caused by an obstructed conversion from functionings to capability could be interpreted as an aspect of market obstruction, or of imperfect markets, as discussed in Chapter 2.[3] Indeed, this reading is encouraged by Sen's explicit endorsement of market freedom as one of his five freedoms that are both instrumental for and constitutive of development. In his work (Sen 1999, p. 26), he elaborates:

> [The argument] that markets typically work to expand income and wealth and economic opportunities that people have ...
> is certainly strong, in general, and there is plenty of empirical evidence that the market system can be an engine of fast economic growth and expansion of living standards. Policies that restrict market opportunities can have the effect of restraining the expansion of substantive freedoms that would have been generated through the market system, mainly through overall economic prosperity. This is not to deny that markets can sometimes be counterproductive ... But by and large the

positive effects of the market system are now much more widely recognized than they were even a few decades ago.

He then makes the standard case for market efficiency that is common to the neoclassical tradition and, in particular, is emphasised by the Austrian school, such as Friedrich Hayek's principle of price discovery. He argues that:

> a competitive market mechanism can achieve a type of efficiency that a centralized system cannot plausibly achieve both because of the economy of information (each person acting in the market does not have to know very much) and the compatibility of incentives (each person's canny actions can merge nicely with those of others). (Ibid., p. 27)

Such rhetorical use of deductive dichotomies is typical in many neoliberal defences for liberalisation, in which the only alternative to free and unfettered trade is autarky, rather than any intermediate gradations of regulation or intervention within a market system. For instance, Bhagwati and Srinivasan (2002) make use of the same rhetorical technique of referring to autarky in their defence for trade liberalisation. Sen also adds intrinsic value to this defence for market freedoms, arguing that even if central planning could achieve the same outcomes, free markets are nonetheless superior because the outcomes are derived through freedom. He also draws a comparison to slavery, although again this arguably creates a straw-man case for markets based on extreme dichotomies.

Sen is obviously liberal, but not neoliberal. He is probably best understood as belonging to the social-democratic tradition of Western liberalism. This is apparent in his endorsement of universal social policy and of the regulation of finance, as well as his caution against poverty targeting (which his prodigy seemingly ignore in their enthusiasm to design targeting devices, as discussed above). However, he makes these cases through a particular liberal, neoclassical logic, as is typical of many mainstream economists of social-democratic or even socialist persuasion, such as Joseph Stiglitz or Dani Rodrik, who also arguably remain within the neoclassical paradigm. As I have argued in Fischer (2014b), the marker is that their theoretical formulations accept the perfect market outcome as the deductive abstract reference point against which government intervention is to be justified.[4] In other words, while the ideal perfect market, as described above by Sen, is accepted as an abstract principle, in reality most markets are characterised by intrinsic information asymmetries between buyers and sellers, or by other 'imperfections' or transaction costs, which ultimately result in obstructions to the axiomatic pure market equilibrium.

Along similar lines, Sen's approach to development falls within this family of liberal theorisation. Various freedoms are seen as mutually compatible and reinforcing, rather than at odds. In this philosophical sense, Sen would find himself more at home with Hayek, who similarly argued that various freedoms are compatible and mutually reinforcing, than with Karl Polanyi, who argued that economic freedom is fundamentally at odds with social and political freedom. Polanyi's warning was that economic freedom tends towards fascism while social and political freedom tend towards socialism, which is part of the reason why his thinking has struck such a resonance in the current context of rising right-wing populism lead by oligarchs in the US and elsewhere.

Moreover, as with the deductive individualist approaches common to liberal theories, Sen's ontology can be best described as individualist. He is sometimes described in terms of methodological individualism (e.g., Fine 2004, Dean 2009), but ontology is arguably the better term. In Sen's conception of development as freedom, the entity that is being developed is the capability of an individual, not necessarily the capability of a society or a group within a society (although in the 2013 HDR, the concept of 'social competencies' was introduced, which might represent a timid step towards a conception of societal capability, although perhaps not – see UNDP 2013). Rather, societal development is simply an aggregation of individual developments. This works well in certain dimensions such as literacy. For instance, if every person in a society becomes literate, then the society as a whole benefits from a more literate population, as was commonly observed in the rapid developments of East Asian societies, from Japan, South Korea and Taiwan to China.

However, this ontological position is much more problematic in situations that do not add up well. As noted by Corbridge (2002), the most obvious are situations of conflicting freedoms, when the life that you value living undermines the capability of others to do the same. It is also problematic in situations where fallacies of composition complicate the adding-up process, such as when everyone invests in commodity production or handicraft production, but then unit prices fall for these commodities as a result and no one is better-off and investments are wasted. Or, as classically postulated by Keynes, when one person saves, they are richer, but when the society as a whole saves, everyone ends up poorer.

These insights on fallacies of composition in particular were at the foundation of both Keynesian and early development economics for at least the first decades of the postwar era. Both schools of thought challenged the simplistic method of aggregating micro-level behaviour or observations to draw macro conclusions, given that the adding-up often leads to unexpected and counterintuitive types of dynamics, particularly when money is introduced into the equation. The neo-classical revival in economics from the 1970s onwards rejected much of this with the call for a return to 'micro-foundations', although the challenge is really the other way around. How do we take observations of compositional fallacies at the macro level and work these back into our understanding and conceptualisation of individual- or firm-level behaviour at the micro level given the simultaneity by which both micro and macro dimensions co-exist and interact? Such an approach might indeed prove to be very incisive for understanding individual behaviour that, from a restricted and partial micro view, might otherwise be perceived as non-rational or otherwise not predicted by micro-theoretical foundations operating in isolation of broader systemic contexts.[5]

Examples of conflicting freedoms are also especially rife in settings of development, particularly in peripheral societies or regions that have strong centripetal forces driving wealth, people and resources away from local communities, or, as Gunnar Myrdal (1957) once called it, backwash effects. A simple example can be drawn from the health sector. If a person in, say, Malawi obtains a degree in medicine or nursing, but then migrates abroad and ends up working for the National Health Service in the UK, they will earn substantially more income as a result of their enhanced capability through education. This can be seen as a form of individual development, whereby education mutually reinforces income and capability for the individual. We need to question whether such an individual path of development makes that person happier, although Sen rightly questions whether objective wellbeing is necessarily associated with subjective states such as happiness. Indeed, studies have revealed a high prevalence of depression among university students in the UK.

Nonetheless, the individual development in this case works against the development of societal capabilities in the Malawian health system, not only in terms of the loss of skilled labour but also in terms of the loss of the previous investment of scarce financial and human resources that went into educating the person who then migrated abroad. Indeed, even the HDRs regularly document inequalities of this sort, such as the fact that there are more Ethiopian-trained doctors in the US than in Ethiopia, which is a situation that has been going on for decades, particularly since structural adjustment programmes in the 1980s and 1990s crippled the fiscal ability of many national governments in poorer countries to retain staff. The point is that poor countries have proven themselves very capable of generating highly skilled 'functionings' in their populations for decades, but given scarce resources and other constraints, combined with the freedom of exit through migration, substantial obstacles persist in converting these individual functionings into societal or state and administrative capability. Similarly, financial freedom might encourage nationals to hold their assets and savings abroad. This might be perfectly rational behaviour for those with access to this option, but it has the effect of exacerbating the vulnerability of domestic financial systems to crisis. In the event of crisis, people who do not possess this international financial mobility generally bear the brunt of subsequent austerity and adjustment, as has been the case in international debt crises since the 1980s.

It is this liberal theoretical stance and ontological individualism in Sen's work that has made it very amenable to mainstream adoption, in particular by the dominant international financial institutions that, at least since the 1980s, have been vanguards in the neoclassical revival in economics and neoliberalism in economic policy. It is in this sense that Amiya Kumar Bagchi (2000) has argued that this stance has acted as a Trojan Horse for more neoliberal ideas. Others, such as Polanyi Levitt (2000), have similarly criticised such thinking for contributing to undermining the idea of development as a social or collective transformative project, in which the realisation of individual rights or freedoms necessarily must be advanced through collective efforts, in particular through the leadership of states, in the absence of which the assertion of individual freedoms or rights rings hollow.

Such points of criticism lead us more clearly into debates about what is required to develop. For instance, as noted by Corbridge (2002), the end of freedom is generally not questioned (indeed, even Marxists would agree with that), but Sen is often criticised because his idea of freedom as means is not consistent with the experience of countries like South Korea or China. Indeed, all countries, including the UK, were not effectively democratic – not in the modern sense of universal suffrage – during their phases of intensive industrial and social transformation.

This in turn relates to the use of coercion in development, or of unfree means to achieve ends of freedom. As emphasised by Bagchi (2000) and other critical scholars, capitalism has been as much about coercion as freedom (see a similar point by Dean 2009). Indeed, how is factory production or mass consumption and marketing about freedom? Are we really free in what Polanyi once called the factory system and market society? And is freedom the most important message for poor societies, with already highly informal and unregulated labour forces, when in fact the rich nations of the world are highly regulated, if not by governments then by large monopolistic corporations. Even with respect to the end result, we need to ask, as per Foucauldian notions of governmentality, whether development has indeed resulted in 'freedom' or, rather, in more complex forms of social organisation based on myths of freedom as powerful self-disciplining ideologies. Indeed, this was also fundamental to Polanyi's message, that liberalism essentially operated as the ideology for the self-regulating market society.

This raises deeper questions about the application of liberal deductive modes of analysis to complex historical and social phenomena, as has long been a source of debate in the social sciences. Can conceptions of justice, rights or freedom be abstracted from their historical, social and cultural context? Deductive theory does not tell us how we got to where we are, which is very important when it comes to explaining poverty and development. This is a philosophical issue that lies at the heart of poverty measurement precisely because the determination of acceptable standards of living is invariably rooted in such social and historical contexts, and changes within those contexts alongside development, in often complex, convoluted and contradictory ways.

Indeed, a fundamental problem with the deductive individualist method of Sen is that the theory is unable to deal with systems, structure, and inequality. In other words, social inequality cannot be conceived individually – at least two people are needed for social inequality, whether in terms of income distribution or in terms of groups in society, such as with respect to class, race, ethnicity, gender, etc. Hence, an individualist ontology of development is in tension with integrating issues of inequality into subsequent theorisation.

The same applies to issues of power, which, as often noted, is relational. It is often claimed or celebrated that Sen does offer a relational theory of poverty and development, although this is arguably not found in the internal logic of his theorisation. Rather, while Sen does discuss issues of inequality at length, he approaches these in a deductive manner. Inequalities are assumed or imposed on the theoretical model, as if exogenous occurences, but their emergence is not explained from within the causal dynamics informing the model (as would be the case, for instance, in Marxist theory). Such deduction is shared with liberal theories of justice more generally, such as that of John Rawls, with whom Sen sees himself in critical dialogue.

In this respect, development, understood as processes of structural transformation, requires an understanding and mode of analysis that embrace broader systems and patterns of structural integration, among other considerations, and brings these into the core of analysis. This is crucial for understanding the reproduction of modern poverty within these processes, which cannot be perceived through the abstraction of deduction.

Rather, the danger of the deductive bubble is that it encourages circular reasoning. This is more clearly revealed if the logic of capability failure is inverted and we suggest that the rich are rich because they have greater capability, which also results in greater capability. That the rich can do what they want with their wealth within legal (or even illegal) limits is stating the obvious. That they derived their wealth through their individual capability is problematic, especially at a time when we know from the work of Piketty (2014) and many others that a huge proportion of the lifetime wealth of the rich is inherited and not earned. Unless of course we define such wealth itself as a functioning, but then we are dealing with a tautology: that being rich makes you rich. None of this circular reasoning and play on words is particularly useful for learning about how the rich actually became rich (or inversely, how the poor became or remained poor). For this, we need induction and history.

Conclusion

This chapter started with a discussion of direct measures of poverty and/or illbeing, as the precursor to multidimensional measures of poverty. Similar to food income lines in money-metric approaches, these are considered as the gold standard of absolute non-monetary measures even though they are also fundamentally arbitrary and relative, particularly with respect to the determination of thresholds. The chapter then continued with a critical examination of human development and multidimensional measures, focusing on the project of constructing composite indices such as the HDI and the MPI, and how these actually compound and multiply many of the problems associated with money-metric lines rather than correcting or attenuating them. Three problems were highlighted: problems of meaning, both with regard to the choice of variables and the resultant indices that are abstracted from any tangible social or economic meaning; problems of obscuration through aggregation; and problems of priority, in terms of the way that these agendas have been channelled into and influencing statistical and policy agendas.

The third section then engaged in a more theoretical discussion around the work of Amartya Sen to clarify how these agendas have been sliding into or are susceptible to being coopted by mainstream supply-side and targeted agendas of social provisioning and poverty alleviation. These conceptual and theoretical perspectives are important because of the way that they feed back into practice, especially in terms of how we view the causes of poverty as primarily individual failings versus as structural outcomes. Similarly, they influence how we view poverty reduction strategies and whether these should be mainly focused on the accumulation of individual functionings, so to speak, and their liberal integration into broader social and economic systems, or whether these should start by addressing broader and systemic issues of inequality and power that so often undermine existing or ongoing accumulations of functionings, capability and so forth.

The former perspective has been arguably reinforced by the capability approach and by the MPI project, as revealed by the proclivity by which they have been taken up by existing mainstream agendas without significantly altering these agendas, certainly not in terms of actual policy conception and design. This is most clearly evidenced by the way that these measurement projects have been taken up as threshold-based targeting devices. Even though Sen himself argues against targeting, the MPI in particular has been fully drawn into a logic of targeting, perhaps as a way to justify its practical credibility with powerful patrons, even while it seeks its theoretical legitimacy from Sen and the capability approach.

These implications of targeting are discussed further in Chapter 6 and some practical alternatives are also discussed in the concluding chapter. Suffice to say here that when capability (or capabilities) is turned into a threshold practice, we effectively extend the scope of criteria by which we target people beyond income, to determine whether they are deserving and so forth. It thereby encourages a tendency to multiply the focus on the deficiencies of the poor, and the spaces within which they can be disciplined by elite-led state policy. It also exacerbates the complexity of the measurement exercise, which becomes particularly crucial when measurement and evaluation are turned towards the actual distribution of resources and benefits, in which purportedly scientific processes of selection invariably break down under the pressures of local power relations and the imperfections of actual administrative practices.

There is also a close fit between these measures and behavioural approaches, particularly with the use of conditionalities in policy. Conditionalities in social protection, for instance, are mostly focused on behaviour within these 'human dimensions', such as school attendance or clinic visits (although also increasingly in terms of work requirements, especially in richer OECD countries). While no one can argue against the virtues of children attending (good-quality) schools and women and children visiting (good-quality) health clinics, these should not be substitutes for a broader understanding of how structures and relations of power influence and condition the broader context within which poor people behave and make choices in highly constrained ways. Such matters are more explicitly addressed by the social exclusion approach, as discussed in the following chapter.

5 | THE SOCIAL EXCLUSION APPROACH

The other major concept in poverty studies that has stood the test of time and of fleeting fads of self-promotion is that of social exclusion. The concept emerged in the 1970s and has become a central reference in the lexicon of poverty studies since the 1990s, to the extent that poverty and social exclusion are often used inseparably. It is one of the three approaches dealt with in this book because of its prevailing usage as a poverty concept in official policy documents, especially in the UK and Europe, and also in scholarship the world over. It is also the antithesis of social inclusion, which has become a cornerstone theme for the World Bank as well as for current global development agendas. In this sense, common definitions of inclusion within the discourse of inclusive growth or development are essentially mirror images of previous attempts to define exclusion in the 1990s.

Both concepts, however, are politically contested and suffer from vagueness, even while they garner wide appeal. Early discussions around inclusive growth or development in the late 2000s revolved around the tension between absolute poverty reduction (roughly represented by the World Bank position) and relative poverty or inequality reduction (roughly represented by the UN position), thereby reproducing the frame of debate in the idea of pro-poor growth that preceded it in the early 2000s. However, within this frame, inclusion is definitely juxtaposed with the idea of exclusion, by both the World Bank and the UN. This is clearly evident in what appears to be the most recent effort by the World Bank to give substance to the idea of social inclusion (WB 2013), as linked on their website at the time of writing.[1]

Debates around social exclusion in the 1990s nonetheless offered more nuance. The exciting potential presented by the concept was the chance to bring in subtler sociological analyses into the existing field of poverty studies, such as notions of social integration, ordering, segregation, stratification and subordination. It is also commonly said that the attractions of the concept of social exclusion are that it brings attention to relational dimensions of poverty, highlights the types of processes that cause entitlement or capability failures (as discussed in the previous chapter), and brings to the fore issues of discrimination or disadvantage in the discussion of poverty. For these reasons, it is generally valued as a concept, even though it is never very clear how, exactly, it should be differentiated from poverty. In the policy literature, such as in documents by the European Commission that have officially adopted the concept, it is generally defined as a type of poverty.

This leads to the perennial question of whether the concept of social exclusion adds any value if it is essentially synonymous with poverty. Why not just talk about poverty? Amartya Sen (2000) argues that the concept is essentially redundant, perhaps semantically useful for the reasons mentioned above, but already implicit within various existing approaches to studying poverty, especially the capability approach that already deals with issues of relationality. Social exclusion can therefore be seen as an adjunct to this and other poverty approaches, describing various contextualised social causes and/or social consequences of poverty, albeit with an extra emphasis on coercion and discrimination than is usually made in the more liberal strands of the poverty studies literature. After a period of debate about the usefulness of the concept in the 1990s and early 2000s, many seem to have settled with this compromise.

Others, however, have raised more polemic critiques. The identification of exclusion as a principle characteristic of poverty encourages policy approaches that seek inclusion as the solution. Mistrust with the concept has been due to the fact that this is usually interpreted more specifically as market inclusion, thereby harmonising with neo-liberal obsessions of extending and deepening markets. The problem that has often been raised since the 1990s is that much of what is identified as exclusion, especially in developing countries, might in fact represent impoverished or even exploitative forms of inclusion, or inclusion on poor terms, as synthesised by Gore and Figueiredo (1997). DuToit (2004) coined this as adverse incorporation and Du Toit and Hickey re-coined it as adverse incorporation and social exclusion. However, the idea is as old as theories about capitalism itself, whereby the exploitation of labour is understood to occur through their inclusion into capitalist processes, not their exclusion.

Li (2007) nonetheless raises the spectre that contemporary capitalism might be evolving towards greater degrees of exclusion than in the past through the creation of 'surplus populations', although the question again is whether she is simply referring to the widespread informalisation of labour in developing countries that, as in the past, plays a functional role within capitalism of keeping wages low and workers disciplined.

To the extent that the problem is with the terms of inclusion and not with exclusion *per se*, simplistic promotions of inclusion might actually make matters worse. This is perhaps best exemplified by programmes of financial inclusion for the poor that are in effect predicated on quite exploitative terms (e.g., see Dymski 2005). Examples include the subprime crisis in the US (Dymski 2010; Dymski et al. 2011) or else many of the varieties of microfinance currently in practice, as discussed by Bateman (2010, 2012), Roy (2010) and Mader (2015, 2018), as well as in a compilation of articles edited by Bateman (2017).

These criticisms more or less accept the location of social exclusion within the space of poverty but then challenge whether notions of exclusion are necessarily the most appropriate to understand the cases of poverty that they are associated with. Another, subtler critique of the social exclusion approach questions its association with poverty and, in this sense, pushes back on the assertions made by Amartya Sen, as mentioned above. In other words, the concept might be redundant according to the ways it is conventionally defined and operationalised, but it nonetheless remains popular in both policy and academic discourse precisely because it captures the idea of something that is not quite the same as poverty. It is like an itch that we keep calling poverty but often is not. Indeed, the potential of this realisation is that it helps to move poverty studies away from its obsession with thresholds and into broader considerations of social integration.

This critique of both the dominant conceptions and the dominant criticisms of social exclusion can be clarified by situations where what we call social exclusion does not overlap with poverty, however conceptualised and measured, or where such exclusions worsen with movements out of poverty, such as among relatively non-poor and/ or upwardly mobile people. As discussed below, examples include international migrants who face subordinating exclusions in their attempts to integrate into their host countries, or university graduates from disadvantaged minorities who struggle to compete for employment in the upper strata of the labour market, in accordance with their levels of education, and yet who are not necessarily poor as a result. Both examples would not necessarily fall under the rubric of capability or relative poverty (unless, of course, we tautologically define an exclusion as a capability failure, which is a danger of the capability approach, as discussed in the previous chapter). They might not even be reflected as rising inequality. In such cases, it would be wrong to assume that social exclusion is the same as poverty, whether absolute or relative.

This critique is also clarified by what I refer to as causal and positional relativity (Fischer 2008a, 2011a). The causal refers to the idea that there are multiple often contradictory processes at work within any condition or state of being, such that a person might face both exclusionary and inclusionary processes at the same time. Some of this might be conceived in terms of multidimensionality, such as exclusion from health insurance but not from labour markets, but not necessarily all, given that these multiple causalities can even occur within a single dimension. As a result, the identification of exclusion in these situations depends on which causal process we decide to focus on. It is not necessarily possible to essentialise the characteristics of this exclusion onto an overall identity or condition of the person or group in question. This point is similar to the often-noted insight that exclusion is usually predicated on patterns of inclusion, or vice versa, as referred to in Gore and Figueiredo (1997). It is not exactly the same as the adverse incorporation point made by Du Toit (2004), insofar as it recognises characteristics of exclusion as distinct from inclusion, operating together rather than being conflated. As such, it bears more similarity with some of the French sociological scholarship (e.g., Roulleau-Berger 1999), as discussed further below.

Positional relativity means that what we call exclusion is relative to a person's position in a social hierarchy, both objectively and subjectively. In other words, a person can be an excludee and an excluder at the same time and will tend to perceive their exclusion (or inclusion) relative to the social strata immediately surrounding them. This is analogous to insights from the wellbeing literature that one's subjective perception of wellbeing depends in part on one's position or situation relative to one's immediate surrounding, which serves as a basis of social comparison.[2] It also ties into feminist notions of intersectionality in that positional relativity can apply across many dimensions of comparison, such as ethnicity, class, caste, clan, occupations, gender, generation or location.

In these respects, various poverty approaches are only capable of reflecting what we call exclusions operating at the bottom of a social hierarchy. They do not capture similar processes operating higher up in a social hierarchy among non-poor people, even though these dynamics might be crucial for understanding processes of social stratification, marginalisation, disadvantage and discrimination, all of which can occur in the absence of poverty. Overlaps obviously occur between these processes and poverty, which merit our urgent attention, although we render a disservice to our ability to understand and address the interactions if we merge concepts together.

Differentiating poverty from what we call social exclusion is also important from a policy perspective. As has been noted with respect to gender, such as by Jackson (1996), policies that are designed to address poverty might not be appropriate to address things such as disadvantage or discrimination. Indeed, the policy objectives of addressing each might be quite distinct, such as when addressing ethnic disadvantages that do not necessarily overlap neatly with socio-economic disparities.

If differentiated from poverty, the social exclusion approach might provide additional analytical insight to understand these processes that overlap but also extend beyond the space of poverty. However, the question then is that, for all of the vagueness, confusion and politically loaded insinuations associated with the concept, why not jettison it altogether? How does the concept of social exclusion add to our understanding of processes of stratification, subordination and segregation, or of disadvantage and discrimination, more than we are already able to obtain through these existing sociological concepts? This has been debated intensely in the literature, but with no convincing or conclusive results. In effect, the enticement of the concept is that it permits a discrete consideration of social power relations – the ways in which social power relations work to confer or deny access to resources or opportunities – with a jargon that does not cause alarm to the establishment. But, then, what are the costs of trying to assuage the establishment, such as the cooptation of the concept into market inclusion agendas, as noted above, versus calling a spade and spade and being done with it? The danger, as usual, is in replacing existing, established and relatively clear social-scientific concepts and methods with vague and unspecified new ones.

These arguments are made in four sections. The first offers a brief introduction to the concept of social exclusion and the second synthesises the many ambiguities surrounding the concept. The third elaborates on the point about differentiating what we have come to call social exclusion from poverty and the fourth provides some practical examples of why it is important to do so. The conclusion returns to the fundamental point that other, more precise social science concepts are arguably better-suited for the purpose of studying and addressing the range of issues that have been stuffed under the social exclusion umbrella, and with clearer political and policy implications.

A synthesis of the social exclusion approach

In the canonical accounts of the social exclusion approach, the concept is generally said to have been coined by Réné Lenoir (1974) in his seminal book, *Les Exclus*. His work essentially referred to the increasing inability of European welfare states (and, in particular, that of France) to deal with cases of people falling through the cracks of the welfare system because they were not able to work. Work was crucial because these systems were designed on the basis of full employment, whereby at least one member of every family would establish the basis for welfare entitlements through regular, full-time, formal employment. Lenoir identified those who were unable to work for either physical or mental reasons as the excluded, who accounted for a minor but significant and growing proportion of the population.

The idea was then increasingly taken up in 1970s and 1980s in Europe, although with somewhat different interpretations. Instead of dealing with the marginals who could not work, it was increasingly applied to the emergence of chronic, long-term, involuntary unemployment, in the context of economic crisis and restructuring and the increasingly inability of the welfare states to deal with the rising trend of people who were able to work but could not find work. This interpretation of social exclusion then became increasingly mainstreamed in the EU and the UK in the 1990s, as discussed further below.

The International Institute of Labour Studies (IILS) of the International Labour Office (ILO) then launched a research project on social exclusion in 1993 with the support of the UNDP. The aim was to refashion the concept from its roots in European social policy discourse to a wider, less Eurocentric global application, for application to anti-poverty policy in particular (see Rodgers et al. 1995, p. vi). Attempts were made to re-interpret the concept from a way of describing processes of marginalisation and deprivation in rich countries with comprehensive welfare systems and where the vast majority of the workforce is integrated into formal employment, to developing countries where universal welfare provisioning is mostly absent and formal employment usually only covers a small minority of the workforce. The project was intended to contribute to the discussion at the World Summit for Social Development in 1995 and to explore ways in which the analysis of exclusion could make anti-poverty strategies more effective (ibid).

This need for a more general and generic refashioning was seen as particularly urgent given the economic crises and structural adjustments of the 1980s and early 1990s. These were undermining whatever limited welfare developments had previously been achieved by developing countries, especially in Latin America. Crises and neoliberal responses were also associated with an intensification of informality rather than its attenuation, despite neoliberal arguments that deregulation would facilitate formalisation, as argued, for instance, by De Soto (1989). The fact that structural adjustments were being guided by the same overarching ideology, with comparable dynamics of increasing precarity and insecurity as those occurring in northern welfare states, lent weight to the project of extending the concept of social exclusion to developing countries even despite the absence of similar institutional settings.

The effort to render the concept less Eurocentric was nonetheless criticised as Eurocentric, from the perspective of trying to impose concepts that derive from a European context onto non-European contexts. The criticism is that there is little to be gained from applying a concept formulated in rich post-industrial societies with already-existing comprehensive formal labour markets and welfare systems to poor countries where, if the same metres of identification and measurement were to be used, the majority of the population would be deemed 'excluded'.[3] However, this criticism can be easily dealt with by loosening the institutional specifications of the concept and treating it more generically in terms of the principle that patterns of exclusion are relative to whatever prevailing modes of inclusion are operating in any particular context, whichever the context. This point is similar to arguments made by Hillary Silver (1995), as discussed further below.

The Eurocentric critique can also be turned on its head by simply reversing the charge and noting that the intellectual origins of the concept might have plausibly derived from the South in any case. We need only recall that Latin American structuralist and dependency scholars were using terms that are very analogous to exclusion since the 1950s and 1960s, such as marginalisation and peripheralisation, if indeed they were not already referring directly to the term 'exclusion' itself. As noted by Gore (1995, p. 4):

> it has been suggested that the emerging social problems of Europe reflect a process of 'Latin Americanization', in the sense that European economies and societies are moving closer in their forms of organization to those of Latin America ... As that occurs, the language to describe and analyse the situation in Europe is catching up to one already widely deployed in Latin America, where debates about marginalization were already vigorous in the 1960s.

In terms of lineages of thought, it is also notable that the Brazilian economist Celso Furtado, one of the foremost from the Latin American structuralist school, taught at the Sorbonne from 1965 to 1985, along with many other Latin Americans exiled from their countries during that time (Kay 2005, p. 1204). Furtado would have undoubtedly influenced his French colleagues. The presence in Paris during the 1950s and 1960s of other well-known Third World scholars using similar terminologies is also noteworthy, such as Samir Amin (e.g., 1968, 1970, 1973). Likewise, René Lenoir spent several years as a technical advisor to African governments prior to his 1974 publication, further reinforcing this hypothesis that his ideas might have been the product of creative intellectual fertilisation from South to North.

Irrespective of these debates in the history of thought, the literature has generally settled around a number of conventional definitions of social exclusion. In the IILS project to universalise the concept, Rodgers (1995, p. 44) defined it quite generally and vaguely 'as a way of analysing how or why individuals and groups fail to have access to or benefit from the possibilities offered by societies or economies.' Meanwhile, the way the concept has been defined in the UK and EU policy and academic literature is more in terms of the social aspects of deprivation, such as the isolation that one presumably experiences when one is (relatively) poor, or else how experiences like isolation might cause or reinforce relative poverty (e.g., see the volume edited by Room 1995b). The latter approach is decidedly individual in its identification of attributes, in the sense that the attributes of exclusion are not necessarily based on identity, even though identity could be one cause of exclusion. This is in contrast to some of the approaches of applying the concept to developing countries, which tend to define social exclusion in terms of group-based discriminations, as discussed further below.

The exercise of determining definitions obviously raises a variety of questions. From what should people be considered excluded? Or by what or by whom? Some argue that social exclusion differs from poverty because it begs these types of questions and points towards non-material aspects of poverty, such as status or denial of access, or else highlights concepts such as disadvantage, discrimination, marginalisation and the relational processes that are related to these phenomena. It also highlights the importance of citizenship rights and the importance of institutional analysis in understanding patterns of inclusion, in terms of how formal or informal rules and norms are formed and practised to segregate, stratify, structure and order populations, such that some experience restrictions to the rights enjoyed by others, whether for reasons of identity, property, rights, etc.

In terms of methods, various approaches have also been proposed. In the UK and EU approach mentioned above, the main efforts have been to quantify various social dimensions of poverty. Others propose measures of group representation, such as proportions of a group in particular positions or experiencing particular outcomes versus their population share, such as the percentage of African-Americans in the US prison population versus their population share. Of course, the latter measures do not detect exclusion *per se*. Rather, they are measures of representation aimed at revealing discrimination, which might or might not result from exclusionary practices. Other measures include legal approaches that attempt to identify legally defined exclusions, or sociological analyses of daily practices, in cases where formal legal provisions are inclusive but practices and experiences are not.

Much like the capability approach, one of the main challenges of measuring social exclusion is to actually identify exclusions rather than the spaces in which we might expect exclusions to be occurring, which will be discussed further below. Moreover, the measures that identify discriminations are group-based measures and, much like the challenges facing the HDI discussed in the previous chapter, the challenge is to design measures that are able to identity individual experiences of exclusion.

While there has been some development on individual-based measures, particularly with respect to the UK/EU work on social exclusion as noted above, the problem is that the proposed and adopted individual-based measures are essentially measures of poverty rather than necessarily representing exclusion. For instance, Burchardt et al. (1999) propose a notion of participation in five types of activity, including consumption, savings, production, political and social. However, this essentially boils down to income and asset poverty, and unemployment, with the addition of social isolation and lack of political participation. (The inclusion of political participation is odd and normative, in the sense that there might be many otherwise 'normally' integrated people who are not members of political parties or campaign groups, or who do not vote.)

This constantly leads back to the central criticism in the literature, which is that the social exclusion approach is duplicating or even distracting attention away from poverty, that it is redundant with poverty concepts or that it leads to a different identification of the poor or different anti-poverty policies. Indeed, this last point is a conclusion from Burchardt et al. (ibid.), who identified only a few people in their study who were excluded on all dimensions in any one year and even fewer who experienced multiple exclusions for the whole period, although of course this is not surprising given their inclusion of the political participation variable, as noted above. They argue that this 'supports the view that treating different dimensions of exclusion separately is preferable to thinking about social exclusion in terms of one homogeneous group.' While this is a sensible point, it still begs the question of what, exactly, is different between this approach and multidimensional measures of poverty, as discussed in the previous chapter.

The ambiguities of social exclusion

In order to expand on the last points above, it is useful to clarify three closely related problems in the literature on social exclusion since the early 1990s that result in strong degrees of ambiguity. One is that most authors invariably operationalise social exclusion as a static description of outcomes or a state of being, even though most also agree that the strength of the concept lies in the attention it brings to dynamic processes. Second, as noted above, there is a propensity to treat the concept of social exclusion as a type of poverty, despite the fact that it is often recognised that exclusion can occur in the absence of poverty. The third problem derives from the ambiguous use of the terms 'relative' and 'relational'.

Processes and states

A good starting point to demonstrate the ambiguous reference to processes and states of being is found in the IILS work in the mid-1990s. Most scholars in this project came to agree that the value-added of the social exclusion approach, over other concepts of poverty or deprivation, is its focus on processes, particularly social processes such as disadvantage and/or impoverishment. For instance, in the introduction of their summary of one key debate organised by the IILS, in which they define exclusion as both a situation or a process of marginalisation or the fragmentation of social relations, Gore and Figueiredo (1997, p. v) argue that the concept focuses attention on processes that lead to disadvantage, impoverishment or illbeing, rather than an identification of excluded individuals or groups in an absolute sense. Similarly, in their comprehensive review of four main ways of defining and measuring poverty, Laderchi et al. (2003) conclude that a key strength of the social exclusion approach, in comparison to the monetary, capability or participatory approaches, is that it 'is the only one that focuses intrinsically, rather than as an add-on, on the processes and dynamics that allow deprivation to arise and persist' (p. 260). This position is also reflected in much of the UK-oriented scholarship, such as that by Berghman (1995), who argues that social exclusion needs to be seen as a dynamic process and not a state or outcome. Peter Townsend (2002, p. 7) makes a similar point, that inequality and poverty correspond to an idea of state, whereas polarisation and exclusion correspond to an idea of process.

However, in their attempts to operationalise social exclusion, most scholars invariably end up treating it as a state, outcome or condition of being, rather than as a process. This tendency derives from the unbearable itch to apply thresholds, reproducing the equivalent of poverty lines, as an effort to identify who, exactly, are the excluded, and below what threshold they should be considered excluded. The resultant search for an appropriate set of outcome indicators invariably leads to a static conceptualisation of social exclusion, which is arguably in tension with the emphasis on process. In particular, the outcome indicators mostly do not identify processes but instead the outcomes that are presumed to result from exclusion or that perhaps cause exclusion (such as income or asset poverty, as noted above). This also leads to dangers of tautology whereby causal processes are defined by their results.

Moreover, the outcome-based operationalisation of social exclusion also encourages a methodology-driven influence on the definition of social exclusion. As noted by Levitas (2006) with respect to the work on social exclusion in the UK and EU, 'the necessity of multiple indicators means that it is possible to draw up a provisional set without clarifying underlying definitions and relationships, and without any statement of priorities' (p. 127). In other words, operationalisation sweeps the definitional problems under the carpet rather than solving them. It is therefore no wonder that scholars have had difficulty in determining the applicability of social exclusion outside a European context, given that there is no clarity or precision on the concept even within Europe.

This problem of slipping into static notions is similar to the problem inherent in the capability approach of measuring potentials in terms of functionings, that is, outcomes such as life expectancy, morbidity, literacy and nutrition levels. As noted in the previous chapter, this removes the key philosophical insight of the capability approach on freedom and essentially renders it the same as the basic needs approach it set out to supplant. Social exclusion comes at the problem from a different angle – the measurement of processes rather than potentials – although it ironically ends up in more or less the same predicament of being measured according to various static outcome indicators of functionings or basic needs.

As a result, many definitions of social exclusion lack clarity as to whether social exclusion refers to a state or a process. Most authors compromise by treating it as both. Gore and Figueiredo (1997) accept that the dimensions of state and process overlap and that this is not necessarily contradictory. They suggest that (p. 18):

> the former offers a way of describing social exclusion and can for instance be used to define situations of permanent exclusion. In the latter, the focus is on the mechanisms which create or recreate exclusion, and on how poverty and deprivation are associated with structural economic and social change.

Laderchi et al. (2003) summarise this position by stipulating that 'the definition of [social exclusion] typically includes the process of becoming poor as well as some outcomes of deprivation' (p. 258). Similarly, Beall and Piron (2005) offer an abbreviated working definition of social exclusion as 'a process and a state [deriving from exclusionary relationships based on power] that prevents individuals or groups from full participation in social, economic and political life and from asserting their rights' (p. 9). Besides the recurrent tautology of defining exclusion as exclusion in these attempts at definition, they seek to solve the ambiguity between state and processes by grounding social exclusion in an understanding of poverty.

Social exclusion and poverty

The tension between states versus outcomes is closely intertwined with the common association of exclusion with poverty. As in the example of Burchardt et al. (1999) mentioned above, the definition of social exclusion is usually collapsed into a conception of poverty, either as the aspects of social deprivation involved in multidimensional concepts of poverty, or else as social processes leading to poverty. In other words, many definitions imply that if exclusion does not lead to some impoverishment, it is therefore not exclusion, or else it is not one that warrants our attention, and that it is mostly in the space of overlap where we should focus our concerns. For instance, in their efforts to resolve the debate on how best to differentiate social exclusion from poverty, Gore and Figueiredo (1997, p. 10) argue that the former refers to processes of impoverishment. 'Its value then is that it enables causal analysis of various paths into and out of poverty, getting beyond the unhelpful lumping together of diverse categories of people as "the poor."' Similarly, Laderchi et al. (2003) explicitly treat social exclusion as one of four main ways of defining and measuring poverty.

Gore (1995, pp. 1–2) nonetheless clarifies that the early French debates of the 1970s and 1980s did not necessarily equate social exclusion with poverty as such, but with processes of social disintegration. The concept only became more closely equated with poverty in the early 1990s after the European Commission defined social exclusion in relation to a certain basic standard of living. In the UK, Levitas (2006, p. 126) notes that the distinction between social exclusion and poverty is 'sometimes masked by references to "poverty and social exclusion" as an inseparable dyad'. Pantazis et al. (2006, p. 8) also note that the 1999 Poverty and Social Exclusion Survey for the UK proposed impoverishment as one of four dimensions for measuring social exclusion, alongside labour market exclusion, service exclusion and exclusion from social relations. This selection thereby includes a notion of poverty into its implicit definition of social exclusion. Levitas (2006, pp. 130–131) remarks the same with the indicators adopted by the EU Social Protection Committee in 2001, which included income and labour-market position as well as deprivations in education, housing and health. The EU position has basically not changed since.[4]

In the development studies literature, such as Laderchi et al. (2003), social exclusion is usually defined as poverty or as processes leading to poverty. For instance, all of the working definitions in the series of country studies commissioned by the IILS in the 1990s essentially treat social exclusion as contextually defined forms of relative or capability poverty – see Rodgers et al. (1995) for detailed presentations and a summary by Gore and Figueiredo (1997, pp. 17–18). The India study defined social exclusion as a denial of the basic welfare rights that provide citizens positive freedoms, and Appasamy et al. (1995, p. 238) define these as basic needs in education, health, water and sanitation, and social security. The Thailand study defined it as a non-recognition or disrespect for the citizenship rights on which livelihood and living standards depend. The Russia study defined it as material deprivation and infringement of social rights, defined mainly in terms of employment. The Tanzania study defined it as both a state and process, with the state being equivalent to relative deprivation, while the processes were socially determined impediments to access resources, social goods or institutions. The Yemen study defined it as social segregation, where some individuals and groups are not recognised as full and equal members of society. The Peru study defined it in terms of the inability to participate in aspects of social life considered important (Gore and Figueiredo, 1997, pp. 17–18). Figueroa et al. (1996) deemed that its analytical value comes from its elucidation of social processes which contribute to social inequality (p. 201). The general definitional gist remains consistent throughout; all these studies treat social exclusion as either relative or capability deprivation.

Subsequent elaborations of the concept in development studies scholarship continued along these lines. In a workshop convened by the Institute of Development Studies in Sussex in 1997, De Haan thought that despite its overlap with the concept of poverty, the concept of social exclusion could be useful nonetheless because it focuses on processes and because it is multidimensional in nature. However, he was doubtful whether these aspects made it different from poverty. The distinction was only clear if one adopted a very narrow view of poverty, whereas 'much of the current debate on poverty, especially in developing countries, was concerned with wider concepts of relative deprivation, ill-being, vulnerability and capability', and was thus very similar to the social exclusion approach (cited in O'Brien et al. 1997, p. 3). Bhalla and Lapeyre (1997) operationalise social exclusion by essentially focusing on depth of poverty and income inequality measures, and a variety of social aspects purporting to measure access but that essentially boil down to a measurement of various functionings and outcomes (pp. 425–426). Saith (2001) also explores the feasibility of operationalising the social exclusion concept in developing countries. She notes (p. 1) that efforts

> appear to largely result in a repetition of research that has
> already been conducted within frameworks that have developed
> in developing countries (basic needs, capabilities, sustainable
> livelihoods, risk and vulnerability, participatory approaches)
> in parallel to the 'social exclusion' concept in industrialised
> countries.

In order to avoid the relabelling of poverty studies, she suggests that 'rather than trying to transplant the concept, it might be worth concentrating on incorporating the advantages of "social exclusion" like its emphasis on process into existing frameworks in developing countries' (p. 14). In all these examples, the authors struggle to break free from existing poverty approaches, but ultimately return to the fold.

This point is made by several authors in both the social policy and development studies literatures. Levitas (2006, p. 126) notes that even the aspects of social exclusion dealing with social relations, which are deemed to be among of its most important contributions, such as exclusion from social participation, were part of the earlier conceptualisation of relative deprivation by Townsend (1979). Room (1999) makes the same point, that the multidimensional, dynamic and community aspects often promoted as the novelties of the social exclusion approach all existed in the 'classic' studies on poverty. He suggests that the more original element of social exclusion is found in its emphasis of relational issues (inadequate social participation, lack of social integration, and lack of power), versus the primary emphasis of poverty on distributional issues (pp. 167–169). Bhalla and Lapeyre (1997, p. 417) contend with this distinction – made in earlier papers by Room, e.g., Room (1995a), arguing that the broad concept of poverty (i.e., relative and capability deprivations) covers both the distributional and relational aspects of deprivation referred to by Room (1994, 1995a), hence bringing even these elements back into the poverty fold.

Amartya Sen (2000) makes exactly this point in his own rendition of social exclusion. He argues that, by way of relationality, social exclusion constitutively describes one aspect of capability deprivation and instrumentally causes further diverse capability failures (p. 5). In other words, he paraphrases in the negative what he says about freedom in *Development as Freedom* (1999): the relational features of social exclusion 'enrich the broad approach of seeing poverty as the lack of freedom to do certain valuable things' (ibid.). He notes that this emphasis is nothing new and refers back to Adam Smith's concern with 'deprivation in the form of exclusion from social interaction, such as appearing in public freely, or – more generally – taking part in the life of the community' (p. 7).

However, by reducing the social exclusion approach into an analysis of relationality, Sen argues that its helpfulness does not lie in its conceptual newness, but in the attention it focuses on the role of relational features in deprivation (p. 8). For this reason, if the language of exclusion is to add value to our understanding of deprivation, 'it is crucial to ask whether a relational deprivation has been responsible for a particular case of [deprivation]' (pp. 9–10). He therefore concludes that, if understood in this way, the 'perspective of social exclusion reinforces – rather than competes with – the understanding of poverty as capability deprivation' (p. 46). In other words, he effectively relegates the concept of social exclusion to an adjunct position within his own theoretical agenda.

Unfortunately, Sen seems possessed with establishing the authority of his own capability approach rather than with distinguishing the social exclusion approach in its own right, to the extent that he almost appears defensive. For instance, in his rendition of social exclusion, Sen contends with an implicit criticism of the capability approach made by Gore (1995, p. 9), arguing that there is nothing in the capability approach that would doom it to be excessively individualist and insufficiently social, and thereby causing it to miss a focus on the relational features of deprivation (Sen 2000, p. 8). Indeed, it is ironic that many of the efforts to clarify or elaborate a social exclusion approach, such as the IILS studies, have instead ended out adding operational rigour to the capability approach. Conversely, Sen avoids the concept of relative deprivation, even though it might seem better-suited than the capability approach for dealing with many of the concepts that he discusses in relation to social exclusion, such as the inability to participate in a community due to a lack of means relative to social norms. In any case, he offers no guidance on how to differentiate social exclusion from poverty.

Some authors in the development studies scholarship attempt to avoid an explicit association between social exclusion and poverty but nonetheless use an idea of norms to situate exclusion within a social context. Examples include the reference to 'full participation' mentioned above (cf. Laderchi et al. 2003, p. 257; Beall and Piron 2005, p. 9), or 'normal activities' (Stewart et al. 2006, p. 4). These references are probably influenced by the EU definition of social exclusion in the mid-1990s as a 'process through which individuals or groups are wholly or partially excluded from full participation in the society in which they live' (Laderchi et al. 2003, p. 257). Here again, exclusion is tautologically defined as exclusion and, despite the effort to explicitly define it without reference to poverty, the understanding of 'full participation' or 'normal activities' places the definition into a metre of relative deprivation without explicitly stating this as such.

Similar attempts have been made to refine the concept of social exclusion along the lines of rights or choice. However, once the implications of such an approach become specified, it again becomes difficult to see how it differs in practice from either the capability or relative deprivation approaches, particularly given the emphasis on freedom in the former and the emphasis on norms in the latter. For instance, Schulte (2002) deals with social exclusion within a rights framework, treating it as the denial of a whole range of rights denoted by the concept of social citizenship. He stipulates that these include 'the right to social security and economic wellbeing, to the right to a full share in the social heritage and to the life of a civilised human being according to the normal standards prevailing in that society' (p. 121). In other words, once he stipulates the meaning of social citizenship rights, his approach essentially seems to be a reformulation of the capability approach, with an emphasis on capabilities defined by the relative norms of a society.

Choice was also emphasised in the adoption of an initial definition of social exclusion by the Centre for the Analysis of Social Exclusion (CASE): 'an individual is socially-excluded if he or she does not participate in key activities of the society in which he or she lives; ... the individual is not participating for reasons beyond his/her control; and he or she would like to participate' (Burchardt et al. 2002, pp. 30 and 32). However, it is again not clear how this emphasis on lack of choice (or un-freedom) is simply not a restatement of Sen's position on capability failure, as discussed below. In any case, Levitas notes that once operationalised, this CASE approach becomes limited to the first of their clauses and sidesteps the issue of choice for pragmatic reasons (2006, p. 134). In other words, as noted above, this approach also falls into the same predicament as the capability approach of reducing the measurement of potentials to that of functionings. The definition also runs into problems of determining which 'activities' should be considered 'key', in particular because such considerations are hugely related to one's social position, as discussed further below.

Kabeer (2006) makes a notable attempt to differentiate social exclusion from poverty by treating social exclusion as an analysis of processes of disadvantage, although she does this exclusively through the lens of identity discrimination. She elaborates (p. 3) that it

> reflects the multiple and overlapping nature of the disadvantages experienced by certain groups and categories of the population, with social identity as the central axis of their exclusion. It is thus a *group* or collective phenomena rather than an individual one.

Thus, she contends (p. 2) that

> understanding the social dimensions of inequality, hitherto ignored in mainstream poverty analysis, provides new lens through which to view the issue of chronic disadvantage ... These revolve around social identity and reflect the cultural devaluation of people based on *who they are* (or rather *who they are perceived to be*).

In this sense, Kabeer frames the 'social' of social exclusion in terms of social groups and identities, sharing much in common with the recent scholarship on intersectionalities. This is in contrast to an understanding of the 'social' in most of the UK- or EU-oriented literature, which refers to the social aspects of deprivation, which can operate at the individual level and without the intermediation of identity-based discrimination. Thus, while her approach makes sense within the South Asian context, at least in terms of understanding one aspect of disadvantage, it is hardly encompassing of the broader dimensions of exclusion, particularly in terms of how the concept came to be used in the 1980s with reference to economic restructuring.

Furthermore, her treatment of disadvantage is explicitly connected to an analysis of poverty. She notes in the beginning that the 'durable nature of this form of disadvantage means that people bearing devalued identities are likely to be disproportionately represented among the poor, as well as among the chronic poor' (ibid., p. 2). The rest of her paper therefore looks at social exclusion mostly from the perspective of an enriched processual understanding of the identity-based dynamics of poverty. Thus, it does not as such resolve the ambiguity between social exclusion and a wider multidimensional understanding of poverty, but implicitly accepts the fact that exclusions are only worthy of our attention if they overlap with poverty.

It is not clear, however, why she asserts that these aspects have been ignored in mainstream poverty analysis, given that her approach more or less echoes certain strands of the IILS publications ten years previously. For instance, in the debate summarised in Gore and Figueiredo (1997), there were several suggestions to see social exclusion as the generation of multiple disadvantages. Citing the work of 'Waltzer' (perhaps Michael Walzer?), these can then further evolve into 'destructive synergies' or 'radical disadvantage' (p. 43). It was further suggested that social exclusion be understood as a 'second-tier' concept of risk regime that expresses the interaction between social risk factors (such as unemployment, lack of access to social services or family breakdown), the cumulation of these factors and the diminished capacity of groups to respond to risk.

> The notion of social exclusion is therefore not a broad notion of poverty which encompasses non-material aspects and deprivations which do not arise from lack of resources. Rather poverty is a part of social exclusion. It is one of various risk factors which together cumulate to form a risk regime. (Gore and Figueiredo 1997, pp. 40–41)

While the source of this perspective was not identified, it resembles arguments made by Room (1999) that the element of catastrophic discontinuity in relationships with the rest of society offers the most essential contribution of social exclusion, in combination with its emphasis on relational elements. He argues (p. 171) that

> to use the notion of social exclusion carries the implication we are speaking of people who are suffering from such a degree of multi-dimensional disadvantage, of such duration, and reinforced by such material and cultural degradation of the neighbourhoods in which they live, that their relational links with the wider society are ruptured to a degree which is to some considerable degree irreversible. We may sometimes choose to use the notion of social exclusion in a more general sense than this: but here is its core.

This perspective certainly provides perhaps one of the most convincing distinctions of social exclusion from poverty, although it still ends up treating social exclusion as a catastrophic outcome occurring horizontally at the bottom of a social hierarchy, parallel to poverty.

It also brings us back to the idea of thresholds, in terms of being able to social-scientifically identify a point below which things start to fall apart, as discussed in previous chapters – ironically because the title of Room's 1995 publication is *Beyond the Threshold* (Room, 1995b). Indeed, he argues that it may be better to use the notion this way for it to be 'useful as an analytical concept and as a point of reference for policy design, rather than to use "social exclusion" as no more than a synonym of "disadvantage"' (ibid.). However, his distinction along these lines is not made through precise definition, but rather through a complex consolidation and integration of five elements, most of which already exist in the classic studies of poverty, as he consistently argues. In other words, his own argument that the other aspects of exclusion can be dealt with through a multidimensional approach to understanding poverty could equally apply to his conclusion on catastrophic discontinuity.

Relativity and relationality

The inconsistent meanings implied by the use of the terms 'relativity' and 'relationality' constitute a third problem in the literature, which in turn reinforces the ambiguity between social exclusion and poverty. Relativity is typically used in two closely related ways; relative poverty (exclusion relative to social norms) and contextual relativity (exclusion depending on societal modes of integration or incorporation). Laderchi et al. (2003, p. 258) draw a close connection between these two meanings, in that norms are determined by context.

The latter, contextual meaning of relativity owes much to the work of Hilary Silver (e.g., 1995), who proposes a threefold typology of the multiple meanings of exclusion inspired by the three models of welfare capitalism elaborated by Esping-Anderson (1990). These are situated in three different theoretical perspectives, political ideologies and national discourses (the solidarity, specialisation and monopoly paradigms). Without going into any detail on these paradigms (in part because their substantive content refers mostly to OECD countries), it suffices to note that Silver purposely avoids offering a definition of social exclusion precisely because she sees the ambiguity as offering a window of opportunity through which to view conflicting social-science paradigms and political ideologies. 'This is because at the heart of the question "exclusion from what?" is a more basic one, the "problem of social order" under conditions of profound social change' (Silver 1995, p. 61). Even though her three types refer mostly to European contexts, her work has nonetheless helped to extract the concept of social exclusion out of an association with a specific context and to theorise it in more generic terms.

Her stance in turn inspired the approach of the IILS, particularly considering that she was a central player in its initiatives of the 1990s. Thus, Gore argues that

> a precise definition of social exclusion depends on the paradigms of social integration and citizenship and the cultural environment prevailing in a society. These structure people's sense of belonging and membership and consequently the perception of what is exclusion and inclusion in their society. (Gore 1995, p. 8)

A similar line is taken up in the work of Atkinson (1998), who emphasises relativity as one of the three main characteristics of social exclusion, alongside agency and dynamics. Relativity in this sense refers to the fact that the meaning of exclusion is relative to a particular society, and Atkinson argues that this is an important element that differentiates social exclusion from the concept of poverty (pp. 13–14). Similarly, Laderchi et al. (2003) note that definitional problems 'are especially great in applying the concept to developing countries because "normality" is particularly difficult to define in multipolar societies, and because there can be a conflict between what is normal and what is desirable' (p. 259). Similar to Silver, this sense of relativity is generally seen as one of the principle strengths of the social exclusion approach.

Silver does raise some important interpretative issues, although her avoidance of definition by way of typology runs the risk of giving licence to use the concept as an ad hoc descriptor of any variety of multidimensional deprivation or disadvantage. Or else, it risks rendering the concept into an entirely descriptive template and aborting the analytical project of understanding exclusion as a causal process in its own right. Moreover, the typological approach also avoids the ambiguities between exclusion and poverty, which are not necessarily the result of relativity, but rather of conceptual imprecision. Indeed, as noted above, the allowance for definitional plurality was so loose in the series of IILS studies that that the concept came to mean just about anything to anyone, so long as it generally referred to some negative sense of multidimensional deprivation or disadvantage. Thus, while the various elaborations of social exclusion represent very valuable deepening of our understanding and measurement of deprivation, they do not solve the conceptual problem of differentiating social exclusion from poverty.

On a similar note, there is inconsistency in the literature on the exact meaning of the term 'relational' or 'relationality'. As argued by Room (1999), a relational deprivation need not imply an intentional act of exclusion, but merely a breakdown in social relations due to some deprivation, or else that social isolation leads to other deprivations, such as when a lack of social integration leads to poor health or education. In this sense, 'relational' refers to the absence of social relations, not necessarily that exclusion is caused by a relation between people.

However, others such as Beall and Piron (2005, p. 11) refer to the term 'relational' as an intended act of exclusion by an excluder towards an excludee. This latter usage, which is quite common, is actually closer to the term 'agency' used by Atkinson (1998), as also emphasised by Laderchi et al. (2003). Sen (2000, pp. 14–18) is ambiguous on this point and uses the two meanings interchangeably, noting that 'relationality' is already dealt with in the capability approach. He also refers to 'active' or 'passive' exclusion, which seems to be his way of dealing with agency. Regardless, we have to question whether exclusion necessarily needs to be intentional, insofar as impersonal structural dynamics can equally produce exclusion despite the best of relational intentions, as in the case of neighbourhood gentrification due to rising house prices. Indeed, the earlier conceptions of social exclusion developed in the 1970s and 1980s were precisely in response to such structural processes of social disintegration related to economic restructuring. Any attempt to define the concept should therefore engage with these 'non-relational' structural dimensions. Nonetheless, even if we accept 'relationality' or 'agency' as distinguishing elements of social exclusion, these arguably also play an important role in the capability approach, as noted earlier.

These various meanings of relativity and relationality throw a serious wrench into the definition or identification of exclusion. In particular, it is very difficult to determine norms within highly segmented, heterogeneous and hierarchical settings, where one person's norm is completely different from another's, or is at least perceived to be and accepted as such. However, this perspective also offers a way out of the ambiguity of social exclusion by implying that exclusions (or what we call exclusions) occur vertically across social orders, whereas poverty occurs horizontally at the lower end of social orders. In other words, all individuals or groups can perceive or experience an exclusionary process from whatever their position.

Differentiating social exclusion from poverty

These ambiguities in the scholarship dealing with social exclusion are substantive and not merely semantic. Indeed, ambiguity is a more serious criticism than the charge of Eurocentrism in the application of social exclusion to developing countries. As noted above, the Eurocentric critique can be dealt with by loosening the institutional specifications of the concept, or by reversing the charge and noting that the intellectual origins of the concept might have derived from the Global South in any case. However, the same cannot be said for the ambiguous association of social exclusion with poverty, which applies to both South and North. If the difference is merely semantic, as claimed by Sen (2000), then the whole project of trying to establish social exclusion as more than simply an adjunct way of describing various social aspects of poverty is put into question.

If merely semantic, then the often-noted criticism that the concept of social exclusion deflects political attention away from poverty and inequality would be particularly damning, although this criticism is more oriented towards its usage in the UK and Europe. For the rest of the world, the more significant implication is that, as noted in the Introduction, the association with poverty implies that the solution to poverty is to intensify inclusion. Indeed, this partly explains why the concept has been adopted so enthusiastically by the mainstream of development policy, such as by the World Bank.

The problem with attributing the solution to poverty as one of inclusion is that most cases of poverty in developing countries are better described as arising from the manner by which people are already included (i.e., low wage rates and poor working conditions) rather than exclusion (i.e., unemployment), as noted by a variety of scholars (e.g., Gore and Figueiredo 1997, pp. 41–42; Room 1999, p. 171; Du Toit 2004; Hickey and Du Toit 2007). Policies of inclusion that do not address these existing terms of inclusion might simply end up exacerbating exploitation, particularly when they end up facilitating such practices through liberalisation and deregulation. In contrast, people in such circumstances might well regard their situation as better when they are 'excluded', as highlighted in a study by Beall (2002) of municipal sweepers in Faisalabad, Pakistan, who used their identity-based social exclusion to secure livelihoods. Interestingly, however, the World Bank has recently come to define social inclusion as improving the terms by which individuals and groups can take part in society, particularly with regard to identity disadvantages, perhaps reflecting some influence from these previous contentions.[5] Of course, the devil is in the detail, with respect to how the Bank defines 'terms' and 'participation' within such revised conceptions of inclusion.

It is from this perspective that Byrne (2005, p. 60) warns that the 'babble – no other word is strong enough – by political elites about exclusion can serve as a kind of linguistic trick', on one hand presuming a continued commitment to the values of social democracy, while on the other hand supporting globalisation and neoliberalism. For similar reasons, Clert (1999, p. 195) warns that the coexistence of different ways of using social exclusion discourses can serve to obscure policy orientations and generate false consensus. Indeed, the typical emphasis of agency and relationality can also lend weight to the tendency within mainstream development policy to focus exclusively on the failures and abuses of domestic policies and domestic elites rather than, for instance, the economic austerities imposed by structural adjustment programmes or by international economic integration.[6]

These criticisms would be potentially allayed if we could distinguish between social exclusion (or what we consider to be exclusion) and poverty, or if we can identify exclusions that do not lead to poverty and vice versa. This is recognised by many authors, such as Gore and Figueiredo (1997) or O'Brien et al. (1997), who note that it is possible to be poor and not socially excluded or vice versa. Examples of the latter can be drawn from the Indian caste system, or else from classic cases of discriminated minority groups specialising in trade and commerce. Stewart et al. (2006, p. 5) elaborate on this, in tune with their focus on horizontal inequalities as a cause for conflict. They note that there are some groups who are privileged in some respects, yet still excluded from some important aspects of societal activity, particularly political participation, such as the Chinese in Southeast Asia or the Jews in Europe for many centuries. However, they make a distinction that those who are socially excluded are usually identified as having multiple deprivations, whereas these privileged groups suffer mainly from political exclusion, but they do not suffer multiple exclusions (ibid.). By making this distinction, they seem to reduce social exclusion (as opposed to 'exclusion' more generally) back into a metre of poverty, thereby discounting the valuable insight that derives from these examples, which is that exclusion and poverty do not always work together.

Similar observations have also been made in OECD countries. Atkinson (1998) makes the point that poverty does not necessarily always go together with social exclusion, and he argues that confusion of the two concepts is one reason for differences of view about the role of social security benefits (p. 9). Levitas (2006) also notes that, even in the UK, paid work itself may in some cases limit social 'inclusion' or that 'economic inactivity' does not necessarily lead to exclusion from social relations (pp. 123, 147). In such cases, when exclusion is associated with poverty, we are dealing with an overlap. However, it would be wrong to then integrate this overlap into the very definition of exclusion, thereby reducing social exclusion to its most restrictive case. That being said, once this distinction is recognised, there is still a tendency among these authors to reduce social exclusion back into some metre of poverty, similar to the case of Stewart et al. (2006) mentioned above.

In this regard, caution is also needed for the propensity to elaborate binary typologies of overlaps (e.g., poor and excluded; poor and not excluded; not poor and excluded; and not poor and not excluded), as this also succumbs to the tendency to treat exclusion as a state, similar to that of poverty, as discussed previously. This would also tend to compound the conceptual and methodological quagmires already associated with poverty and aggregated composite indicators. For instance, are we to develop a multidimensional 'exclusion line', distinct from a multidimensional poverty line? Many of these operational issues are the focus of contributions in Atkinson and Hills (1998), Burchardt et al. (1999), Hills et al. (2002) and Pantazis et al. (2006), among others. Notably, most of these authors tend to treat social exclusion as an outcome, which in turn leads us back to the slippery slope of ambiguous synonymy with poverty.

Causal and positional relativity

Indeed, this tendency to treat the identification of social exclusion in a similar manner as poverty leads to an arbitrariness that is far more intractable than the arbitrariness of threshold-setting in poverty measurement. Two often-overlooked dimensions of relativity help to shed light on this, which can be called causal and positional relativity. They are to be differentiated from the two meanings of relativity commonly referred to in the literature as mentioned in the last section, i.e., relative poverty (as per Sen) and contextual relativity (as per Silver).

Causal relativity refers to the observation that that there are multiple often contradictory processes at work within any condition or state of being, such that a person might face both exclusionary and inclusionary processes at the same time. In the IILS debate (Gore and Figueiredo 1997), this point was made by noting that processes of exclusion are not independent from processes of inclusion and patterns of integration; the 'excluded' are almost always 'included' in a variety of ways, such as *Dalits* in India who nonetheless serve important functions in the labour hierarchy, even if these are subordinated and exploited functions. Similarly, the inclusion of landless peasants into poorly paid and exploitative wage labour might be predicated on their exclusion from land assets. DuToit (2004) later contended that this is an issue of adverse incorporation rather than exclusion, which was then coined by Hickey and Du Toit (2007) as 'adverse incorporation and social exclusion'. Across the linguistic divide of scholarship, however, Roulleau-Berger (1999) was making much subtler points in French, by describing how young minority people in France pass several times a day, and on a daily basis, through situations that could be described as either 'excluded' or 'included'. Hence, the identification of exclusion in these situations depends on which causal process or situation, or even moment, we decide to focus on.

This is not simply another perspective on the multidimensionality of poverty. The conception of poverty as a state of being is more or less straightforward even if its measurement is not (i.e., lack of means or outcomes in relation to a relative or absolute metre, however measured). If exclusion is treated in the same way, thereby requiring a partial selection of criteria from which to determine whether someone is excluded or not, the risk is that the simultaneous and dialectical modes of integration and segregation that operate within social processes might be overlooked, particularly if these do not necessarily result in states that we might caricaturise as social exclusion in our abstractions. Even if we would wish to prioritise one process in order to characterise a person as 'excluded' in an absolute sense, such as ethnic segregation, how should we determine this priority over other contradictory processes? In some cases, the choice is made obvious by our normative concerns, although in many cases it is not.

Nor is this necessarily an issue of multidimensionality within exclusion itself. As noted in the beginning of this chapter, social exclusion is generally conceived as multidimensional, such as exclusion in various dimensions like health insurance but not from labour markets, etc. This point is also made in much of the scholarship and, indeed, some of the above examples above would fit into this mould, such as how exclusion from land assets can allow for exploitative inclusion in labour markets. Burchardt et al. (1999) also make a similar point with regard to their five dimensions of social exclusion in the UK (although the choice of these dimensions is debatable, as noted above). However, the multiple contradictory tensions could also be experienced within a single dimension, such as going in and out of situations of social integration or social isolation on a regular basis, as noted above in the studies by Rouleau-Berger (1999). As a result, the identification of exclusion possibly depends on the choice of process even within a single dimension.

The latter point is reinforced by positional relativity, meaning that exclusion is relative to a person's position in a social hierarchy, both objectively and subjectively. In other words, a person can be an excludee and an excluder at the same time and will tend to perceive their exclusion (or inclusion) relative to the social strata immediately surrounding them. This is analogous to insights from the wellbeing literature that one's subjective perception of wellbeing depends in part on one's position or situation relative to one's immediate surrounding, which serves as a basis of social comparison.[7]

This latter relativity can apply across many dimensions of comparison, such as ethnicity, class, caste, clan, occupations, gender, generation or location. For instance, a man might face forms of exclusion outside a household while at the same time practising forms of exclusion towards women within the household. Similarly, anti-Muslim activism by Tibetans in Western China presents a classic case of a subordinated minority group practising various forms of exclusion towards another subordinated minority group, partly as a reaction to their own perceptions of exclusion (see Fischer 2008a, 2009a, 2014a). Notably, to further complicate matters, Muslims are targeted precisely because of their economic success, and thus their own exclusion is difficult to corroborate with poverty.

In this sense, concepts of exclusion and inclusion reflect the constant jostling for social position within hierarchical social orderings. This conforms with the suggestion made by Room (1999, p. 172) that society can be seen as

> a battleground of different social groups (based on social background, ethnicity, economic interest, gender, age, etc.), seeking to maintain and extend their power and influence, in a zero-sum struggle with other groups who they seek to exclude. 'Exclusion' is the result of this struggle, rather than a label to be attached to the casualties of some impersonal process of urban-industrial change. Social exclusion is a normal and integral part of the power dynamics of modern society.[8]

One (unidentified) participant the IILS debate summarised in Gore and Figueiredo (1997) made a very similar point, referring to the grey area between social exclusion and social inclusion, within which most people in the real world live most of their lives at one point or another.

> In another formulation, which was classically Weberian, it was suggested that society could be seen as multi-layered, like a kind of staircase, with processes of exclusion and inclusion occurring at all levels and executed by various kinds of organized groups and associations who are seeking on the one hand to exclude others, to defend privilege and limit competition, and on the other hand to counter exclusion ... It also implied that in seeing social exclusion as a cause of poverty, it was important to focus on the exclusionary and inclusionary processes occurring 'at the bottom of the staircase. (Gore and Figueiredo 1997, p. 42–43)

This formulation is useful to think through how processes that we might identify as exclusionary can be constantly present for even those who live well above the poverty threshold, whether defined in relative or absolute terms, including among elites.

In other words, even a relatively secure person (from a poverty perspective) can psychologically experience insecurity in a manner similar to a poor person, even if, objectively speaking, they would be considered far from vulnerable.[9] We treat the insecurity of a poor person with greater normative legitimacy, although from an analytical point of view we cannot assume that subjective emotive insecurity necessarily correlates with socio-economic insecurity. In some cases, there can even be an inverse relationship, when privilege induces grasping or implies having more to lose, whereas poor people might be more inclined to accept change (for a discussion of this in relation to rural subsistence economies, see Fischer 2008b, 2014a).

Both meanings of relativity throw a serious wrench into the definition or identification of exclusion, even once the norms of a society have been context-specified. However, they also clarify that exclusionary processes occur vertically across a social order, whereas poverty occurs horizontally at the lower end of a social order. In other words, all individuals or groups can perceive or experience an exclusionary process from whatever their position. Without belittling the normative importance of situations where exclusion overlaps with poverty, this clarification is important from an analytical perspective, that even the rich can experience exclusion. Hence, to focus on one aspect or process for the purpose of identification risks missing the simultaneous and dialectical modes of integration and segregation that operate within actions and events, the results of which may or may not lead to states of poverty – relative or absolute.

Dynamic divergences

A further observation that compounds the distinction between poverty and what we have come to call exclusion is that some exclusionary processes might in fact intensify with movements out of poverty. Migration in China serves as an intuitive example. The poorest in China today are typically characterised as rural residents whose livelihoods are based exclusively on agriculture and who possess some of the worst functionings or basic needs in China, such as in education, health or social security. In contrast, processes of exclusion – i.e., obstructed access to certain sectors of employment or social services (rather than a lack of employment or services) – are arguably faced most strongly during the migration of rural residents to urban areas through institutionalised systems of residency status (Ch. *hukou*). While these migrants might be relatively poor in urban areas (although in many cases they are not),[10] in general they were relatively wealthy in rural areas before migration, in line with the widely accepted observation in migration studies that migrants, on average, tend to be wealthier, more educated and more entrepreneurial than the norm in their sources of emigration. In contrast, the rural poorest avoid these urban exclusions by virtue of remaining in agriculture. According to this logic, wealthier rural households – which tend to be more integrated into urban employment systems via one or more family members – would be more exposed to exclusion than poorer rural households. Similarly, movements out of poverty through the predominant vehicles of education and migration (both of which require considerable resources) might intensify rather than alleviate experiences of exclusion among rural households, which anti-poverty policies predicated on urbanisation would also tend to aggravate. These implications would be difficult to capture through standard income, basic needs, capability or relative measures of poverty, or even through inequality measures, given that they would occur at middle rather than lower social strata.

This point – that the dynamics of poverty and exclusion are often poorly correlated – is similar to criticisms of the 'feminisation of poverty' made by certain gender scholars, particularly Jackson (1996).[11] Her arguments hold a strong parallel with the treatment of social exclusion elaborated here, although elsewhere she also cautions against the integration of gender analysis with social exclusion (Jackson, 1999). However, this caution is based on her analysis of the way social exclusion has come to be conceived as a 'binary and polarised formulation of inclusion and exclusion' (ibid., p. 132). This caution is therefore very much in line with my own arguments regarding social exclusion.

Jackson (1996) provides a compelling argument for why gender is distinct from, and sometimes contradictory to, poverty and class. She contends that the 'arguments which show how women's subordination is not derived from poverty need to be excavated to demonstrate the (liberal) fallacy that poverty alleviation will lead to gender equity' (p. 491). This is not to say that gender cannot overlap and reinforce poverty, as is variously emphasised by the scholarship on social reproduction or intersectionalities. Jackson acknowledges the importance of a gendered analysis of poverty, such as in the case of Indian households headed by widows that face higher-than-average levels of vulnerability and impoverishment (p. 493). However, she also quali-fies that there is considerable evidence that gender relations are more equitable in poor Indian households than in wealthier households, in terms of women's engagement with labour markets, contribution to total household income, control over income, and physical mobil-ity. As a result, gender equity often appears to be inversely related to household income. She notes that studies of the Green Revolution have 'shown a pattern of withdrawal of women's labor from farm work and increasing dependence of women on men as household incomes rise'. Other studies have shown that 'some of the most severe dis-crimination against the girl child in India is found in high-caste rural groups, characteristically also high income'; and her own research in Bihar found that 'higher caste farmers had very few surviving daugh-ters whilst the juvenile sex ratios in low caste and tribal households of the same village were much more balanced' (p. 497).

She offers some explanations for these findings, based on a lon-gitudinal study of a village of Uttar Pradesh in the context of the Green Revolution. These explanations place much emphasis on processes of structural change associated with development, such as employment changes due to crop changes and mechanisation, which reduced employment for women. As a result, rising prosperity led to the withdrawal or displacement of women from wage work, the strengthening of *purdah* norms and the inflation of dowries. The increasing dependence of women in upwardly mobile households therefore brought deeper aversion and higher mortality rates for girl children in these households (pp. 497–498).

Jackson clarifies that these findings are not to suggest that women are better off poor, but that this 'is one way of looking at the limited degree to which poverty and gender development can be approached synergistically with the same policy instruments' (p. 498). In other words, gender justice is not a poverty issue and this distinction is important to make given the tendency of development organisations to collapse all forms of disadvantage into poverty. She argues that rescuing gender from poverty analysis 'involves poverty-independent gender analyses and policies which recognize that poverty policies are not necessarily appropriate to tackling gender issues because the subordination of women is not caused by poverty' (p. 501). Moreover, she notes that non-poor women 'experience

subordination of different kinds ... which make them important categories in their own right' (ibid.).

Similarly, non-poor people experience exclusions of various
kinds, which also make them important categories in their own right,
without requiring an overlap with poverty in order to legitimate our
attention. In particular, an exclusion that does not necessarily lead to
any particular poverty outcome might still have a very powerful effect
on various social processes of integration, even when it occurs at the
middle or upper end of a social hierarchy.

In recognising this distinction, however, we must also beware
of the contrasting danger of treating exclusion as synonymous with
disadvantage, as warned by Room (1999, pp. 171–172). The challenge, then, is to differentiate social exclusion from disadvantage
rather than from poverty. Similar to the circular logic associated
with the capability approach, an exclusion may or may not arise
from or lead to a disadvantage. Exclusion can create disadvantages
(say, by excluding certain people from certain types of education,
thereby leading to later disadvantages in labour markets), or else
can be reinforced by existing disadvantages (such as when linguistic
competency is used as a selection criterion in a multilingual setting
dominated by one hegemonic linguistic culture, such as Chinese in
China or English in the US). Distinctions between exclusion and
discrimination could be made in a similar manner, although, in both
cases, it brings us back to the question of why throw in the concept
of social exclusion at all, rather than just dealing head-on with disadvantage and discrimination?

The benefits of differentiation

To give the benefit of the doubt, distinguishing social exclusion
from poverty does provide some remediating potential to the concept
of social exclusion by opening up potent avenues for the analysis of
stratification, segregation and subordination, especially within contexts of high or rising inequality. These include at least three. The
first is situations where exclusions lead to stratifying and potentially
impoverishing trajectories without any obvious short-term poverty
outcomes. The second is situations where exclusions among the non-
poor shed light on obstacles to upward mobility faced by the poor.
Finally, this distinction corrects the association between exclusion
and conflict, as promoted scholars working on the closely related

idea of 'horizontal inequality', and the tendency that derives from this to blame inequality-induced conflict on poor people.

Exclusions as processes of stratification and subordinated inclusion

The first avenue deals with understanding how processes of subordination, stratification and segregation can lead to various forms of disadvantage, discrimination or long-term poverty trajectories even when there are no obvious short-term poverty impacts. Such considerations are especially important in contexts of structural change such as urbanisation and migration, rising education levels or changing livelihoods patterns, during which the exact distributional implications of such changes might not be obvious, but where powerful stratifying social processes might nonetheless be at work. They also apply to situations where exclusions in certain domains allow for subordinated (or adverse) inclusion/integration in other domains, such as in labour markets or in cases of financial exclusion/inclusion, as noted earlier. This latter point is similar to the concept of 'adverse incorporation and social exclusion' proposed by Hickey and Du Toit (2007), except that their treatment is restricted to the space of poverty. The approach proposed here widens consideration to processes occurring vertically across social hierarchies.

This strength particularly applies in contexts of rising inequality or polarisation. In terms of income distribution, rising inequality effectively results in a flattening-out of the income distribution, with fewer people in the middle of the distribution and more at the tail ends (mostly the bottom tail end). In the process, middle strata potentially face the greatest relative downward displacements. Lower strata will experience more competitive pressures due to the downward displacements of those from above, or reduced opportunities for upward mobility, and this will induce considerable churning within the lower strata.[12] However, as discussed previously, many poor might be insulated from churning at higher levels, such as rural dwellers with little or no integration into urban labour markets. Among those in the lower strata who do experience exclusion, they will more likely experience it as obstruction of upward mobility, while their relative position within a social hierarchy might remain unchanged. Rather, the greatest insecurity in terms of loss of relative position (rather than poverty) is usually faced by various middle strata. It is in this sense that we often see intensifying exclusionary pressures among middle strata in contexts of rising inequality.

An example of this comes out of my own work on Tibetan areas in Western China, in my attempt to understand intensifying exclusionary processes within a context of rapid but dis-equalising growth, falling poverty, rising education levels and other developmental improvements (see Fischer 2009a, 2014a). Most conventional measures of exclusion offer little insight into this situation, except perhaps inequality-based measures given rapidly rising inequalities alongside rapid growth. However, inequality measures put the focus on the poorest strata of Tibetan society, whereas I came to realise during my fieldwork that some of the most intense exclusionary pressures – as well as grievances and political frustrations – were faced by relatively elite and/or upwardly mobile Tibetans, such as Tibetan high school and university graduates (only about five per cent of the population had a high school or university level of education at the time, in the early to mid-2000s). In particular, the implementation of competitive labour market reforms and educational campaigns exacerbated exclusionary pressures among this elite educational stratum by accentuating the linguistic and cultural disadvantages faced by these graduates in competing for public employment correspondent with their educational achievements and employment expectations. Notably, these particular pressures were not faced by Tibetans with lower levels of education. The 'excludees' in this case had among the highest educational achievements of their respective communities, they came from families with the resources to be able to finance these levels of education and they had the ability to perform relatively well at these levels (although not enough to compete with Chinese graduates). As discussed below, the resultant exclusions offer important insights into recent tensions in this region, in addition to the more blatant proximate causes such as discrimination or political repression.

Indeed, it was these observations that led me to rethink the social exclusion approach, precisely because the concept of exclusion seemed salient to describe experiences on the ground, even though these experiences were not reflected through any of the conventional absolute or relative poverty measures. Moreover, while this example definitely implicates practices of discrimination, it also brings to light how processes of structural and institutional disjunctures can lead to effective discrimination, even though discrimination might not be necessarily intentional. The methodological challenge, then, is to find ways of identifying these structural and institutional disjunctures across hierarchies and to differentiate them from intentional practices of discrimination. Notably, similar challenges also confront work on identifying social and economic rights abuses or on structural violence more generally.

Another poignant example of this application is in the study of immigration. For instance, when more stringent rules and procedures are imposed on immigrants to North America or Europe, including profiling or the criminalisation of illegal immigration, it is unlikely that the increased stringency stops – or is even intended to stop – such immigration. Immigrants continue to be demanded in a widening variety of sectors of employment, from agriculture to services (exemplified, for instance, but President Trump's use of migrant labour despite his anti-immigrant rhetoric). Hence, the tightening rules are unlikely to exclude immigrants, in an absolute sense. However, stringency allows for stronger mechanisms of subordination and segregation during the integration of such immigrants into the receiving labour hierarchies. This result might or might not be the intended purpose of such rules – the rules themselves might have evolved out of impulsive political reactions within the receiving societies, themselves undergoing a variety of exclusionary displacements among middle strata due to rising inequality. The important analytical point of this example is that these processes often have little correlation with poverty, given that the targeted immigrants are often well-educated and are often not poor, even according to the standards of the recipient countries, particularly if they find work. Nonetheless, despite the lack of correlation with various measures of poverty, these exclusionary processes are very important for understanding the resulting stratification of labour hierarchies, which could well lead to future trajectories of impoverishment, discrimination or disadvantage.

Obstacles to mobility

The second related strength of distinguishing exclusion from poverty is that the obstacles faced by poor people attempting to escape poverty through upward mobility are clarified by exclusions occurring in the non-poor social strata that these poor are attempting to enter. This is especially important in situations where poverty reduction strategies are predicated on upward mobility, such as education or entrepreneurship, versus improving the terms of labour. For instance, the idea that education is good for poverty reduction is largely based on the presumption that those receiving education will subsequently move into higher strata of employment, such as from farming, menial wage labour and informal petty trade, to formal white-collar employment, whether in the public or private sector. However, this idea is problematic when these targeted sectors of employment are already subject to strong exclusionary pressures. Indeed, this insight puts into question the mainstream human development emphasis on absolute levels of education without corresponding emphasis on employment generation and upgrading, particularly in contexts of high or rising inequality, as noted in the first point above.

This perspective is different from the more common assertion that we need to understand the relationship of more advantaged groups to the socially excluded, as suggested by Room (1999, p. 172), which is still based on a binary conceptualisation of excluders and excludees. Rather, here the emphasis is on how exclusions experienced by those higher up in a social hierarchy can lead to a variety of knock-on effects lower down in the social hierarchy. Warren and Tyagi (2004) make this point with regard to the importance of looking at the pressures on the middle classes in the US in terms of how this affects poor people aspiring to that middle-class status. It is also evidenced in my Tibet research mentioned above, whereby the difficulties experienced by Tibetan and other minority graduates in obtaining appropriate formal employment were in part due to labour market reforms occurring more generally across China, which intensified competition within such employment between more advantaged Chinese graduates. Related points have also been made with regard to gender by Jackson (1996, p. 501), who argues that the experiences of non-poor women are relevant to poor women through role-modelling and changing social norms, in both positive and negative ways. Similarly, exclusions occurring within middle strata could have ideational and demonstrative influences on the poor, such as by signalling the importance of cultural assimilation versus political assertions of language rights and affirmative action.

Inequality-induced conflict

The third avenue is in the study of conflict, particularly with respect to correcting the common tendency in much of the literature to implicitly blame inequality-induced conflict on poor people. For instance, if increasing inequality is evoked as a cause of conflict without any further qualification, the implied presumption is that rising inequality raises the relative disparity of the poorer sections of the society in question, thus raising their discontent and their propensity for engaging in conflict.

Perhaps the best example of this is found in the 'horizontal inequality' approach, referring to inequalities between groups rather than between individuals, as laid out by Stewart (2002). More specifically, Stewart et al. (2006) make an explicit effort to connect social exclusion to their broader project of identifying 'horizontal inequalities' as a critical determinant of inter-group conflict. However, they operationalise social exclusion as involving multiple overlapping deprivations and argue that, because of economic deprivation, the '[socially excluded] appear to have little to lose by taking violent action' (Stewart et al. 2006, p. 6). Interestingly, the only solid examples used by the authors to substantiate this contention are cases of discriminated, typically minority, cultural or religious groups, including, among others, Tibetans. Here again, we must question whether those who do agitate are necessarily suffering from severe deprivations due to multiple exclusions. For instance, as discussed above, the Tibetan case actually suggests that the aggrieved socially excluded are, in many cases, people who are best characterised as middle strata, squeezed by both downward competitive pressures and obstructions to upward mobility.

Moreover, we know from actual studies of conflict that most conflicts involve a considerable degree of elite participation, especially in leadership and also in core support. Obviously, there is no doubt that the poor often serve as a reserve army, literally or financially. But the very poor are often too poor or too unhealthy to engage in sustained violent conflicts. Similar to migration, such engagement usually requires resources and organizational capacity, things that the very poor presumably lack.

Indeed, Stewart et al. (2006) qualify their argument in this respect, noting that leadership plays a critical role in emphasising and accentuating particular identities, and that leadership emerges out of the middle classes rather than the deprived in most of the conflicts they studied (ibid., pp. 7–8). However, the problem is that they end up treating different strata in arbitrarily different ways with respect to how common grievances might coalesce within a common cross-strata group cause. Lower strata tend to be treated in a functionalist or even primordial manner with respect to grievances or cultural affinities, while leadership is treated in an instrumentalist manner, using these grievances and affinities to enact political ends (e.g., see pp. 9–10). Perhaps as a means to overcome this dualism, the authors refer to a complicated mixture of exclusions, although in their attempts to operationalise social exclusion as poverty, they appear to convolute rather than enhance their otherwise-interesting discussion of conflict.

Rather, by focusing our attention to include exclusionary processes occurring in the middle and at the upper ends of a social hierarchy, we can understand why the non-poor might also come to be aggrieved by rising inequality, thereby clarifying inequality-induced social dynamics that might contribute to conflict. In particular, as discussed above, the dislocating effects of rising inequality can be seen to be most intense at the middle strata of a social hierarchy in terms of relative downward displacements. In the event that these displacements are caused by exclusion, whether perceived or real, these experiences can turn into potent focal points for grievance and rallying points for political agitation, particularly when they occur among politically active people. This perspective is important because it implicates middle classes and elites into an understanding of how inequality might induce conflict. Indeed, it resonates with the theses of Polanyi (1944) and Arendt (1951) regarding the social origins of fascism in Germany – they both identified economic insecurity among the middle classes as a critical factor. It is precisely this angle that gives a concept of exclusion that is differentiated from poverty an edge over poverty and inequality approaches in understanding social conflict, given that the methodologies of poverty and inequality analysis tend to divert attention away from vertically occurring processes that cut across hierarchical social orderings and, in particular, away from elites.

Instead, by conceiving social exclusion as vertically occurring processes of obstruction or repulsion, we come closer to prying open the puzzle of how social dislocations might occur in very different ways across different strata of an intra-group hierarchy, yet still might provide for a basis of common grievances within the group. For instance, this approach addresses the puzzle posed by Mann (2005, p. 5), regarding why, in situations of murderous ethnic cleansing, class-like sentiments come to be channelled into ethno-nationalist ones. This requires an understanding of the possibility for vertical social bonds to form in the face of a commonly perceived adversity, crossing over the horizontal loyalties that are presumed to exist in conceptualisations of class and other forms of socio-economic status. The actual experience of exclusion or insecurity would differ considerably across these horizontal strata, but processes of exclusion that cause deprivation at the lower end of a social order can, in many cases, also cause an erosion of economic or political power or social status among certain elites.

Hence, a heightened sense of insecurity can occur among upper social strata in line with multiple deprivations among lower social strata, thereby allowing for a perception of shared adversity that forges vertical bonds of solidarity within a group, in contrast to differences in actual experiences faced by various social strata within the group. Common perceptions of cause, rather than common outcomes, allow for common narratives to emerge across social strata, which can then be used as mobilising focal points for organising common remedial strategies. This can be observed, for instance, with the rise of populist right-wing parties around the world, which tap into classic working-class concerns while also finding support and leadership among various elite factions (as did fascism in the 1930s, for that matter). This understanding of exclusionary processes therefore helps to move towards a more nuanced position that understands the actions and ideologies of both rich and poor alike as both instrumental and normative at the same time.

Conclusion

This chapter has sought to highlight the conceptual ambiguities of the social exclusion approach through a deconstruction of the concept. Despite the fact that most of the literature agrees that the value-added of social exclusion is found in its treatment of processes and that social exclusion can occur without poverty, most attempts to operationalise the concept end out reducing it to a description of certain aspects of poverty. It is usually formulated in terms of multiple and cumulative disadvantages that lead to or reinforce multiple deprivations, or else as a description of various social aspects of deprivation. This opens the way for valid criticisms that the concept is redundant with respect to already-existing concepts of poverty, particularly more multidimensional and processual concepts of poverty such as relative or capability deprivation.

However, similar to criticisms of the feminisation of poverty by certain gender scholars, social exclusion must be differentiated from poverty in order to do justice to the study of exclusion (or what we call exclusion), given that exclusion and poverty do not always go together. This insight is important because an exclusion that does not necessarily lead to poverty might still have a very powerful effect on social processes such as stratification, segregation, subordination, discrimination or conflict. Indeed, exclusionary processes at the upper end of a social hierarchy are especially powerful. Such processes are therefore pressing concerns in their own right and should not require an overlap with poverty in order to legitimise our attention.

The remediating benefits of making this distinction are on the insights that it can provide on many processes of subordination, stratification and segregation, particularly within contexts of high or rising inequality, which are not effectively captured by poverty or even inequality methods of analysis. In other words, absolute and even relative indicators often tell us little about processes of exclusion and marginalisation. If they do, they usually only do so by providing clues about the spaces within which exclusionary processes might be operating. Indeed, standard statistical sampling methods based on outcome indicators might be poorly suited for capturing the processual emphasis of the social exclusion approach, which would be better served by more inductive methods that are able to trace subtle social dynamics rather than cross-correlations across divergent people. This would include interdisciplinary analyses of structural and institutional disjunctures and asymmetries operating not only across social hierarchies, but also among comparable cohorts within a social hierarchy, for instance, with similar levels of educational achievements and employment expectations. Ultimately, the social exclusion approach also calls for a shift of methodological and even epistemological dimensions.

Most importantly, exclusion understood in this way avoids the tendency to blame poor people for a variety of perverse social dynamics that emerge across social hierarchies in response to rising inequality, which can be easily misattributed as stemming from poverty due precisely to their association with inequality. Conflict is an obvious example given the common assertion in academic, policy and journalistic circles that increasing inequality will exacerbate conflict. While this might be true, it is equally important – indeed, it is an ethical responsibility – to also remind ourselves that the conflicts to which we refer usually involve substantial elite participation, particularly in leadership positions. Hence, we need social theory to address how elites themselves might find grievance with inequality, lest we fall into a trap of crude instrumentalism. The poor have enough to deal with; they do not need the additional burden of our implicit blame or paranoia.

The question still remains whether all of these functions of the social exclusion approach could be even more effectively analysed with existing sociological concepts, such as many of those mentioned above. The addition of the concept of 'social exclusion' serves no obvious additional purpose and brings no obvious value added to these concepts. Indeed, whereas we can resolve the issue of whether social exclusion is redundant with poverty, we are then left with the question of whether it is redundant with concepts of disadvantage or discrimination. Moreover, the approach has brought a lot of vagueness and confusion, and even though it initially seemed to offer some exciting potential for bringing in more critical perspectives into the field of poverty studies, it has also exhibited a strong propensity to be coopted into various mainstream agendas around inclusion. Since most of the debates of the 1990s and early 2000s were wrapped up, its application with respect to developing countries has been mostly through these agendas.

The challenge to rehabilitate the approach is to emphasise the potential for a critical political economy element within it, such as through an understanding of exclusion as part of the exercise of power within social relations, or that exclusion in certain spheres or dimensions creates dependence in others, which becomes a basis for exercising power. In this way, it permits a discrete consideration of social power relations and the ways these work to confer or deny access to resources or opportunities. Nonetheless, the danger in even this emphasis is in replacing existing, established and relatively clear social-scientific concepts and methods with vague and unspecified new ones, particularly when these new ones are so easily coopted away from their original intent.

6 | LOCATING MODERN POVERTY WITHIN THE CREATION AND DIVISION OF WEALTH: TOWARDS A STRUCTURALIST AND INSTITUTIONALIST POLITICAL ECONOMY APPROACH IN POVERTY STUDIES

In most approaches within the field of poverty studies, the focus has been overwhelmingly on enumeration and descriptions of poverty rather than serious attempts to explain causality, or what has lately come to be popularly referred to as 'theories of change'. This avoidance of the causal is not necessarily due to an inductivist impulse of building theory from the detailed observation of facts. Rather, poverty studies scholarship, especially the economics scholarship that dominates the field, is primarily deductive, as epitomised by econometric analyses that, in so many cases, do not even involve any direct observation by the researcher of the people studied. Although glorified, these often boil down to fragile edifices of abstracted axiomatic principles and assumptions, superimposed on data and deploying sophisticated techniques to establish authority. So-called econometric tests for causality are usually so narrow (by necessity, in order to have sufficient control for the test) that the insights they produce are rather banal, especially from a broader perspective of development. As argued by Deaton (2009), they also mostly lack external validity beyond the specific contexts studied. Arguably, they are still measuring associations rather than causality in any case, as is the basic principle of positivist deduction. Broader theorisation does lurk in the background of all of this research as the implicit source of assumptions informing choices that ultimately guide and condition results, but not as the explicit object of scholarship. Broader theorisation is instead left to the fads of grand theories, which of late have come to embody quite simplistic and unsatisfactory approaches to understand the political economy of poverty and development.

The causes of poverty and the ways that poverty transforms and is reproduced over time, particularly within a process of development, can only be fully understood from a broader holistic perspective of all that is involved in the creation and division of wealth within and across societies. Theorisation therefore needs to be placed within broader debates on these questions. The ideal starting points for this are classical political economy as well as so-called heterodox economics perspectives, in particular, Marxian, post-Keynesian, structuralist and institutionalist approaches, which have been the main avenues for perpetuating, adapting and updating these classical perspectives into contemporary scholarship.

These intellectual streams of political economy are emphasised here because they are the main theoretical traditions that seek to integrate an understanding of distribution within an understanding of growth, as opposed to neoclassical economic traditions that mostly separate the two. The neoclassical Solow-Swan growth model, for instance, is based on a one-good model with a representative agent and, hence, by design, is unable to deal with issues of distribution. The Stolper-Samuelson and Arrow-Debreu family of models also do not necessarily deal with distribution *per se*, except by way of collapsing distribution into a theory of exchange and treating profits and wages as factor prices based on relative endowments of capital and labour. However, they do not theorise growth, except by way of the efficiencies gained through a static reallocation of inputs based on comparative advantage. As a more recent example, the theoretical model of Piketty (2014) does not even include labour or capital-labour relations in its attempt to explain inequality through the concept of capital.

In contrast, political economy in the classic sense refers to an understanding that distribution and its interaction with production and hence economic growth are fundamentally political and institutional. The value of labour in particular (and hence of profits in the inverse) is the outcome of power, social relations, and social conflicts (e.g., class, etc.), rather than of market-mediated returns for the marginal productivity of 'factor inputs' (i.e., labour and capital). This leads to explicit questions about who creates value (i.e., labour, the organisation of labour by capitalists, or the owners of assets, etc.) and who controls this creation and subsequent circulation of value. 'Structuralist' in the sense used here refers to an understanding of the economy in terms of its articulations and patterns of integration and circulation, of where value is occurring and how is it occurring, and with the understanding that sustained economic growth and poverty reduction generally involve processes of structural change, fundamentally driven by rising labour productivity.

Accordingly, this chapter proposes a schematic framework for building an integrated structuralist and institutionalist political economy approach for what we might call critical poverty studies. 'Critical' here does not refer to post-structuralism but rather to the more classical principle of political economy that we must critically introspect theoretical, normative and ideological assumptions from the outset and how these are built into our paradigmatic conceptions of – in this case – poverty and development.

The example of inclusive development, as discussed in the previous chapter, can be used to illustrate how different underlying assumptions feed into the conception of policy. If we focus specifically on the case of marginalised groups, an inclusive growth or development perspective would aim for a better 'inclusion' of these marginalised groups into growth or development as a way to lessen inequality and poverty, ideally in a manner that does not undermine the agency, autonomy and dignity of the marginalised, as is often the case in state projects aimed at such groups (e.g., see Fischer 2014a). Indeed, this is roughly the current (at the time of writing) generic definition of social inclusion used by the World Bank, as discussed in the previous chapter.

Accordingly, we can think about inclusion in several ways drawing from the classical divisions from political economy (e.g., production, distribution and redistribution). To start with, from a structural perspective, it is important to think about differences in the basic employment structures that frame marginalisation, such as the proportion of the labour force integrated into formal employment, from less than 10 per cent in many poor countries such as India, to over 80 per cent in most so-called Northern countries. The implications of what constitutes 'marginalisation' and 'inclusion' in each setting would be very different, particularly with respect to contexts where most people are 'marginalised' and 'excluded' from formal employment, as discussed in the previous chapter. Hence, policies would have very different implications and consequences in each of these types of contexts, particularly given that much of the distributional struggles waged by organised labour in formal employment might be quite disassociated from conditions among more marginalised and/ or informalised workers. Transformations in these contexts over time are also crucial considerations.

Following on from this, we can think of three dominant approaches to address marginalisation. The first is the productionist approach, which aims to help marginalised groups to become more productive by giving them productive assets, education, microfinance, land titles and so forth. The idea is that the marginalised people become richer and/or more empowered – and, hence, less marginalised – by becoming more productive, as if, by operating as microentrepreneurs and small businesses, they gradually grow into the norm of the economy. Such approaches are fairly typical in mainstream development policy (besides land reform, which is generally regarded as more radical). When advocated in isolation, they can be characterized as 'supply-side', in the sense that policy focuses on providing the inputs (human capital, financial capital, etc.), whereas it is assumed that demand works itself out in due course (as discussed in Chapter 4 and elaborated below).

A redistributive approach might focus on taxing profits and formal wages (and other incomes and assets via consumption or other taxes) and using part of the revenue to spend on services or cash transfers to the marginalised communities. Much of social policy falls into this category, which encompasses both more mainstream approaches (i.e., targeting) as well as less mainstream approaches (i.e., universalistic social policies). Here, the general principle is that you 'include' the marginalised through redistributive transfers and social provisioning – giving them education, health, cash, etc. The question with such demand-side approaches is whether such provisioning actually allows for any substantive form of improved inclusion, rather than simply reproducing marginalisation on new terms. The intervention of the state can also involve aspects of top-down impositions or stimulate changes in the regulation or governance of the poor that can also have both positive and negative effects on marginalisation.

A distributive approach would emphasise the integration of marginalised groups into (decent and ideally formal) employment, or to raise their wages and working conditions if employed, with the understanding that most of them will not become microentrepreneurs. Notably, most of the labour force – at least in most rich countries – is composed of employees, not entrepreneurs or business owners. So, policies like affirmative action reservation policies in public employment might actually be considered as distributive, in the sense that they constitute efforts to effect marginalisation through this channel. Redistributive policies can also have an indirect distributive effect. For instance, public spending can have the effect of raising aggregate demand, which presumably raises demand for labour and hence wages. Employment guarantee schemes are probably best characterised as a combination of distributive (increasing employment) and redistributive (because the employment is subsidised and effectively replaces cash transfers).

As discussed in the previous chapter on social exclusion, sociological approaches cut across all three of these political economy approaches – particularly the second and third – by focusing on the processes and pathways that people actually take according to each approach to inclusion. For instance, discrimination might act as an obstacle to asset and productive accumulation, or to effective inclusion through education systems or to achieving decent employment.

Following on from this illustration and as a means of placing these issues within broader debates about how wealth is created and shared within and across societies, I propose a holistic framework for engaging with such perspectives in this chapter. The framework is based on two conceptual dimensions that are implicit in much of the ideas and policies relating to poverty and social needs. Each of the two dimensions is in turn composed of three elements. This two-by-three framework can then be examined in terms of the more conventional discussion of policy realms, such as the division suggested by Cornea (2006) for examining inclusive growth in terms of social policy, developmental policy and macroeconomic policy. The theme of social policy in particular is taken up in the next, penultimate chapter, given its centrality to understanding processes of social integration and ordering.

The first dimension deals with the creation and division of wealth, which can be conceived in classical political economy terms as production, distribution and redistribution (similar but not identical to the idea of spheres of production and circulation). The second deals with the more secondary, indirect and aggregated factors influencing the first. These can be divided into supply-side factors, demand-side factors and factors dealing with terms of trade or wages (or the relative valuing of labour and its fruits). The latter dimension can also be considered in terms of indirect policy means to influence production and distribution, as opposed to direct policy interventions in production or employment, or else direct use of fiscal policy to redistribute resources.

These interacting dimensions help to clarify how different approaches to conceptualising poverty and its reduction, as well as theoretical perspectives in economics and social sciences more generally, usually place selective emphasis on different combinations of elements across these two dimensions, even though all elements are needed to understand the evolution of social needs and the reproduction of poverty. While each approach might have its own insights, the causes of poverty can only be fully understood from a broader holistic perspective of all that is involved in the creation and division of wealth. More specifically, prevailing approaches to understanding poverty, which implicitly rely on neoclassical theoretical approaches, generally overlook several key dimensions. This latter point will be elaborated throughout and in the conclusion.

Production, distribution and redistribution: The classical triad

The conceptual distinction of production, distribution and redistribution is rooted in the foundational division between production, distribution and exchange in classical political economy, or between the spheres of production and circulation in Marxist political economy. These in turn have influenced the conception of twentieth-century national accounting, i.e., GDP, with a similar division between production, income and expenditure approaches to understanding the creation and circulation of monetary value-added in an economy.

Production

Production focuses on the creation of value-added. It is associated with the production approach of national accounting (gross domestic product, or GDP), represented by the primary, secondary and tertiary sectors. The central concern is labour productivity, understood as output per unit of labour, although because output is mostly valued in monetary terms, the more appropriate term is 'monetary value-added productivity', in order to keep this point clear. As discussed below with respect to the terms of trade/wages, this actually has problematic implications for our understanding of productivity and hence poverty, particularly as labour increasingly moves out of physical production and into non-physical services.

The importance of a production or productivity focus in poverty studies is that it frames poverty as deficient productivity, and poverty reduction as fundamentally driven by increasing productivity. It therefore emphasises that the primary effort of poverty reduction policy is to increase the productivity of the poor. Indeed, productivity determines the upper possible threshold for incomes and/ or wages, regardless of how output is distributed and prior to any redistributions.

This is most easily conceived in agrarian economies, where physical productivity creates a ceiling for how much farmers can earn (or else ceilings on the value that can be appropriated from their labour, as discussed below under distribution). If a farmer harvests 1000 kilograms of grain in a year, net of the inputs of grain used for planting, and has no other source of income, his or her income can be no greater than the value of this harvest, however this value is calculated (e.g., in terms of its monetary value based on market prices, or in terms of its subsistence value if consumed by the farming household, as discussed in Chapter 3).

This easy conceptualisation invariably becomes complicated, however, as soon as nuance is brought into the example. For instance, in the case of a small-holder farmer, labour productivity is constrained by the amount of land, more so than by access to capital and technology, given that there is only so much that can be produced per unit of land even under the best of circumstances. Moreover, strategies to increase land productivity when land is constrained are often predicated on increasing the labour intensity of production and hence on reducing labour productivity. This must then be evaluated relative to other uses of household labour, particularly when households are engaged in off-farm activities and employment (or, conversely, if they experience substantial levels of unemployment or underemployment).

Indeed, many income generation projects devised for poor people by various governmental and non-governmental organisations often receive an unenthusiastic reception from the intended beneficiaries, but not because of behavioural resistance to change, as is often assumed or argued. Rather, lack of enthusiasm is often related to the fact that the projects are very labour-intensive and the implicit returns for labour time have not been well estimated (if at all), with returns that might be well below the effective minimum wages on offer in local labour markets. While those who devise such projects might assume that any rupee or peso earned by a poor person is better than none, poor people are in fact quite sensitive to their own – perhaps qualitative, but nonetheless roughly accurate – evaluations of the relative returns for their labour time.[1] In particular, unlike the unemployed in Northern welfare states, poor people in most developing countries are often very time-constrained. This is especially problematic with many interventions that require substantial voluntary time commitments, such as with microfinance or social protection schemes requiring regular meetings and visits.

Despite the rapid proliferation of complexity as one approaches real-world settings, a production focus is nonetheless essential to understand the structural sources of inequality. An important foundation of inequality rests on differences of productivity across sectors or groups of people. The easiest example is the difference between labour productivity in small-scale peasant agriculture versus labour productivity in modern highly capital-intensive large-scale farming, or in modern manufacturing. Productivity measures in this sense can be disaggregated across different sectors of an economy, and even within sectors if both value-added and employment data are available for such disaggregation. With this information, it is possible to identify low- and high-'productivity' sectors or even sub-sectors of an economy, again, measured by monetary value-added produced per unit of labour.

This was the basis, for instance, of the well-known pioneering studies by Simon Kuznets on inequality in the process of structural change. His inverted-U hypothesis – that inequality rises during early phases of development, stabilises in the middle and then falls at more advanced phases – specifically referred to the effects of a structural shift between different sectors of an economy with different levels of productivity and inequality. In his classic article, Kuznets (1955, pp. 7–8) posited that rural areas are less unequal than urban areas because there is greater potential for productivity increases in urban industry than in rural agriculture. In other words, rural inequality is more restricted by the upper bound of productivity that can be achieved in agriculture, whereas urban inequality is much less so. He did not argue, as misrepresented by Milanovic (2011, p. 9), that inequality is low in preindustrial societies because almost everybody is equally poor. Rather, he pointed out that, according to the available evidence at the time, 'underdeveloped' countries were actually more unequal than developed countries and, on this basis, he already suggested at that time that his insights would probably have limited applicability for developing countries (e.g., see Kuznets 1955, p. 20).

As noted above, measures of productivity face the dilemma that they are generally based on monetary value-added measures, not actual output. Output-based measures of productivity can only be analysed with reference to single homogeneous physical goods (e.g., kilograms of soya beans). However, value-added measures must necessarily be used as soon as productivity is compared across more than one physical good (e.g., kilograms of soya beans versus kilograms of cherries, versus cars produced in a factory, etc.). The problem is that value-added is a combination of output and price, and already includes within it the value of wages. Hence, measuring productivity with value-added data could reflect as much differences in prices and wages as anything specifically related to actual differences in physical output or efficiencies in the use of labour. Indeed, in service sectors where there is no physical output, value-added measures are completely a reflection of wages and prices.

As discussed further below, it is therefore important to exercise caution and a degree of critical distance from ideas that productivity necessarily sets the value of labour, that poverty is due to 'low productivity' or that increasing productivity necessarily needs to be at the forefront of poverty reduction strategies. Monetary value-added measures of low productivity might, in fact, be reflecting something else. I have called this a 'fallacy of productivity reductionism' (Fischer 2011c), referring to the assumption that monetary valuation can be used as an accurate approximation of productivity in a complex modern economy. The logic might apply in a farm-based economy, although, even then, simple strategies of income generation are notoriously susceptible to the fallacy of composition. For instance, when everyone starts producing handicrafts, this then creates a glut in the market for handicrafts, lowering their price and then eliminating the potential gains of increasing the physical output of handicrafts at the individual level. Indeed, such an outcome occurred in the coffee sector in the 1990s, when the investments of millions of small-scale producers to increase coffee production were cancelled out by collapsing prices, particularly as several large-scale investments came into production in the mid-1990s. In other words, the logic that monetary valuation can represent actual effort or output breaks down in more complex economic interactions or aggregations, even within agrarian settings and where people are owner-producers. Things become even more complex when dealing with wage earners instead, or as we move away from relatively simple agrarian economies to more complex urban-industrial ones.

Distribution

Distribution in turn deals with how the surplus – or the value-added of output – is divided into various income streams across different sets of people involved in the production process, or who own and/or control the production and distribution process, including assets used in production such as land or loans. In modern economics parlance, these are referred to as payments to the factors of production. According to the income approach of modern national accounting (gross domestic income or GDI), these income streams are generally categorised as wages, profits, rents, interest payments and taxes on production, with some of the value-added produced also deducted for depreciation and for payments to foreign factors of production.

Recently, it has also become common to refer 'pre-distribution', made popular by Ed Miliband in 2012, then the Labour Party leader in the UK, among others (e.g., see O'Neill and Williamson 2012). For earlier academic references, see Plotnick (1982); more recently, the term has also been taken up by Wade (2014) – see Kerr (2016) for a good overview. However, in both classical political economy and modern national accounting terms, this runs the risk of conflating the term 'distribution' with 'redistribution', as is common in the less-attentive uses of the term. The use of the term by O'Neill and Williamson (2012) does imply more than simply the distribution of the economic product, and is used in a way that implies a political strategy of dealing with distributive struggles in property-owning democracies or, as Wade (2014, p. 1079) suggests, 'changes in institutions and policies to make pre-tax income distribution less unequal, including in laws of corporate governance, employee protection, consumer protection, environmental protection'. Nonetheless, many people simply juxtapose pre-distribution against redistribution, as if implying distribution.

Distribution in this sense refers to the initial division of the product or income, which can then become the object of redistribution. This is also related to the concepts of market wages versus net wages, or pre- and post-tax and transfers. Market wages reflect the amount initially given to different categories of labour, whereas redistribution is generally treated in terms of taxes and transfer payments, which are reflected in net wages. In some Northern welfare states, the differences can be striking, such as in Sweden or Belgium, where inequality before taxes and transfers is among the highest in OECD countries,[2] whereas after taxes and transfers is among the lowest (see Brys et al. 2013, p. 30).

In classical political economy terms, wages, profits and rents are related to the abstracted class notions of labour, capital and rentiers, which formed the basis of most classical economic models, from David Ricardo to Karl Marx. As such, this dimension is closely related to and determined by class relations, which is precisely why it is so central to political economy, especially with regard to the social relations and class conflicts that determine the value of labour and of rents. This is also why classical economists referred to themselves as *political* economists, in addition to the fact that they also understood the study of an economy to be a study about statecraft. As noted in the Introduction of this book, classical economists up to Marx assumed that the value of working-class labour – then the large majority of the work force – would always be pushed down to a level of subsistence, whether due to the forces of population (as per Thomas Malthus and followed by David Ricardo) or due to the nature of class conflict (as per Karl Marx).

It is also useful to clarify that in this classical political economy conception, which also informs modern national accounting, rents are conceived as income earned from ownership and/or control over assets rather than from investment into production, which generates profits. This conception contrasts from the modern neoclassical conception of rents as excess profits earned through the obstruction of markets (relative to a hypothesised 'market-clearing' equilibrium). The neoclassical conception places the onus of rent-seeking, so to speak, on state actors or else others holding relatively monopolistic positions over relatively inelastic goods and services, instead of recognising rent-seeking as primarily a private activity endemic to modern capitalism. Rents in the latter sense are literal, i.e. earning rent from property, or earning interest or profits from financial assets. This distinction is often confused in the adoption of rent-seeking as an analytical frame in much of contemporary political economy scholarship, such as with respect to political settlements, probably because some of the lead authors such as Mustaq Khan usually imply a neoclassical conception of rents despite their general Marxist orientation (e.g., Khan 2002, 2006).

Again, distribution (and its national accounting correlates) can be conceived quite intuitively in terms of a simplified farm economy, with a representative agent and abstracting from class relations (as in the conceptual framework of foundational neoclassical economic models, such as in the one-good world of the Solow growth model). If a farmer plants 10 kilograms of grain and harvests 110 kilograms, the value-added is 100 kilograms. The grain that the farmer eats is wages. The grain taken by the landlord is rent. The grain paid to the moneylender is interest, or to the state is tax. The grain that is eaten by mice or that rots is depreciation, and the grain left over is profit, which in this case accrues to the farmer owner-producer (the profit in this sense is the residual). There is effectively nothing else that the grain can be distributed to. The profit can be saved, given or lent to neighbours, or traded, although these activities fall outside of the realm of initial distribution, given that they are subsequent (secondary) uses of the initial product. Some of these secondary uses would also have their own logic of distribution, such as with the value-added generated by trade, etc. It is also clear through this example how the inclusion of class relations creates a fundamental tension given that profits are inversely related to wages, all else held constant.

The importance of distribution for the study of poverty is that it places the focus on wages, or on the net value of own-production in the case of farmers who farm for themselves (either on their own land or on share-cropped or rented land). In other words, it frames poverty as deficient wages, or as a deficient share or value of output. It also identifies the other major source of inequality next to structural sources, which is the functional income distribution, or the distribution of income across different groups, most fundamentally expressed as the profit/wage share. This differs from the household or personal income distribution, depending on how factoral incomes are distributed across individuals and households. Personal income distribution is effectively the outcome of all sources of inequality.

Redistribution

Last, redistribution (or 'secondary distribution' in the most recent national accounting terminology) involves shifting value from its initial distribution. This can either be progressive (taking from the richer and giving to the poorer) or regressive (the opposite), thereby either improving or worsening the initial inequalities created by the structural and distributional dimensions (or by the idiosyncratic characteristics of individuals). Redistribution as such is largely constituted by state or collective action, such as fiscal and social policy, or else by community-organised systems of sharing, charity, and so forth. In this sense, it falls into the Polanyian notions of both redistribution and reciprocity.

Redistribution is central to the study of poverty primarily in terms of public policy to address poverty directly through transfers or subsidies, or indirectly through general fiscal spending. While this is perhaps less fundamental in determining poverty than production and distribution, it nonetheless occupies a large part of the attention in poverty studies and policies. The current social protection agenda, which to a large extent refers to cash transfers to the poor, is one of the most obvious current examples. Of course, these must be measured against the tax burden also faced by the poor. In particular, cash transfers are often funded from value-added taxes (VAT), which the poor pay and are generally seen as regressive towards them (meaning that the poor pay a higher tax rate than the rich because a greater proportion of their income is spent on consumption rather than being saved and invested). Indeed, in this sense it is a misnomer to call these programmes 'non-contributory', as has become standard, and the net balance between taxes and transfers might in some cases not even be redistributive. Beyond such programmes, other less-explicit forms of redistribution can include all sorts of public spending, such as education spending prioritised towards disadvantaged groups and areas, or regional redistribution, whereby regions receive more spending than they provide to the government in revenue.

A parallel concept that is often referred to in classical (especially Marxist) political economy is the sphere of circulation or exchange, in contrast to the sphere of production (e.g., see Fine and Saad-Filho

1975; Weeks 1977; Passinetti 2007). The distinction might be seen in terms of whether value is created through the initial production of a good or service, or whether value is created through the subsequent circulation of that good or service already produced. Again, a simplified farm economy serves to illustrate this point: the fully specialised function of a doctor, teacher or priest can only be afforded by a community when all other households produce enough surplus and set aside part of this surplus in order to pay for (i.e., feed) such a specialised service within the community. However, this is not the same as redistribution because activities such as finance, trade and commerce are generally conceived as part of the sphere of circulation in this alternative conception (also expressed, for instance, in the distinction between financial and productive capital). Indeed, the example of other services such as health and education are ambiguous within this conception given that they constitute both the original creation of value (of a service) and yet they would typically be included as part of the sphere of circulation, for the reason that they are afforded through a surplus in production, as noted above. It is perhaps due to these ambiguities that this categorisation has not gained much traction in modern national accounting, in which all services are simply included as part of the tertiary sector of production.

The concept of the sphere of circulation nonetheless raises some interesting further questions. For instance, to what degree should finance be considered a redistributive process, in the sense that there are some who gain more than others in the reallocation of savings and/or money, and some who lose quite substantially? Or is it better conceived as simply part of the sphere of circulation, or as an additional service, with its own generation of value added in the economy and hence its own productive, distributive and redistributive implications? As mentioned above, modern national accounting treats it as the latter. Similarly, monetary policy is never neutral, in the sense that it affects debtors and creditors differently, and it can have an important impact on inequalities. Should this role be conceived as one of redistributing primary values created in the economy, or as something more fundamental, particularly through its effect on the valuation of economic activities, prices and so forth? The latter does not fall well into the categories of distribution and redistribution, but is rather part of the regulative functions of states that can also have important impacts on poor people.

Supply, demand and terms of trade and wages

The second dimension deals with the more secondary, indirect and aggregated factors that influence the primary creation and division of wealth. These can be roughly divided into supply-side and demand-side factors, and the terms of trade and wages. Note that the uses of the first two terms can refer to different positions within the demanding and supplying, although here it refers primarily to aggregate processes driving or influencing growth and/or poverty, rather than with respect to service provisioning.

For instance, demand and supply sides are often referred to in the social sector, such as with respect to the demand for education or health by the users of those services (and hence people demanding these services). Similarly, supply-side in the education or health sector refers to how the actual services are provided, in what quantity and quality, by which providers (public or private), with what infrastructure and human resources, etc.

This provisioning usage is common, for instance, in the social protection literature. Cash transfers are seen as 'demand-side' interventions given that they augment the ability of those receiving the transfers to pay for education or health services, and to thereby exert 'demand' on these services. One of the principle critiques of these strategies (and of the human capital presumptions that come with them as the rationale for conditionalities) is that augmenting demand in such a manner is unlikely to have any significant effect on educational performance or outcomes if and when the supply of education services remains poor (e.g., see this critique in Fischer 2012). Indeed, most of the focus in this cash transfer agenda, of just giving money to the poor (e.g., Hanlon et al. 2010), has been on such demand enhancement rather than on investments in the supply of services and better quality services, or on a better integration and unification of the provisioning systems that service the poor with those that service the middle classes. From a social policy perspective, the latter strategies are arguably the strongest ways to guarantee quality services for the poor, and hence for genuine and broad rather than minimalist universalistic provisioning for the poor. In the absence of attention to such supply-side issues in provisioning or to broader aspects of institutional integration, critics (such as myself) have warned that cash transfers, or similar policy agendas such as basic income schemes, could actually serve as Trojan Horses to advance privatisation agendas in the social sector, whereby demand-side interventions are used to support poor people in their purchase of privatised services (see the next chapter for further discussion of this and related points).

Here, however, the principal reference to demand- and supply-side is in terms of how they have come to be used in macroeconomics, unless otherwise specified. 'Demand' refers to effective aggregate demand, as the crucial macroeconomic variable governing demand for labour through its effect on output and economic cycles. 'Supply' in turn refers to an economy's output of goods and services to meet aggregate demand, as well as the supply of labour.

The idea of supply-side economics became famous when it was endorsed and promoted by Ronald Reagan in the 1980s, basically as a free-market ideological attack on Keynesian demand-management, which had been the establishment view up to that time. As discussed in Chapters 2 and 4, it essentially refers to the idea, known as 'Say's Law', that supply creates its own demand. In other words, increasing supplies of goods and services will find buyers, and increasing supplies of labour will find gainful employment, as long as the government does not interfere with the market system that allows the economy to manifest demand for its output or factor inputs. As such, it is usually associated with neoliberalism.

An alternative perspective is that employment transitions and urbanization are primarily driven by social need rather than economic incentives, and that optimal quantities (and qualities) of employment are not guaranteed by the free and flexible operation of labour markets. This requires that governments must actively engage with development and related public policies to mediate the changing supply of labour generated by rapid social structural transformations.[3] If not, governments risk exacerbating employment disjunctures in both rural and urban areas, which labour market flexibility might in fact offer little potential to redress.

Continuing with the example of cash transfers, this policy instrument is conceived as demand-side from a service user perspective (the user uses the cash to 'demand' services) and also from a macroeconomic perspective (augmenting the aggregate demand of the poor). However, the human capital justification for the policy – which finds its zenith in the promotion of conditionalities or 'co-responsibilities' – is better described as deriving from a supply-side logic, with respect to the employment and poverty reduction dynamics beyond the one-off transfer of cash. The cash provided is often seen as just the carrot to induce people to make 'good' choices about 'investing' in such human capital (that is, school attendance and health checks), rather than as income support. As with human capital theory more generally, the argument is that long-term poverty reduction, beyond the immediate and negligible impact of the cash transferred, is driven by such increases in human capital. The assumption is that the increased supply of human capital, or increased number of people with augmented human capital, creates its own demand, presumably in the form of more employment that corresponds to the increased embodied capital, with higher wages and non-wage conditions, etc.

The problem, as has been recognised since some of the earliest studies of cash transfers in the noughties, even by their proponents, is that these outcomes rarely occur in any significant or systemic manner in the absence of other interventions (this will be discussed further in the next chapter). Few long-term employment impacts are observed among cash transfer recipients that can be attributable to the conditionalities and their effects on enrolments. Arguably, this has been due in large part to the fact that the demand-side factors of employment creation are generally neglected, including the role of government interventions in the labour market, and also because social provisioning to the poor is generally of poor quality, hence unable to produce much transformative punch despite improvements in utilisation indicators. If anything, quality of education or health care might actually deteriorate in the face of increasing usage if insufficiently supported on the infrastructural supply side.

However, if we strip away the human capital supply-side jargon, cash transfers themselves are essentially (albeit fairly marginal) demand-side interventions, arguably best conceived as income support or as a 'non-contributory' substitute for social security for those sections of the population who do not have access to social security. As noted above with respect to redistribution, 'non-contributory' is of course a misnomer because the poor or informal do contribute significantly through indirect taxes such as VAT, even though they usually do not pay direct taxes or contributions to social security. In other words, they do contribute, just not through the direct institutional channels generally conceived as being appropriate forms of contribution by more privileged parts of the labour force.

Policy obviously needs to consider both supply and demand holistically, as there are good reasons for both supply- and demand-side approaches, from various angles. Indeed, whereas the notion of supply-side accrued a negative association with supply-side economics, the idea of public supply-side interventions is especially relevant for development, in terms of supplying human resources and physical infrastructure, and supporting productive capacity. Without such supply-side interventions, demand-side interventions such as cash transfers can risk running up against supply-side constraints and bottlenecks when scaled up. These constraints could be in food supply (a classical concern), in terms of foreign exchange (depending on the import intensity of the increased consumption) or in terms of an ability to provide quality schooling, in the case of scaling up enrolments. These were some of the classic criticisms of Keynesian demand-management posed by the early structuralists of development economics, i.e. that poor countries are generally supply-constrained, rather than demand-deficient as in the case of rich economies. Conversely, an excessive focus on supply-side accumulation might result in lots of infrastructure or employment but with low rates of utilisation or value, as was a common criticism of the Soviet Union in terms of its neglect of consumer demand. Ironically, however, both the supply-side emphasis of structuralists and socialists as well as the demand-side emphasis of Keynesians came under attack with the rise of neoliberalism from the 1970s onwards, which was adamantly against any form of public intervention from either side. 'Supply-side economics' is, in this sense, a misnomer.

Terms of trade and wages

Underlying both supply and demand are the questions of what fundamentally determines the relative value of output and labour in an economy, or what is referred to here as the terms of trade or wages. In other words, if a farmer produces 100 kilograms of surplus grain and decides to trade it, the value of this surplus needs to be measured relative to what it can buy, thereby setting relative prices, such as 1 kilogram of grain for 100 grams of butter. Alternatively, if the farmer decides to work for a wage, then, as classically postulated by Arthur Lewis (1954), the wage must be set slightly above the amount of food the farmer can produce, because otherwise there would be little incentive for him or her to seek wage employment as an alternative to farming (assuming, of course, that labour is free to choose and farmers have land).

The introduction of new products into the mix similarly shakes up these relative price and wage structures, particularly as new products come to be seen as necessities, as has been common with the industrialisation of consumption across the world over the last century. This is why industrialisation is so important even for countries that are effectively non-industrial, because their consumption has, over the course of the century, become increasingly industrialised and hence dependent on the terms of trade of their local non-industrial production in comparison with industrial imports, or else by the prices set by industrial processes in the broader global economy even for their own non-industrial output (such as with grains). Under such circumstances, the value of labour can be easily eroded even while workers and entrepreneurs are making efforts to increase productivity.

This predicament was eloquently elaborated by Arthur Lewis in his classic (and often poorly regurgitated and understood) pioneering contribution to development economics. One of the two key puzzles that he was trying to solve in his 1954 article was the question of 'why tropical produce is so cheap'.

> Take for example the case of sugar. This is an industry in which productivity is extremely high ... [with] a rate of growth of productivity which is unparalleled by any other major industry in the world – certainly not by the wheat industry. Nevertheless workers in the sugar industry continue to walk barefooted and to live in shacks, while workers in wheat enjoy among the highest living standards in the world. (Lewis 1954, p. 442)

To answer this question, he focused on factoral terms of trade in the open economy version of his model of economic growth with unlimited supplies of labour. 'Factoral' in this sense means that he was not focused on the terms of trade between the prices of commodities, which is how it is generally treated (such as the price of bananas or sugar compared to the price of wheat or cars). Instead, he was looking at the terms of the price of labour in the respective sectors of these export commodities, or wages in (Southern) sugar production versus wages in (Northern) wheat or car production.

He argued that because wages are set in what he called 'subsistence sectors' rather than in capitalist export sectors, and, more importantly, that the supply of labour from these subsistence sectors is unlimited at a wage that is set sufficiently higher than what can be earned in these sectors, the benefits of increasing productivity in the capitalist sector accrue chiefly to the (Northern) importers of these exports by way of lower prices, rather than rising wages for the (Southern) producers. Hence, he contended that 'the prices of tropical commercial crops will always permit only subsistence wages until, for a change, capital and knowledge are put at the disposal of the subsistence producers to increase the productivity of tropical food production for home consumption.' The implication of his argument, which is now usually overlooked in deference to a caricature of his theory of growth with unlimited supplies of labour, is that wages are not reflected by productivity, even in physical production, and that increasing productivity in physical production will not necessarily result in rising wages, at least not under the conditions of an open and poor economy with substantial supplies of labour available to work in the so-called 'capitalist' sectors.

Later in his life, Lewis (1978, p. 36) similarly predicted that even as developing countries would move into manufacturing exports, these new exports would function in a manner similar to the previous agricultural export commodities, in the sense that increasing productivity would simply reduce the prices of such manufacturing exports, thereby continuing to exhibit declining terms of trade. This prediction appears to have borne true for Southern countries that have moved massively into manufacturing through their integration into international production networks dominated by transnational corporations, including China (for a detailed discussion of this point, see Erten 2011; Fischer 2015, pp. 717–718).

Lewis' theoretical provocations were pointing towards fundamental debates about what, precisely, determines prices and wages. As discussed above in the section on production, attributes of physical productivity to a certain degree create floors and ceilings for the valuation of labour (or else ceilings on the value that can be appropriated from such labour), especially in relation to rural economies. Economic considerations of supply and demand also operate at the margin, that is, they affect how prices or wages might move higher or lower from a certain position. Indeed, it is in this sense that early neoclassical economics in the late nineteenth century was referred to as the 'marginal revolution'. However, these marginal effects do not fundamentally determine the price, except perhaps with pure commodities, but labour is definitely not one of these. Change at the margin is arguably not a primary determinant of why wages are set at certain levels and how they change over time. Of course, neoclassical theory did provide an answer (marginal productivity theory, that wages are set by the level at which marginal costs equal marginal revenues), but this does not solve the problem of what the actual wage would then be. It is presumably set by the average productivity of all workers once that equilibrium point has been reached, although because this is also conceived in terms of a system of relative prices, it is again difficult to say, exactly, what that wage might actually be. These questions have been at the core of contestation between different major modern schools of economic thought up to the present (for instance, with reference to theories of price, see Nicholas 2011). Economic science, so to speak, has not solved the question of how labour is fundamentally valued, even though this is fundamental to understand the causes and influences of poverty.

Lewis' return to the classics was based on his assumption that wages were set by the levels of productivity in the 'subsistence sector' rather than by marginal productivities in the capitalist sector. Subsistence productivity set the terms that capitalists had to offer in order to draw people out of this sector in order to work in capitalist production (unless, of course, we assume that these workers were drawn from among the destitute and dispossessed, but he does not seem to accept this idea based on his own scholarship in the economic history of the UK and the Caribbean). He similarly argues that the value of goods produced by such labour must reflect such valuation of labour. Hence, the groundwork of his theorisation was established by the assumption that factoral terms of trade between temperate and tropical commodities are set by the difference in agricultural productivity between Europe and the 'tropics'. In particular, the great waves of migration of both Europeans and Asians in the late nineteenth century, during a time of unprecedented trade expansion and integration, set the terms of trade for tropical and temperate agricultural commodities respectively. This was because 'for temperate commodities the market forces set prices that could attract European migrants, while for tropical commodities they set prices that would sustain indentured Indians' (Lewis 1978, p. 14).

Indeed, the only sector where very clear labour productivity differences can be observed between North and South today – enough to explain the wealth differences between North and South today – is in agriculture (e.g., Canadian farming versus Indian farming). Such labour productivity differences cannot even be seen in manufacturing anymore (e.g., 'first-world productivity at third world-wages', whereby Chinese factory workers are as productive in producing the same manufactured good as workers in the US or Europe, despite much lower wages). Rather, value in manufacturing today is accrued more in terms of product differentiation, or component differentiation along value chains, and control over production and distribution networks, including control over the more technological and knowledge intensive parts of the value chain. The point here is that wage differences cannot be discerned through simple comparisons of labour productivity in the physical output of the same or comparable goods, besides perhaps in agriculture.

Part of the controversy in these debates derives from different ways of understanding the nuanced and complex consequences of structural integration, while part derives from the contention that the valuation of labour is fundamentally determined by social and power relations (within structural constraints, as noted above), and not by market intermediation. With respect to the structural, the tendency in most of the contemporary literature on structural change is to treat issues such as productivity and valuation in a rather simplistic manner, more or less assuming or accepting the proposition that the monetary valuation of labour is a roughly accurate measure of labour productivity and that labour productivity is a relatively straightforward function of efficiency and capital accumulation. However, within complex, increasingly integrated economies, the relevant question is about the relative valuation of labour, in which many of the simple linear assumptions about productivity break down, as highlighted by Lewis.

The fallacy of productivity reductionism and development

The idea of what I have called a 'fallacy of productivity reductionism' (Fischer 2011c) was already briefly introduced in the section on production. This refers to the assumption that monetary valuation can be used as an accurate approximation of productivity in a complex modern economy. This modern neoclassical assumption contributes to the myth that the rich are rich due to their greater productivity than the less-rich and thus, by implication, that their wealth is a fair and just reward for effort. It is similar to early neoclassical theory in the late nineteenth century, which collapsed the distributional concerns of classical economics into a calculus of market allocation. The assumption arguably lies at the heart of ideological efforts to legitimate the inequalities of the current world economic order, particularly with respect to the increasingly transnationalised networks that regulate the valuation of output produced by poor people working within these networks.

This insight draws in part from the post-Keynesian school of economics. Perhaps the most practical insight that can be distilled from the otherwise-highly abstract 'Cambridge capital controversies' of the 1960s is the point that, in a monetary world with heterogeneous goods and services, 'capital' is effectively almost impossible to measure in any coherent aggregate sense. In contrast neoclassical assumptions treat capital as substitutable and, hence, more or less identical with consumption goods (such as corn for planting and corn for consumption, if we return again to the highly simplified neoclassical farm economy with only one good, as referred to earlier with respect to the Solow growth model). Accordingly, aggregate 'productivity' can only be understood in terms of monetary valuation (i.e., through prices), not in physical terms – this point should be obvious with respect to most services. It should be recalled that Paul Samuelson (1966) implicitly conceded defeat in these debates to Joan Robinson and Piero Sraffa, although this concession was subsequently ignored by most of the profession, particularly from the 1980s onwards.[4] Instead, the profession has continued to assume that complex modern industrial economies essentially function in the manner suggested by the one-good (or identical two-good) world imagined in the production functions of standard modern neoclassical theoretical models (and the so-called New Keynesian variants). In these models, capital and productivity are treated as if they can be measured in physical terms, such as in the total factor productivity measures derived from one-good moneyless growth models of the Solow variant. It is in this sense that the bulk of contemporary economics can be described as a faith-based discipline, in the sense that a leap of faith is required to enter its temple of logic.

In consequence, most mainstream approaches to measuring productivity almost always rely on value-added accounting data in various ways as a means to approximate aggregate productivity, whether at industry, sectoral or economy levels. The justification for this was partly based on early econometric work by Kenneth Arrow, Hollis Chenery, Singh Minhas and Robert Solow. Starting with the 'empirical observation that the value added per unit of labour used within a given industry varies across countries with the wage rate', these authors concluded that most of 'the variation in labour productivity is explained by variation in wage rates alone' (Arrow et al. 1961, pp. 225 and 228). In other words, the implication is that variations in wage rates are mostly due to labour productivity. However, as pointed out by Felipe and McCombie (2001, p. 1222), these results were essentially the product of tautology in that 'the estimations of production functions [are simply] capturing an underlying accounting identity [that value added equals the wage bill plus profits] ... Hence, regressing output on the inputs is bound, almost by definition, to give a very good statistical fit.' In other words, it is basically saying that there is a very strong correlation between wages and the sum of wages and profits, particularly given that profits are generally a fairly stable and consistent share of the total. To the extent that their contention is true, it undermines the whole edifice of aggregate productivity measures that have since been elaborated on the basis of the results of Arrow et al. (1961), as noted in subsequent work by Felipe and McCombie (e.g., Felipe and McCombie 2003, 2006, 2012, 2013).

The use of value-added as a shorthand for productivity leads to absurd logical implications. For instance, it suggests that a barber in the US is 30 or more times more productive than a barber in India, even though they both 'produce' the same number of haircuts per hour (according to the tastes and expectations of their clients), simply because the wage of the barber in the US is 30 or more times higher. Or else, within the US, that the 'productivity' of a lawyer is ten times higher than that of a barber. The lawyer's labour is certainly more valued than the barber's, whether or not for good reason, but this has little to do with productivity (e.g., what is the output of a lawyer or a bureaucrat?). We might consider that the power to leverage higher value for one's labour is, in itself, a form of productivity, but this is more accurately represented as power, as discussed further below.

Indeed, the rising value of labour in financial services, and hence of 'productivity' in this sector, is related to processes of financialization, whereby levels of remuneration in the financial sector are allowed to rise to unheard-of heights (and then might be interpreted as improving 'productivity' within that sector as a result). The differences across different types of labour are usually explained in terms of 'human capital', referring mostly to years of schooling, and to skills premiums, although similar wage differentials can also be observed between employees with more or less equivalent levels of education, such as teachers versus lawyers, or a computer engineer in California versus one in Bangalore. In other words, much of what we are picking up in most conventional measures of productivity actually amounts to price or wage differences, not actual effort, output or even skill, especially in economies that are increasingly based on services.

The idea that monetary valuation can represent productivity is especially problematic with respect to the tertiary sector, given the notorious difficulties of measuring productivity in services. For instance, while some dimensions of productivity can be measured in some aspects of tertiary work, such as patients treated per doctor, students taught per teacher, numbers of sheets cleaned per domestic worker or merchandise sold in a supermarket per cashier, such productivity measures are often deceptive in that the quality of the good regularly changes through the process of increasing outputs (such as more children per classroom leading to worse learning outcomes, or less care in serving hospital patients). Hence, such measures are not necessarily measuring a consistently comparable good (as would be the case with physical measures of identical goods, such as tonnes of wheat). Even in the case of wholesale and retail trade where productivity measures bear some relevance (i.e., merchandise sold per employee per unit of time) and where the application of technology is also relevant, increases in productivity – especially in retail trade – often imply shifting labour and time costs onto customers, which makes them profitable but not necessarily more productive from a broader holistic perspective that includes all of the labour involved in the process.

It is also somewhat nonsensical and arbitrary to use the standard lexicon of 'labour intensity' (versus capital intensity) to explain wage differentials within the tertiary sector or in comparison to other sectors given that service-sector activities are largely – or in many cases entirely – based on labour inputs rather than capital inputs, except again in the activities of trade or transport, where we can conceive of capital inputs, including automation and robotisation. Tertiary-sector professionals such as lawyers are not usually referred to as labour-intensive even though, in capital-labour terms, most if not all of the input of legal services is labour.[5] Presumably, they are not referred to as labour-intensive because they generate high value per unit of labour time, or else because their education is taken to be a proxy for capital (unlike nurses or school teachers, who have similar levels of education in terms of degree types but at much lower levels of value-added and, hence, are often referred to as labour-intensive).

The logic of differentiating capital intensity in service activities through the designation of 'human capital' is problematic for these and similar reasons. Human capital is usually proxied by years of schooling and hence is basically referring to formal education. However, the evidence that differences in education can predict wage differences – particularly across countries but also across service sectors within a country – is increasingly weak, especially as populations attain higher and broader schooling levels. Much of the earlier assumptions on this were based on cross-country regressions whereby richer countries generally had much higher levels of formal schooling. However, this association becomes progressively weak the more poorer countries (or lower social classes) progress in levels of formal schooling without necessarily experiencing the economic benefits that were associated with equivalent levels in the earlier cases. Hence, like with fertility in demography as discussed in Chapter 4, human development has become increasingly disassociated from economic development. It is a classic case of misattributing causality with association.[6]

In other words, there is a degree of tautology at work. Labour-intensity is associated with relatively lower wages, and hence when relatively lower wages are observed, the labour is assumed to be more labour-intensive, even though both labour intensity and labour productivity are nonsensical reference points in the measurement of the outputs of intangible services, the value of which is mostly based on the value of the labour inputs.

The mainstream response to the quandary of productivity in services has usually been with reference Baumol's 'cost disease'. This refers to the work of Baumol and Bowen (1966), who attempted to explain the apparent paradox of rising salaries in jobs that experience no increase in labour productivity (such as in the performing arts, where the same number of people are required to play a symphony as a century earlier), in comparison to rising salaries in jobs that do experience labour productivity increases (such as in manufacturing). They deduced that this seemingly contradicts the standard assumption that wages are closely associated with changes in labour productivity (as discussed above). Their answer was essentially that wages in sectors without productivity gains increase because they must compete for employees with the sectors that do experience productivity gains. The analysis is notably built on differentiating physical production from services and presumes that productivity in services can be measured using standard total-factor productivity techniques. The very fact that wage equalisation across the economy might be seen as a 'disease' is itself indicative of the particular perspective informing this approach.

Triplett and Bosworth (2003) claim that the disease had been cured on the basis of evidence of rising productivity growth in service sectors in the US economy after 1995, although their measurement of such productivity continues to rely on the standard productivity-growth accounting framework originating from the work of Solow (1957), whereby labour productivity is measured as the value-added output per person engaged in production. It also remains bogged down in a variety of theoretical and methodological issues, many of which they admittedly acknowledge. For instance, they exclude social services from their calculations because of difficulties surrounding the treatment of capital in such industries. On the treatment of capital in other service industries, they acknowledge the problems of relying on capital stock data at the industry level as a measure of capital input given that it is dominated by financial wealth, not simply 'productive' capital stock that is used as an input to production. They propose a resolution of this problem by combining such data with flow data on capital services by industry, although, as pointed out by Andersen et al. (2009) in their review of methods commonly used to measure capital service flows, a variety of important assumptions are used in constructing such measures and, even in the case of the relatively easy-to-measure capital inputs of agriculture in the USA, they demonstrate that substantial differences in these measures can be computed depending on which assumptions are chosen.

In other words, the more one tries to narrow the problem to make it tractable, the more it becomes problematic.

The fallacy of productivity reductionism becomes especially pertinent when considered in light of the increasing transnationalisation of production and distribution in the postwar era (although it was also very pertinent during the colonial era, for similar reasons). For instance, when an increase in the value-added of the tertiary sector is recorded in the US or Europe – such as in the categories of management, finance, marketing, trade or research and development – this is usually interpreted as increasing productivity in those sectors (and increasing economy-wide productivity if this results in overall economic growth). Yet at least part of such an increase represents the inflows of profits and concentration of value in the headquarters of lead corporations (such as Apple, Google or Amazon) from across diverse networks of subsidiaries, affiliates and sub-contractors, many of which are based in the Global South, especially those based in actual physical production. When a transnational corporation practises transfer pricing or equivalent practices that have become standard in international accountancy,[7] as a means of transferring profits from a Southern subsidiary or affiliate to a head office in New York or London (usually via various offshore financial centres), the subsidiary appears less productive as a result, whereas the head office appears more productive. Moreover, most of the activities of the head office would be in services, not physical production, which doesn't seem to factor into the Baumolian concerns of service-sector productivity, presumably because these are seen as 'business services' rather than, say, orchestra performers (even though orchestra performers do tend to perform for the beneficiaries of high wages in such business services and might even derive from a similar social class).

Ironically, the actual producers of goods – who are increasingly located in the Global South – might well be accused of being inefficient (in value terms) and in need of extra structural adjusting, even though the appearance of such inefficiency is in many cases the product of accountancy practices that reduce reported measures of value-added to a functional minimum and thereby maintain subsidiaries in a perpetual profitless existence. Such producers might be otherwise working very diligently and investing in a whole myriad of ways in order to keep up with the competition. In such circumstances, the precise meaning of 'being productive' is difficult to pin down, except in cases of the physical output of comparable goods. The idea that inter-country differences in wage rates can be explained by obstructions to the free flow of goods, services and capital across borders also becomes increasingly absurd the more the global economy liberalises and becomes increasingly unequal.

These issues also highlight the importance of ownership and/ or control over processes of value circulation in monetary economies, and the insidious siphoning of wealth that usually results from a dominance of foreign ownership in the peripheral economies of the Global South.[8] Effective outflows of wealth, whether through licit or elicit capital flows or else through subtle processes such as transfer pricing, undermine the monetary aggregate demand in these economies that would otherwise contribute towards enhancing employment generation as well as the fiscal revenues required to finance comprehensive social policies. It is also in this sense that national ownership plays a hugely important role in efforts to retain wealth within national economies, thereby capturing the benefits of productivity increases when and where these take place. For similar reasons, national ownership has been one of the principle targets of ideological attack under the last 30 years of neoliberalism, with the frontline currently targeting China under the guise of accusations of currency manipulation or other unfair trade practices.[9]

Raising productivity in the Global South through efforts to support farmers or through industrial policies to support fledgling industrialists is obviously an important component of development strategy and of efforts to reduce poverty and inequality, particularly if the resulting benefits are used in ways that genuinely improve wellbeing among the poor. For instance, small-scale farmers would obviously benefit from raising their output on both their existing plots of land and, ideally, on enlarged land holdings (which, by implication, would require land reform), at least so long as the costs of increasing their output would not exceed the benefits. However, such self-evident examples are often used to simplify and legitimise the more generalised patterns of inequality in our world today, which are much more obscure in terms of a direct connection between effort or output and poverty. The underlying fallacy of productivity reductionism is imperative to recognise because, otherwise, an obsession with raising productivity risks being turned into a powerful ethos for disciplining an increasingly Southern global workforce together with nationally based productive capitalists, both subordinated into global networks of production and distribution that increasingly control the most lucrative flows of value in our world economy.

Social relations and structure in the determination of value within development

These issues surrounding the valuing of labour are generally ignored by prevailing mainstream approaches to poverty studies, except when viewed through a particular neoclassical lens drawn from the marginal productivity theory of wages. However, as the fallacy of productivity reductionism reveals, the processes involved in valuing the labour of a poor person are arguably influenced by a variety of broader political economy and sociological factors, both structural and institutional. Correspondingly, the question of modern poverty is not necessarily about how to make poor people work harder and better, but about how their work is valued within a context of development.

In this regard, the other part of the controversy about how labour is relatively valued is the contention that the valuation of labour is fundamentally determined by social and power relations (within structural limits). In other words, especially but not only in the service sector, wage differences are arguably related to social and institutional processes of valuing various categories of labour, which are driven by power relations, ideological factors, socialisation and related processes of social stratification and differentiation, instead of considerations ostensibly related to labour productivities within the production of comparable goods or services.

Real markets and other economic processes, such as exchange operating through administered state channels or reciprocally through family and community channels, are embedded within these social and power relations. Or, as asserted by Furtado (1983), market operations 'are, as a rule, transactions between agents exercising unequal power' (p. 15). Competitive markets are always embedded in this sense, even though, as argued by Polanyi (2001 [1944]), non-market forms of social organisation come to be subordinated to the demands of 'market society' under capitalism – a process he calls 'disembedding', although there has been much debate over the precise meaning of this term (e.g., see Goodwin 2018, Levien 2018). Accordingly, the valuing of labour itself needs to be understood as an intrinsically social process.

This point was poignantly made in the seminal work by Celso Furtado (1983; translated from the Portuguese edition of 1978), one of the founders of the Latin American school of structuralist economics and a colleague of Raul Prebisch. Furtado identified the rise of industrial capitalism with the rise of unified planning – referred to as economic policy – which was achieved through the emergence of modern nation-states from the mid-eighteenth century onwards. This showed two relevant countervailing features: a progressive concentration of economic power and the highly effective organisation of the wage-earning masses (ibid., p. 17). Within such 'organised capitalism', which is best conceived as a system of social organisation rather than simply a form of organising production, 'political power – conceived as capable of changing the behaviour of broad social groups – emerges as a complex structure in which the institutions comprising the State interact with the groups that dominate the accumulation process and with the social organizations capable of intervening in a significant way in the distribution of income' (ibid., p. 17).

The challenge for contemporary developing countries, he argued, is that the increasing transnationalisation of production weakens the ability of increasingly effective forms of social organisation to exert pressure on the growing power of enterprises for a more immediate distribution of income (ibid., p. 21). While the power of 'social organizations engaged in the struggle to raise the value of labour, that is, to bring about a more widespread social distribution of the benefits of the growing productivity of labour generated by accumulation' (ibid., p. 27) was historically enhanced by the tendency of the state to broaden its social bases of support, the same tendency today is undercut by the fact that the power responsible for coordinating increasingly complex international economic relations has shifted, to a large extent, from the national state to the large enterprise (ibid., p. 23). From this somewhat-prophetic perspective, written well in advance of the globalisation literature of the 1990s, the subsequent emphasis on deregulation during the neoliberal years from the 1980s onwards can be understood as a further privatisation of this macro-regulatory capacity rather than deregulation *per se*.

However, as economies become transnationalised, many of these relations become increasingly opaque and hard to decipher. To a certain degree, this has led to a sort of neo-naïveté in poverty studies, treating poverty reduction as if it is still primarily concerned with poverty traps in traditional subsistence despite decades worth of criticism of such conceptions and even while the conditions governing the poor have long moved beyond such traditional states, if ever they were.

It is important to move beyond such naïveté and towards more systemic understandings of how poor people and regions are integrated into larger economic and social systems. Whether a process whereby people remain poor and do not experience any apparent rising productivity should be called a 'structural transformation' or 'development' is of course open to question. What is important, however, is that the experiences of poor people who are integrated into broader systems must be considered as integral parts of the transformations of those systems, even if there appears to be nothing particularly transformational in their own particular part (although there usually is, insofar as the reproductions of poverty are driven by the broader transformations).

This preference for a macro-systemic view versus a micro-view is an important antidote for micro-fundamentalism or for methodological nationalism and localism. At sub-national or local levels, the precise combinations of the factors that lead economic development – such as increasing labour productivity and capital accumulation, based on increasing scale and degrees of specialisation – will vary depending on regional patterns of integration into national and global economies. Indeed, some regional economies might possess few or none of the attributes of increasing productivity in agriculture or manufacturing, but benefit nonetheless from a rise in national labour productivity, in particular through the supply of cheap mass-produced goods, the circulation of monetary aggregate demand and the dissemination of wage norms throughout the national economy supported by government fiscal policy. Furtado (1973) referred to this as modernisation without economic development, in the sense that modern goods are inserted into the consumption basket of an economy without the capital accumulation or the adoption of more effective productive processes that are associated with the production of these modern goods. He posited that such new forms of consumption could be afforded by increases of income earned through either the depletion of natural resources or else through static reallocations and specialisations of production according to comparative advantage, both of which do not necessarily entail economic development.

We might include aid transfers as another way to raise incomes and hence modern consumption without economic development. From this more systemic perspective, it is difficult to know where to draw the regional boundaries of economic development, that is, the boundaries within which a region can be considered to be developing economically. Notably, there are usually wide swaths of territory and large proportions of population even in advanced industrial countries that are based mostly on the consumption of modern goods rather than their production (increasingly so as employment continues to shift into tertiary activities).

In this respect, remote peripheral rural economies generally transform through consumption-driven integrations into 'industrial civilisation' without necessarily being involved in industrial modes of production. Such situations would describe well much of sub-Saharan Africa, outside specific enclave sectors such as mining where industrial processes are definitely in use, although usually under the control and/or ownership of foreign (or non-local) corporations, which subsequently divert much of the value-added out of the national economy. Ignoring the role of fiscal and other transfers, the relative purchasing power of such a peripheral economy would be determined by the terms of trade between its non-industrial, mostly rural or artisanal, labour-intensive output, versus the industrial goods (and related services) that are consumed in the economy, mostly through import. This relative purchasing power then moderates differences in labour productivity, or what Arthur Lewis (1954) called the 'factoral terms of trade' (labour being a factor of production), as well as the distributive outcomes of production and circulation.

For instance, even if prices for meat increase relative to mass-consumption goods such as instant noodles or mobile phones, the wealth of a herder is nonetheless limited by the size of the herd he or she is able to sustain, and the disposable income by the number of cattle he or she is able to sell in a year. The number remains limited so long as herding is based on household and non-industrial forms of organisation. Indeed, this is the reason why many governments and development agencies have often been intent on making herders become ranchers as a means of poverty alleviation, although less so after environmental concerns have taken precedence since the late 1990s and small has again become beautiful, at least for the poor. Conversely, a factory worker involved in the production of instant noodles or mobile phones most likely contributes to the production of much more output and value-added in a year than the herder, particularly in a highly mechanised and automated factory. The worker's income might not be better than the herder's, not because of productivity considerations but because his or her wages are squeezed through the process of distributing the surplus (i.e., value-added) between profits, taxes, wages and other income payments such as interest payments on the debt used to purchase factory machines or rent. Hence, it is not obvious that the herder would become better-off by becoming a factory worker (or, along the same logic, a rancher), as is often blithely assumed by scholars and policy-makers. However, it is quite likely that, in economic terms, the worker produces more value-added than the herder (i.e., the worker has a higher level of labour productivity), which is then circulated throughout the economy through various processes. (Or else, as noted above, the value-added is circulated out of the economy altogether, thereby not contributing to local process of accumulation, as is the perennial problem of peripheral, externally oriented and externally dependent poorer countries.) Industrialisation is thereby usually seen as a significant driver of economic growth, whereas 'peasant' production is not, even though the 'peasant' might not necessarily become better-off by becoming a worker within an industrial system of production, at least not until that system starts to produce rising wages. The delicate balance, particularly in peripheral economies, can lead to many paradoxical dynamics within the labour transitions of such peripheral economies, that is, paradoxical from the perspective of our stylised understanding of classical labour transitions in Europe.

In this sense, it is important to break out of simplistic normative binaries regarding development. It is not as if negative attributes (such as persistent poverty) or even a lack of structural transformation in some sub-sections or sub-regions of an economic system (such as the persistence of low-productivity economic activities in rural areas or entire economies) somehow invalidate the existence or possibility of development or structural transformation. Rather, from a broader perspective, it is important to consider how such negative attributes are the dialectical parts of a developmental whole, especially with regard to the integration of peripheral regions within wider economic systems. In particular, the ways that development manifests in peripheral settings can be quite different from the ways it manifests in more central locations. Nonetheless, insofar as they are integrated parts, they need to be considered as part of a holistic conception of structural transformation.

Conclusion

This chapter presented a schematic framework for building an integrated structuralist and institutionalist political economy approach for what we might call critical poverty studies, followed by an elaboration on how this relates to development. The proposed framework is based on two conceptual dimensions that are implicit in much of the ideas and policies relating to poverty and social needs. The first dimension deals the creation and division of wealth, which can be conceived in classical political economy terms as production, distribution and redistribution. The second deals with the more secondary, indirect and aggregated factors influencing the first, which can be divided into supply-side factors, demand-side factors and terms of trade or wages (or the relative valuing of labour and its fruits). The last of this second set was elaborated by placing terms of trade within theoretical debates around productivity, or what I call the fallacy of productivity reductionism.

These interacting dimensions help to clarify how different approaches to conceptualising poverty and its reduction, as well as theoretical perspectives in economics and social sciences more generally, usually place selective emphasis on different combinations of elements across these two dimensions, even though all elements are needed to understand the evolution of social needs and the reproduction of poverty. While each approach might have its own insights, the causes of poverty can only be fully understood from a broader holistic perspective of all that is involved in the creation and division of wealth.

More specifically, prevailing approaches to understanding poverty, which implicitly rely on neoclassical theoretical approaches, generally overlook several key dimensions, such as demand-side factors (with respect to employment and growth) and supply-side factors (with respect to social provisioning). They do emphasise the productivity of individuals, often through discourses of self-discipline and self-responsibility, but without more complex consideration of developmentalist strategies for increasing national productivity, to support individual efforts and to avoid them becoming undermined through fallacies of composition (that is, when everyone does the same thing, everyone's investment is lost through falling prices). Instead, free markets and private property rights are generally emphasised as being the driving forces of productivity, usually with reference to the theoretically abstract and empirically problematic, but hugely influential New Institutionalist Economics literature, perhaps best represented by North (1990) and Acemoglu et al. (2001). Or else, behavioural approaches, such as that of Banerjee and Duflo (2011), tend to have a narrow conception of the social reproduction of poverty and assume that behavioural fixes are largely sufficient or at least expedient ways to overcome 'poverty traps' and launch poor people into virtuous cycles of rising prosperity, which becomes growth in the aggregate. The fact that they rarely deal with the aggregate and how aggregate convolutions might express themselves at the micro-level is perhaps one of the weakest links in the argument for relying exclusively on 'micro-foundations', which is invariably made in reference to abstracted neoclassical conceptions of how individuals and firms act.

These two dimensions and their elements also underpin and overlap the more conventional consideration of policy realms as mentioned above. Social policy is often thought of in terms of the spending side of redistribution. However, it also serves important distributive functions and, as seminally highlighted by Mkandawire (2004, 2005), has also played important functions in supporting productive development policies in past cases of late industrialisation. It also needs to be examined from both demand and supply sides, from multiple angles. Development policies, while generally seen as supply-side and productive in nature given their focus on increasing productivity and output, also carry important distributive and redistributive functions that, if ignored, are often their undoing. The general realm of macroeconomic policy identified by Cornia (2006) contains several functions and would be better divided into monetary and fiscal policy, because the two are quite distinct. Fiscal policy has an obvious central role in redistribution and in production, and strong influences over distribution, as well as on demand and supply sides. Monetary policy in turn is never neutral, in the sense that it effects debtors and creditors differently, and in this respect it is fundamentally redistributive (just not in the way that we conventionally conceive of redistribution). It can also have important impacts production (through influencing the cost of borrowing and hence investment) and even distribution through its effects on wages and profits.

Social policy, however, is the realm in which much of poverty alleviation strategy is practised. As such, it reserves special attention in the penultimate chapter of this book. In particular, it is central to understanding processes of social integration and ordering that are so crucial to understanding of the reproduction of poverty and the changing nature of social needs within a context of development, as highlighted in this and in previous chapters.

7 | SOCIAL POLICY AND THE TENSION BETWEEN IDENTIFICATION AND SEGREGATION WITHIN SOCIAL ORDERING AND DEVELOPMENT

The dilemma of all approaches to the study of poverty, including social exclusion in terms of how it is conventionally conceived, can be summed up as a tension between identification and segregation. Poverty approaches derive from a fundamental concern with the wellbeing of the poor and are designed to evaluate their situation and/or to provide information for guiding actual policy-making, which boils down to an exercise of identification. However, the institutionalisation of this exercise tends to lead to a vision and practice of segregating the poor, both in terms of how their place in society is conceived, and in terms of how policy and social provisioning is directed towards them. Even if the intentions are otherwise, the inertia of the logic consistently tugs in this latter direction.

This tension is usually framed in terms of universalism versus targeting. The debate essentially refers to the challenges of treating people the same while at the same time differentiating them in order to redistribute income and wealth across society, and to address disadvantage and discrimination. This classic debate, however, often tends to get somewhat convoluted and easily dismissed, if only because some targeting is usually required in most policy-making, especially in areas of poverty reduction and social assistance.

There has also been a subtle shift in the way that universalism has been referred to in recent years, towards a connotation of universal coverage or access, such as sending all children to school, regardless of how such schooling is provided or financed, or else everyone having some sort of health insurance, regardless of whether the insurance offers complete coverage or whether health care provisioning is unified or segregated. Martinez and Sanchez-Ancochea (2016) refer to this as a minimalist understanding of universalism and give examples of its prominence, particularly among various organs of the UN system, such as the ILO, that are in part guilty for the normalisation of this minimalist meaning.

However, the strongest influence on this shift of meaning probably comes from the World Bank, which explicitly takes the position that universalism is achieved as long as everyone has access to something, regardless of how this is provided. In other words, even if the middle and upper classes access health and education services privately, this is considered to be part of a 'universal' system.[1] This interpretation is also implicit in the special issue of *The Economist* (2018) on universal health care. It thereby includes the vast swath of private provisioning in health and education to the unsecured middle 50–60 per cent of populations in most lower- and middle-income countries as part of a 'universal' provisioning system. Given that almost all systems, even in the poorest countries, usually have at least some very rudimentary public health and schooling systems for the poorest, alongside private provisioning for the rich, this makes it very easy to pre-maturely celebrate the achievement of universal health and education for all, as has become a common platitude.[2] Such sleights of narrative are impressive in the way that they coopt or hijack progressive concepts. Indeed, this is similar to the way that 'pro-poor growth' was defined by the World Bank in the early 2000s as growth with any absolute poverty reduction, which effectively includes most growth episodes as pro-poor.

In the midst of this confusion, a certain reframing is necessary. The fundamental problem is not necessarily with targeting *per se*, but with the increasing normalisation of a segregationist approach to policy-making and social organisation, whereby poor people are not necessarily un-serviced but are treated differently, and often quite poorly. Much of the criticism of targeting in social policy scholarship is implicitly about this aspect of segregation. It is discussed in terms of how targeting severs cross-class solidarities and interests, thereby reducing political support for maintaining service quality to the poor and often resulting in a worsening quality of social provisioning to the poor, and also how it encourages stigmatism of welfare recipients or else perverse incentives. Indeed, even though the argument of perverse incentives has typically been made from the right as a criticism of universal welfare, the irony is that its logic actually applies to targeting – the least universalistic aspects of welfare systems – given that the perversion is the result of the use of thresholds and means-testing, not welfare *per se*. Nonetheless, the challenge remains with regard to how to treat poor people the same as anyone else, without stigmatisation or segregation, while at the same time differentially directing resources towards them in a way that ideally generates a degree of redistribution from rich to poor and otherwise improves their prospects in society. The dilemma encapsulates classical concerns of both liberalism and socialism.

The problem with the de-politicisation of poverty debates, as elaborated in Chapter 2, is that it allows for orthodox agendas to frame the narrative about the optimal ways of solving this dilemma, and about the possibilities and constraints of public action. This has been evident in both the MDGs and the SDGs, neither of which address the policy means that should or could be used to achieve their proliferating goals and indicators. While some might argue that these policy means should not be specified, the void nonetheless gets avidly filled by the most powerful and assertive voices.

Since the beginning of the so-called neoliberal era, from the early 1980s onwards, these orthodox voices have strongly adhered to the idea of targeting in social policy as an overall institutional modality of social provisioning, rather than as just a particular policy tool within a larger profile of more comprehensive programmes and interventions. As pointed out by Mkandawire (2005), this ironically contradicts their opposition to targeting in trade or production policy. The emphasis in turn has tended to reinforce fragmentation and segregation in social provisioning systems, in many cases already existing but in others created anew. The irony is that the 'liberal' in neoliberalism would, in principle, be against creating systems of differentiated citizenship rights, but it appears that this is where neoliberalism shows its reactionary bias. Of course, care must again be taken with the twists of word play, because the World Bank also puts much emphasis on overcoming fragmentation, although by this they do not refer to social fragmentation across classes and different social groups, but sectoral fragmentation, such as with respect to health, education and social assistance services that are targeted to the poor in a fragmented rather than coordinated manner.[3]

A good example of this mainstream position is found in the various *World Development Reports* (WDR) of the World Bank. I have discussed the 2003 WDR on services in Fischer (2010a, 2013a) and the 2013 WDR on jobs in Fischer (2012) alongside *The Economist*'s position on inequality, as discussed in Chapter 2. With regard to the latter WDR (World Bank 2012), besides the regular advocacy of macroeconomic 'fundamentals', trade liberalisation, deregulation and the virtues of special economic zones and foreign takeovers of domestic firms, the position of the WDR on matters related to social policy or poverty alleviation remain remarkably in line with the targeting approach promoted by the World Bank for decades. This typically enters as a corollary to labour market deregulation and social security reforms, with social protection to support the most vulnerable and least able to adjust to the dislocations wrought by these policies (e.g., see WB 2012, p. 257 and pp. 307–309). Indeed, a similar view is expressed in the recent *IMF Framework on Social Spending* (IMF 2017), which created widespread reaction among the academic and policy communities, specifically in relation to the priority given to fiscal concerns over the rights to social security in the IMF suggestions for reforms of the latter.[4]

The absences in the 2013 WDR are also telling, such as on matters related to industrial policy or other forms of government intervention into production or employment.[5] Similarly, the role of universal public provisioning of health care and education is absent from the discussion on human capital. The only brief discussions of 'universalism' address the role of social protection in inducing formalisation of labour forces, although the report advises caution in this regard (e.g., pp. 210–212 and 276). That both state-led industrial policy and universal provisioning of basic health care and education were keys to the employment and growth successes in countries such as South Korea and Taiwan is generally ignored (except one qualified mention of universal education in South Korea on p. 177).

The reasoning of these policy positions remains clearly orthodox. As discussed in Chapter 2, it is founded on the deductive principle that perfect markets – if ever these could exist – lead to the most efficient and pareto-optimal outcome possible. In this sense, there is nothing new under the Chicago sun. This logic has been at the core of the dominant policy paradigm that has arguably induced much of the rising inequality over the last 30 years. In their defence, proponents of this paradigm would retort that it has been the continued obstruction of markets by government policies or other collective actors such as trade unions that has been preventing the outcomes predicted by theory. This is the reason why government spending and policy are repeatedly emphasised in *The Economist* (2012) as the big drivers of inequalities today. To paraphrase Karl Polanyi's criticism of the laissez-faire utopia of economic liberalism: because the ideal free market is never attainable as a reality in a complex modern economy, it can always be argued that the failures of economic liberalism are not because markets were liberalised, but that they were not liberalised enough.

From the perspective of the dilemma mentioned above, the important point here is that these orthodox positions do present themselves – and possibly honestly see themselves – as the progressive option. Despite decades of critique, targeting is still presented as a logical win-win for redistribution; transfers will have much more poverty-reducing effect if concentrated on the poor rather than being dispersed across whole populations and among many non-poor who do not need the transfers or should not have them. Indeed, it appears as a straightforward Robin Hood scenario of taking from the rich and giving to the poor, which is reinforced with the impression that universal-type policies also lead to state largesse as well as corruption, and therefore need to be tightly reigned in and managed. The position appears impervious to decades of critique of targeting, which at best have merely dented its armour in battles with greater demons from the neoliberal imaginary. The critique has also become entangled in confusions surrounding the meaning of universalism, as mentioned above, which facilitates the orthodox dismissal of this critique.

In this respect, there is a necessity to insert a holistic social policy perspective into these discussions, regarding the key role of universalistic modes of social policy in both rich and poor countries as some of our most powerful policy tools to date for dealing simultaneously with poverty and inequality, especially in combination with broader developmentalist agendas. This endeavour, which I already elaborated in Fischer (2010a and 2012), joins similar efforts made by Mkandawire (2001, 2005), as well as others such as Martinez and Sanchez-Ancochea (2014, 2016), and institutionally by the United Nations Research Institute for Social Development (e.g., UNRISD 2010).

The contention here is that shifts towards more universalistic principles in social policy (which may include elements of targeting) are crucial to bring about more egalitarian and equitable processes of social integration and citizenship. Of particular importance is the degree to which poorer and middle social strata,[6] or various other social groupings, are integrated (or segregated), given the centrality of this dimension to the longer-term social and political sustainability of any poverty- and/or inequality-reduction strategy. In addition to this common insight from the field of social policy, another problem with the focus on poverty and even some inequality indicators is that these do not necessarily reflect a wide range of adverse social processes occurring across middle social strata and that can have important consequences on mobility, stratification and cohesion, as discussed at the end of Chapter 5 on social exclusion. Indeed, a lack of attention to middle strata can inadvertently reinforce a tendency to attribute various inequality-induced social disorders to poverty, thereby reinforcing conservative phobic impulses to segregate the poor from other social strata, even though the opposite is arguably required in order to move towards lasting socially inclusive development.

However, such issues are fundamentally political, not merely technical. Hence, they require a politicised engagement within current development agendas in order to create the space for serious deliberation of these possibilities, rather than relying on the apparently apolitical moral ground of goals and indicators. The risk of not explicitly anchoring future development agendas within politicised policy debates is that these agendas can be (and are often being) subverted towards policy agendas that possibly undermine inequality reduction and/or fragment citizenship rights in many contexts.

This is argued in three sections. The first presents a background to conceptions of social policy, particularly with a context of development and with respect to criticisms of targeting. The second offers an attempt to conceptualise universalism in social policy in a manner that bears more general and practical applicability beyond ideal-type Northern welfare states, and that clarifies much of the conceptual confusion surrounding the term, particularly with respect to its application to developing countries or development goals. Accordingly, universalism in social policy needs to be understood as an umbrella term reflecting a set of guiding principles along three dimensions: provisioning modalities, which includes issues of access and coverage; costing and pricing, which relate to commodification; and financing, which involves the principle of (social) insurance.

Within each dimension, we can think in terms of a spectrum from strong to weak (or absent) universalistic principles underpinning various institutional systems of social provisioning. In the third section, this understanding is then brought back into the question of placing poverty and inequality within broader questions of social integration and social needs within development. The conclusion offers some reflections on the necessity of politicising the policy debates along these lines.

Social policy and social ordering in development

The idea of social policy lies at the core of our understanding of modern institutional processes of social ordering and inequality. Social policy generally refers to the range of publicly or collectively provided, funded and/or regulated forms of services and interventions in a society, such as schooling, health care and social protection. The function or purpose is not only to provide these public or social goods, but also to affect various social outcomes through such provisioning (such as learning or health) or else to influence the access to and the incidence of adequate and secure livelihoods and income (as per Mkandawire 2004, p. 1).[7] It is also generally considered to include several other areas such as housing policy, as well as more legal or regulatory aspects such as in child protection or labour market regulation.

Within this broad understanding, social protection has received most of the recent attention as a more narrow view of social policy, whereas it is properly understood as a subset of social policy. It has been commonly divided according to three categories: social insurance; social assistance (i.e., welfare); and standards and regulations (formal and/or informal), such as labour standards and regulations, or child protection.[8] However, health and education provisioning play a central role in both social policy and inequality dynamics. These two social services usually constitute the largest shares of government expenditure in most countries (education is usually the largest, more than three times health care spending in the case of China, for instance). They involve potentially large impacts on household expenditures (particularly if commoditised), for both poor and non-poor, however defined, and thereby have a large bearing on poverty (especially health). Education has huge implications for social mobility and the structuring of education systems goes to the heart of social stratification and the social reproduction of inequality. Both health and education systems touch a core nerve of social politics because they structure the ways that various social groups and classes might come into contact with each other in moments of intimacy and vulnerability.

From the political economy perspective of the previous chapter, social policy can be understood as playing an important redistributive (or circulative) role in an economy, particularly through education and health spending. It has served as the primary policy realm in which most direct public action on poverty reduction is implemented (poverty reduction via growth can be considered indirect, i.e., trickle-down via the employment and demand effects of growth). Social policy also plays an important role in regulating distributive outcomes via its effect on wages and other aspects of employment (such as the role of child care and early school provisioning on women's labour force participation).[9] In the productive realm, social policy and associated policy approaches (such as fiscal policy) also play synergistic roles with productionist development strategies such as industrial policy. Its redistributive function is important in this respect given the exclusionary tendencies of such development strategies (e.g., see Sumner 2017). However, it also plays a direct role in productionist strategies in terms of providing skilled labour inputs, and also a political economy role in terms of forging cross-class alliances in support of such strategies. In all of these senses, social policies are fundamentally political given that they serve as the basis for defining and instituting citizenship rights, distributing public goods, redistributing wealth and articulating some of the main mechanisms of integration and segregation within societies.

Indeed, Mkandawire (2005) highlights the paradox that, historically, poverty alleviation was most successful when it was not necessarily the primary focus of social policies, as opposed to other priorities such as late industrialisation, state consolidation, demand stabilisation, political cohesion or else sheer survival. The key to this paradox is found within the choice of provisioning modalities, broadly characterised as universalism versus targeting.

Trials of targeting

In terms of institutional modalities, the formative debates in the field of social policy have been between targeting and universalism.

While targeting often plays a role within universalistic systems,[10] targeting as an institutional modality refers more generally to the abandonment of the guiding principles of universalism and towards more selectivity in publicly funded provisioning and benefits (e.g., means-tested welfare). It is characteristic of the main approach to social policy under the dominant neoliberal economic policy paradigm from the 1980s onwards, in response to the void created by welfare state retrenchment in the North and fiscal crises in the South, and as epitomised by the targeted social safety net approach of the World Bank. According to this approach, publicly funded and/ or provided services or benefits are to be targeted selectively to the (identified) needy, such as means-tested welfare or means-tested free education and health care. In practice, selectivity is usually implemented through differentiated provisioning systems, based on segmentation and even segregation between different social groups (typically, between the poor and the middle classes), such that state-subsidised services or assistance are provided separately from privately or publicly funded systems servicing middle and upper social strata. Indeed, segregation often constitutes much of the political appeal of targeting for middle- and upper-class people, who seek to obtain their own privileged access without needing to rub shoulders with lower classes (and often ethnicised classes – increasingly so in Europe and the US).

Conversely, a universalistic modality essentially (or ideally) implies that all are serviced through the same or similar provisioning systems (usually publicly funded). Martinez and Sanchez-Ancochea (2016, ch. 1), for instance, elaborate what they call a maximalist vision of universalism, as opposed to the minimalist visions described in the introduction of this chapter. These include three dimensions: coverage, generosity and equity. Coverage refers to 'massive coverage', meaning that most people in a given category are covered or have access (depending, of course, on how citizenship rights define who has the right to be covered or have access – Martinez and Sanchez-Ancochea suggest that non-national residents should be included even if this is difficult to sustain politically). Generosity refers to the level and quality of benefits, with universality being associated with more comprehensive and better-quality benefits. By equity, they refer to the distribution of coverage and generosity across beneficiaries (although perhaps this would be better termed as equality, especially since the 2006 WDR framed 'equity' in terms of equality of opportunity, whereas the implication here is more than that). Hence, countries could secure massive access with uneven generosity, as is typical in minimalist versions of universalism, whereas more universalistic systems would have more evenly distributed benefits.

The contention in the seminal work by Mkandawire (2004, 2005) on synthesising debates in social policy with parallel debates in the field of development studies is that universalistic approaches have been much more successful at poverty reduction (and inequality reduction) than targeted approaches. Targeting, he explains, has been variously advocated since the 1970s on grounds of efficiency, expediency and even equity. The equity argument is based on the logic that if the expenditure used to provide universal benefits is focused on the poor instead, the poor will receive more and the non-poor less, hence producing a more redistributive and equalising outcome than if all receive the same, regardless of need.[11]

Drawing from work by Korpi and Palme (1998) and Rothstein (2001), Mkandawire (2005, p. 6) points out that many of these arguments on the greater potential for inequality reduction in targeted versus universalistic policies are partial and misconceived. They tend to focus only on the partial transfer effect of social spending (holding all else constant) rather than also considering the inequality impact of how such spending is funded, and the dynamic political economy interactions between these two as shifts are made towards more targeted approaches. Hence, the fact that universalistic systems are generally funded by progressive taxation makes them particularly effective at reducing inequality, given that even perfect equity in transfers (i.e., when all people are provided with the same benefit) is more than compensated by redistribution in taxation. Indeed, as demonstrated by Rothstein (2001), even a flat-rate tax funding an equal transfer payment to all results in a substantial reduction in income inequality. The inequality reduction effect would be even greater with progressive taxation.

A poignant example of similar misconceptions can be demonstrated, for instance, in an article by Appleton, Song and Xia (2010) with respect to China. The authors inadvertently make a critique of targeted welfare, albeit only after their argument is correctly reinterpreted. They argue that government anti-poverty programmes in China had little impact on urban poverty between 1988 and 2002.

Instead, through an econometric analysis of urban household survey data, they contend that urban poverty had fallen almost entirely due to overall economic growth rather than 'redistribution.' The misconstrued element in their argument is that they refer not so much to redistribution but, more specifically, to targeting, given that China's urban anti-poverty programmes were heavily oriented towards means-tested targeting within an overall retreat from more universalistic principles over the 1980s and 1990s, including the rapid erosion of most pre-existing redistributive and/or social security systems, and a notably regressive shift in the burden of taxation (e.g., see Khan and Riskin 2001). In this context, it can hardly be said that targeted poverty-reduction programmes constituted a strong case for redistribution. Rather, targeted social assistance probably represented one of the few marginal factors compensating an overall regressive shift in the social policy regime of China, as well as rising inequality. Hence, it comes as no surprise that most poverty reduction could be shown through econometrics to have come from growth, although this can hardly be used as a case against redistributive polices. With this corrective in mind, the argument of these authors otherwise corroborates well with the insights from the social policy literature discussed here.

Obviously, according to this logic, the redistributive potential for targeting could be strong if integrated within a broadly universalistic social policy regime, including progressive taxation. Indeed, this is the logic behind the idea of 'targeting within universalism' (Skocpol 1991), both in terms of its redistributive potential as well as its ability to address diversity, disadvantage and special needs without eroding broader universalistic principles. However, as Mkandawire (2005, p. 7) points out, targeting and selectivity without this universalistic basis usually undermines political support for both progressivity in taxation and for maintaining the size of transfers directed towards the poor. Hence, according to the 'paradox of redistribution' (Korpi and Palme 1998, p. 681), the more benefits are targeted to the poor rather than being equally distributed to all, the less likely poverty and inequality will be reduced.

Mkandawire (2005) also synthesises how targeting can lead to a variety of perverse outcomes. The errors of under-coverage (missing the legitimate poor, also referred to as 'exclusion errors') and leakage (including the non-poor, or 'inclusion errors') are the most commonly discussed in the literature. Indeed, precision in poverty measurement becomes ever more crucial precisely when social policy regimes shift towards greater selectivity, such as under the social safety net approach promoted by the World Bank in the 1980s and 1990s. Such shifts usually involve the erosion of more generalised social security provisions that could cover people in the event that they are not effectively identified by a means-testing approach (i.e., in the event that targeting fails). For instance, some estimates of exclusion rates in the *Bolsa Familia*, the flagship cash transfer programme in Brazil, a country with relatively strong administrative state capacity, were as high as 46 per cent in the 2006 data and 59 per cent in earlier data (Kerstenetzky 2011). Exclusion errors were apparently even higher in the *Oportunidades* programme in Mexico, another flagship cash transfer programme that arguably originated the fad (ibid.).

These problems of accuracy become all the more acute in contexts of rapid socio-economic change, such as urbanisation, whereby many of the more traditional rural-based social security systems – which are often taken for granted by urban policy-makers and economists – become ineffective or break down, and where states might not even have accurate or complete civil registers of the population. As Mkandawire notes, poor countries also have among the least administrative capacity to be able to target precisely, especially when shifts to targeting occur in parallel with economic crises and severe fiscal retrenchment, as has been the case in many poor countries since the successive debt crises and structural adjustment programmes of the early 1980s onwards.

Other perversities of targeting reside in its political and social implications. Because targeting usually entrenches segmentation and segregation in provisioning systems, this tends to reinforce social and economic stratification by separating the middle classes from the services accessed by the poor. As a result, the political voice of the middle classes is also removed from these services as well, as was seminally laid out with respect to public policy more generally by Hirschman (1970) in his classic *Exit, Voice and Loyalty*.[12] In the best of pro-poor times this can lead to short-term bouts of poverty reduction and even inequality reduction, as occurred in Brazil under the various targeted poverty-alleviation programmes of the Lula and Dilma Administrations. However, sustaining these gains requires strong political commitment and leadership in order to maintain funding, supply and quality within these provisioning systems servicing the poor. Yet, this condition for sustainability is undermined precisely by the institutionalised segregation of provisioning systems encouraged by these targeting approaches. Sustainability under such settings is particularly fragile once politics turn less pro-poor, as has happened in most of the erstwhile New Left governments in Latin America that have been replaced by the Right in recent years, or else where the shift to the right has taken place within the New Left government itself, as in Ecuador, for instance. The recent exception of Mexico will be very interesting to observe in this respect. The resulting political economy paradox was best expressed by Richard Titmuss (1968) – although often attributed to Amartya Sen – that the targeting of services to the poor usually results in poor services.

Cash through segregation

The danger of reinforcing stratifying and subordinating tendencies can be illustrated by the current agenda of social protection, in particular conditional cash transfers (CCTs), which are now strongly promoted by the World Bank and constitute a major component of the World Bank response to inequality and social inclusion. Besides the problematic moral issues related to the use of conditionalities to manage the behavioural dispositions of 'the poor' (e.g., see Rodger 2012), which are usually directed towards women and children and often imply considerable degrees of unpaid time commitments, CCTs are usually targeted through segmented systems of social provisioning. Evaluations of such programmes usually show a poverty reducing impact via increased consumption at the very least (which is a fairly obvious result to all but the staunchest opponents of welfare), as well as some increase in health care and schooling (although this is also often related to simultaneous improvements in the provisioning of these services). There is also some evidence that the expansion of CCTs can bring about quick reductions in inequality largely through their transfer effect on the bottom end of the income distribution. However, evaluations of the longer-term employment or development impacts are less clear, which is arguably due in part to the fact that such programmes are mostly implemented through often poor-quality and poorly funded systems of segregated social provisioning, aimed at servicing the poor. As a result, they tend to have little transformative power on broader social relations or social mobility, although they do reinforce institutional segregation and policy practices of targeting, in lieu of other potentially more transformative strategies of social policy.

This has precisely been the dilemma of the much-lauded Progresa/Oportunidades conditional cash transfer programme in Mexico. The programme has shown some degree of success in raising consumption levels, certain health outcomes and school attendance and enrolment rates (e.g., see earlier studies in Skoufias 2005). These results were obtained with relatively low operational expenses, in large part because the programme was implemented through an already well-established network of clinics and schools servicing the targeted rural populations (as distinct from the subsidised network servicing the urban middle classes). However, even its proponents such as Levy (2006) admit that increased coverage was achieved at the cost of lower quality within this overstretched and segregated network. At that time the programme had no impact on the academic performance of students or on their later employment prospects. Thus, while it had a positive impact on absolute human development indicators, it did so at the cost of entrenching the segmentation of provisioning systems and probably reinforced social stratification as a result. Similar outcomes have been noted with the Bolsa Familia in Brazil (e.g., see Kerstenetzky 2011). Several more recent literature surveys of cash transfers have also consistently noted the problem of a lack of improving school performance or employment prospects with cash transfers (e.g., see DFID 2011).

The potential for targeting to bring about marginal improvements in poverty, education and/or health is not necessarily in question (if, that is, targeting actually results in an increase in resources transferred to the poor, which sometimes it does not). If a poor person is given ten dollars, it should be no surprise that his or her income would be ten dollars higher by the end of the year than it otherwise would have been without such a transfer. The hope or assumption underlying many cash transfer schemes is that the person's income would increase by more than ten dollars due to some sort of micro-multiplier effect unleashed by the transfer, such as when the extra cash allows the person to overcome other obstacles to increasing their productivity or returns to labour (aka the poverty trap, as in Banerjee and Duflo 2011). The fear of those warning of the perverse incentives induced by welfare is that the income of the person receiving the transfer is less than ten dollars at the end of the year, due to the substitution of some work for the welfare received, to the extreme that the income would not have changed at all due to a perverse threshold effect. This means that the beneficiary would be just below the targeting line and would therefore avoid working so as not to pass above the line. (Of course, as noted in Chapters 3 and 4, it is unlikely that poor people would have any comprehension of such poverty line measures in any case, especially with proxy means testing, which has become the dominant policy tool for targeting in such programmes; e.g., see Brown et al. 2016.) With respect to informality, the fear is also that welfare will create incentives to remain informal, as a means of hiding income in order to continue qualifying for the transfer (aka welfare cheats or queens).[13]

These narrow questions and debates underlie the obsessive attempts to measure the impacts of cash transfer schemes on the overall income of beneficiaries, which have dominated impact evaluations of these programmes.[14] However, that the increment in income might bring the person above a poverty line – say, if their income was previously five dollars below this poverty line and their income increases by ten dollars as a result of the transfer – is so obvious that it is not even interesting. Unless, of course, one is obsessed with the perverse incentives contention, which unfortunately is the case forced upon many policy-makers given the demands to address such concerns among increasingly right-wing electorates and governments.

Rather, the broader concern needs to be the stratifying, segregating and subordinating trajectories brought into play by the institutional modalities used to enact such marginal improvements. These are potentially very counterproductive for any long-term strategy of poverty reduction, particularly if and when resource transfers to the poor decrease rather than increase as a longer-term consequence of targeting, as has often been the case.[15]

The much-noted case of Brazil is also worth highlighting in this respect. There are debates in Brazil concerning the extent to which the *Bolsa Família* – a targeted conditional cash transfer programme – has been the main cause of inequality reduction in recent years, versus other policies such as minimum wage legislation, which might have contributed significantly more.[16] Soares et al. (2010, p. 41) calculate that between 1999 and 2009 – during which the Gini coefficient in Brazil fell from 0.591 to 0.538 – reduction in labour income inequality accounted for 59 per cent of the Gini reduction, whereas the Bolsa accounted for only 16 per cent and the non-contributory indexed (targeted) pension system for 15 per cent. In personal communications with Fabio Veras from the International Poverty Centre in Brazil, where many of these studies have been piloted, he commented that this is no surprise given that labour income accounts for around 70 per cent of total income. Moreover, it remains an open question whether the labour income effect was due to increases in minimum wage, reductions in returns to education (with respect to top incomes), a tighter labour market (the unemployment rate had never been so low), or to the increased formalisation of employment (email communication, 5 July 2011). However, the fact that so much inequality reduction occurred within labour income is, in itself, a notable achievement, given that this source has more usually been dis-equalising rather than equalising in the past.

Hence, this particular pattern of inequality reduction would appear to validate the labourist and developmentalist agenda of the Lula administration, in combination with a favourable climate for primary commodity exports and the impact of Chinese investment and demand over these years (and despite tight monetary policies of high interest rates), much more so than the targeted social protection programmes. The contribution of the latter has nonetheless been significant, even if minor, especially if one would make the argument that cash transfers – conditional or otherwise – raise the reservation wage rates of the recipients and reduce labour supply, thereby tightening the labour market and putting upward pressure on wages for low-skilled labour. (However, care must be taken with the logic of such arguments because they easily slip into a discourse of perverse incentives.)

Commenting on earlier inequality decomposition analyses by Soares et al., Kerstenetzky (2011, p. 5) also notes that the inequality-reduction impact of the Bolsa Familia in those years is considerable given that it accounts for a much smaller share of (average) household incomes than its share in inequality reduction. This is explained by the fact that the transfers of the Bolsa are targeted to the poorest households; their appearance in average household incomes would be small even though their weight in the incomes of the poorest households would be large. The immediate impact on inequality is therefore brought about through raising this lower tail-end of the income distribution through the cash transfers (this would be the case even if these poorest households would not necessarily be lifted above the poverty line as a result, which Kerstenetsky notes is often the case). In contrast, the other factors effecting inequality (such as those occurring in the labour market) would be felt much more broadly throughout the income distribution.

From this perspective, the relatively minor contribution of these targeted cash transfers must then be balanced with their potential perverse impacts on social integration. For instance, Lavinas (2006, p. 103) has argued that, despite a law approving the right of a basic income, 'Brazilian social policies are increasingly focused on increasing the number of means-tested income programmes while making them conditional on a proven lack of resources and targeting only the very poorest segments of society for a limited period.' In order to counteract this tendency, she proposed that the government should move from means-tested programmes such as the Bolsa to basic income programmes such as the adoption of a universal child benefit scheme. Lavinas (2013, 2017) subsequently has made much more incisive and critical evaluations of what actually happened under the PT government, more or less confirming her initial fears, compounded by alarm at the degree to which the Bolsa had been coopted by a neoliberal financialisation agenda.

Similarly, Kerstenetzky (2009) presciently argued that less selectivity in the scheme, and hence less separation between those who pay for the scheme and the beneficiaries, as well as paradoxically higher expenditures, would ensure wider adoption and political support for the scheme, whereas the-then current emphasis on selectivity in the scheme would result in financial and political constraints to its expansion. In Kerstenetzky (2011, pp. 9–11), she noted that, to a certain respect, political processes undermining the Bolsa had already come into play as early as 2007 when the Brazilian Senate rejected a government proposal for maintaining one of the main sources of funding for social programmes such as the Bolsa, which was supported by a concerted attack on the Bolsa in the media. The rejection 'represented a concrete threat of stagnation for existing social programs, for it impaired the planned and announced expansions, leaving to the executive the conception of alternatives.' She thus suggests that 'we must inevitably ask if the conflict over the [proposal] would in some way anticipate a reversion or saturation of the solidarity indirectly revealed by opinion polls and would constitute a permanent challenge for social programs (especially Bolsa Família), their continuity and necessary expansion.'

Notably, in contexts where the political conditions for maintaining support for redistribution are not as optimal as in Brazil under Lulu and Dilma, such erosions can even be built into cash transfer schemes. For instance, in some cases funding is only mandated for a temporary duration (say, five years). In many others, transfers are not indexed to inflation (this is the case of most cash transfer programmes that I have researched in the course of my recent fieldwork). Or else, a strong emphasis might be put on the 'graduation' of recipients from the schemes, as occurred, for instance, in the case of Ecuador from 2013 onwards (see Palacio 2017).

Depoliticisation redux

Viewed in this way, it is clear how the de-politicising allure promised by various global development goals can obfuscate these very political (and politicised) choices about the ways that societies provide public goods and social security to their citizens. The seductively technocratic appeal of the MDGs and SDGs, for instance, with clear goals and indicators grounded in an authoritative and scientifically informed battery of poverty measures, potentially serves to depoliticise these choices among the general lay public, if only through the force of incomprehension and resulting deference to presumably better-informed experts (who are often poorly informed in these wider social policy debates). De-politicisation serves to veil underlying agendas, particularly with respect to the normalisation of targeting and segmentation within social provisioning systems.

Moreover, these agendas cannot be said to be unbiased towards these choices. They are well-served by targeting given their focus on absolute indicators (whether in income, health or education) rather than relative (i.e., inequality) indicators, as well as by the immediacy they compel. For instance, it is relatively easy to raise school enrolments, but much more difficult to raise the quality of schooling, particularly in ways that would significantly alter the employment trajectories of students. This is especially the case when increased enrolments are achieved in stigmatised and lower-quality underfunded schools designated for poor people within a segmented education system.

Indeed, if the quantity and quality of employment and the level of wages faced by the poor are not addressed by poverty reduction strategies, the expectations raised by educational improvements might lead to frustration and alienation in the medium term.[17] This has precisely been the dilemma of the much-lauded Progresa/Oportunidades conditional cash transfer programme in Mexico, which, as noted above, has had little impact on the academic performance of students or on their later employment prospects. Thus, while it had a positive impact on absolute human development indicators, it did so at the cost of entrenching the segmentation of provisioning systems and probably accentuated social stratification as a result.

While human rights-based approaches are less obviously associated to this tendency of depoliticisation to veer towards orthodoxy, it is important to caution that they can also carry a similar propensity to be coopted due to their ambiguity on a variety of policy fronts, as already discussed in Chapter 2. Human rights-based approaches are arguably founded on a universalistic agenda of social provisioning and social security, as pointed out by Langford (2009). However, in the quest to operationalise these approaches, a degree of ambiguity enters into the translation from ethics to practice. For instance, does the principle of non-discrimination imply universalism (i.e., the same treatment for all) or targeting? Universalism has been criticised, in that purportedly universalistic policies have often reflected fundamental underlying societal biases, such as racial or gender biases. In turn, this implies that a degree of selectivity is required in order to allow for the practice of affirmative/positive action and other forms of preferentiality for disadvantaged or discriminated groups.

Similarly, in the good programming practices specified in the UN Common Understanding (see UNDG 2003), the principle that programmes should focus on marginalised, disadvantaged and excluded groups can be easily construed as a rationale for targeting, particularly when asserted in absence of any substantive discussion of policy. The emphasis on reducing disparity does not, in itself, resolve debates between targeting and universalism given that targeting has been posed by its proponents as more equalising than universalism, as noted above. The principle that people should be recognised as key actors in their own development, rather than passive recipients of commodities and services, can also be attributed as a rationale for using conditionalities in cash transfers, for labour market activation policies or for other means of restricting welfare more generally. This logic – that welfare renders people as 'passive recipients' – has been typical in right-wing political attacks against universalism over the past decades. The point is that all of these policy options are fundamentally political in the choices that they elicit; the ethical principles offered by human rights-based approaches do not necessarily resolve these politicised choices along any predictable path.

Indeed, many advocates of human rights-based approaches appear to acquiesce to targeting as the de facto status quo.[18] Although the potential fragmentation of citizenship rights that targeting can entail should be a major bone of contention for human rights advocates, this specific but powerful dimension rarely figures in many of their analyses, albeit with some exceptions.[19] While such avoidance – perhaps by oversight – provides the appearance of politically neutral moral authority, it also misses a valuable opportunity to explicitly re-embed human rights-based approaches into their earlier postwar association with welfare states and Keynesian commitments to full employment. Instead, human rights approaches risk being subverted as monitoring and disciplinary devices for policy agendas that are otherwise quite antithetical to the spirit of universal rights.[20]

Universalising universalism

In light of this confusion, in which the potentials for cooptation under the guise of depoliticisation are great, it is important to elaborate on the meaning of universalism in social policy and how it might apply to the context of most developing countries. As noted previously, universalism has been at the core of modern social policy since it emerged in the nineteenth century alongside modern nation-states and modern notions of rights.[21] Universalism has also been central to development studies given that the first countries to move towards more universalistic principles in social policy were not industrial leaders such as the UK but industrial latecomers such as Germany, Japan and Sweden, and universalistic social policy played a key role in their strategies of late industrialisation, as classically discussed by Gerschenkron (1962). Universalistic principles in health and education were also central to the development strategies of South Korea and Taiwan from the outset of their industrialisation efforts in the 1950s, even whilst their social protection systems remained very familial-based up until recently.[22] Indeed, it is misguided – at least from historical experience – to state that poor countries cannot afford universal social policy given that successful industrialisers have relied on it in various ways from very poor starting points. Instead, there is arguably an historical precedent that the later an industrialiser, the greater the imperative to innovate shifts towards more universalistic forms of social provisioning earlier than would be predicted by the past experiences of more industrialised countries.[23]

However, the basic principle of universalism – that all are treated the same – quickly becomes complicated in practice, especially in polarised societies, as noted in the previous section. Indeed, the classical dichotomy between targeting and universalism has led to a certain degree of confusion in the recent policy literature, in particular the recent social protection literature. For instance, targeting often plays a role within universalistic systems, as classically articulated by Skocpol (1991) with reference to the targeting of special needs or disadvantages, or else to allow for diversity within integrated universalistic systems of provisioning, or what she calls targeting within universalism. Moreover, some degree of targeting is almost always required for certain aspects of social protection, such as food relief, and even some of the most universalistic systems include important elements of means-tested targeting, such as welfare in Canada or Sweden. However, this understanding of targeting as a specific policy instrument is different from the broader understanding of targeting as an institutional modality, whereby an entire system of publicly funded provisioning is organised along the lines of selectivity, as discussed in the previous section. It is this latter meaning that has been the focus of criticism by authors such as Mkandawire (2005).

Similarly, the terminology of universalism is often used to refer to an ideal type located in one world region at one point in time (e.g., the UK circa 1970 or Sweden circa 1980) and hence it is argued that it is not applicable to poor countries today. Alternatively, it has come to be used in certain contexts in such a generic way that its meaning has been rendered nebulous. For instance, as noted in the introduction and first section of this chapter, there has been a subtle shift in the implied meaning of universalism towards a narrower connotation of universal coverage or access, such as all children attending school, regardless of how such schooling is provided or financed, or all people accessing health insurance, regardless of whether this insurance covers the totality of health care expenditure needs.

In this regard, debates about universalism and targeting in social policy have exhausted themselves, at least in the realm of social protection, despite efforts to revive criticisms of targeting in the 2000s. The impasse in scholarship has been reached despite the fact that targeting is still very much *en rigeur* in actual social protection practice. If anything, despite these debates and the ample evidence of the perverse consequences of targeting, the emphasis in current policy agendas is on sharpening and refining targeting as the accepted best or second-best way forward in achieving so-called 'universal' social protection, as well as health or education. Indeed, part of the problem emerges from confusions about what, exactly, universalism entails. As noted previously, the World Bank, for instance, has coopted the term by including just about any sort of access to any sort of provisioning as falling under the umbrella of universal coverage, even if large parts of such access occur through segregated and privatised forms of provisioning. Even the agenda of universalism in various UN agencies has been whittled down to a minimalist understanding of universal coverage. However, these confusions have also been facilitated by the difficulties of establishing what would be the realistic and practical alternatives to targeting, especially in the field in social protection. There is more clarity about universalism in the policy sectors of education and health given that these are the policy sectors in which universalistic principles have been practised most comprehensively in strong cases of universalism, even though there are few prospects to achieve the same in most countries. This is in contrast to other areas such as public housing or various aspects of social security, where less achievement has been made towards universalistic principles even in 'advanced' countries.[24]

Indeed, there has been much recent confusion with regard to whether the Mahatma Gandhi National Rural Employment Guarantee Scheme in India should be considered a universal programme given that it does not impose means-testing on those who claim their right to receive employment. Many claim that it is universalistic for this reason, although in effect it represents a form of self-targeting – one of the classic forms of targeting. The degree to which universalism should be applied in the direct provisioning of employment is of course debatable – short of the state assuming a collectivist role in the labour market. This is the position of some, such as with the idea of a universal job guarantee programme, with the government acting as employer of last resort, as advocated by scholars at the Levy Institute in the US.[25] Such contention is much less pronounced with respect to health and education, particularly if there is a strong political consensus that public provisioning in these sectors should not be commoditised (which is not the case in the US and in much of the Global South).

Similarly, it is not clear if or how the idea of universalism should be applied in the area of social assistance, which by definition is directed to those in need, not the general population. The position of Barrientos (2013) and Devereux (2016), both leading scholars on the subject of social protection, is that universalism does not apply in this policy sector. But if it would, what would it look like? Devereux (2016) claims that universalism in social protection is sometimes conflated with categorically targeted programmes, such as social pensions for all older persons, although a similar argument could be made with respect to education – the fact that it is categorically targeted towards children does not make the principles of universalism less relevant. But what would universalism be in the area of social protection? Universal basic income is one proposal, but as of yet there are no examples of its implementation beyond a few pilot programmes and there is still much to be answered in the modalities of its implementation – the devil remains in the details still to be revealed. More generally, that elements of targeting are also required even within universalistic systems of provisioning leads some to query what, in the end, is at issue. This leads to the position, in response to the critiques of targeting in otherwise-cherished social protection programmes, that targeting for the time being remains the only available and realistic contingency measure for addressing poverty in contexts of resource scarcity, high levels of informality, political obstacles to more ambitious redistributive agendas, and other constraints.

Some clarification is therefore in order. While universal coverage is obviously a necessary condition of universalism, it is not a sufficient condition. Rather, universalism is best understood as an umbrella term to reflect a set of guiding institutional principles. In an attempt to clarify and systematise these guiding principles in a manner that is attuned to policy-making across the globe, and building on the work by Mkandawire (2004, 2005), I have come to categorise these guiding principles along three dimensions: provisioning modalities, including access/coverage; costing/pricing; and financing. Within each dimension, we can think in terms of a spectrum from strong to weak (or absent) universalistic principles underpinning an institutional system of social provisioning. This approach is useful because it takes us away from the dichotomy of targeting versus universalism and towards a method of identifying shifts towards stronger or weaker universalistic principles, along with their equalising or disequalising potentials, as well as the institutional obstacles potentially blocking such shifts.

Martinez and Sanchez-Ancochea (2014, p. 6) argue that their approach of focusing on coverage, generosity and equity is better than the one I propose here (which draws from Fischer 2012) because mine conflates policy principles with the instruments to achieve these principles, whereas various instruments could be used to achieve these principles. While their point is a valid one and has caused me to reflect, at the same time, the argument tends to come down to splitting hairs about what is a principle and what is an instrument. Their own approach also runs the risk of tautology, that is, bringing results into the definition of causes. Analytically, we should not assume that various instruments associated with universalism would necessarily produce, for instance, greater coverage, generosity and equity/equality. Rather, this should be subjected to empirical inquiry, particularly given that these attributions of universalistic policies are contested by both the Left and Right (especially the Right). Hence, it is important to keep these causal empirical considerations of universalism open to such questions, rather than labelling outcomes as universalistic regardless of the means to achieve them. That being said, as they themselves note, our goals are similar: 'to separate the definition of universalism from a specific historical experience, to establish the possibility of promoting universalism through different channels, and to consider different degrees of universalism' (p. 6). It is for this reason that I have decided to maintain my own approach, in the interests of intellectual diversity and as a complement to their own approach.

Provisioning modalities

As stated above, the universalistic principle is not simply that all people access a social good or service (e.g., education or health care), but that this access is provided through integrated systems. In this manner, all people access the service through the same organisational channels or else different means of access are governed by a unified entity, through which needs and standards can be assessed and managed collectively within the system along principles of equity. Hence, a universalistic health system implies that everyone accesses the same or similar hospitals and clinics, wherein the same quality of service is provided to all without discrimination, and triage is organised according to needs rather than means (meaning the ability to pay or other financial considerations). This is not necessarily a public-versus-private-sector issue given that private-sector provisioning can (and often does) occur within such integrated systems (such as private schools or private clinics). Universalism within such systems is determined by the degree to which private providers are regulated and/or managed as an integrated part of the system and are accessible on the same terms regardless of their ownership status.

For instance, an example of strong universalism within an education system would imply that schools are organised under an integrated and unified organisational structure (such as a ministry of education or school board), which regulates quantity and quality within whole system according to universal criteria applied as equally as possible to all. This does not imply that no streaming or targeting takes place within the system given that all school systems implicitly or explicitly stream students from fairly early ages (e.g., towards academic versus technical education), or they target learning disabilities, etc. The question is whether streaming or targeting is organised in an integrated manner within a unified institutional structure accessed by all students, wherein all students are evaluated according to the same standards and treated according to ability or need rather than status or monetary means.

Conversely, weaker universalism within an education system would imply that the school system is stratified or segmented, such that different school systems serve different categories of people according to different standards and that these parallel systems do not necessarily feed into each other, whether in principle or in practice. Hence, certain students (e.g., poor rural students) are streamed into a school system by virtue of their status (poor and rural), which, by consequence of the type and quality of schooling, locks these students into a segregated and subordinated stream that prevents most of them from entering other streams of education at a later stage (such as more academic streams), regardless of their ability. A strong universalistic principle would seek to correct this by providing mechanisms to correct for the disadvantages faced by schools in poorer localities (through funding and also human resources) and assuring that these schools remain integrated with the more advantaged parts of the system.

Targeting in this sense is not necessarily a useful concept when applied to a system of education provisioning (versus, say, social assistance to help poor people pay for tuition fees or to 'condition' them to send their children to school). Pure targeting as an exclusive institutional modality applied to education provisioning would imply that publicly funded schooling is only provided to certain means-tested categories of people (e.g., the poor) and all others would access schooling through private means, either in separate schools or else in the same schools. In this sense, pure targeting probably rarely exists within the organisation of education systems given that publicly funded schooling usually occurs at all social levels even if segregated. From an inequality perspective, it is more revealing to analyse how and at what levels public funding and/or provisioning occur.[26] The more important principle within sectors such as education or health care is whether the system as a whole is integrated or stratified/segregated, not necessarily whether parts of the service are targeted towards specific groups of people.

This understanding also helps to clarify much of the confusion regarding targeting within universalism, as per Skocpol (1991). There is a world of difference between targeting special needs or disadvantages, such as maternal health needs or learning disabilities, within an integrated system where needs assessments of the population can be managed in a comprehensive and consistent manner, rather than in a fragmented system where different standards are already in force in different parts of the system. High degrees of relatively unregulated private provisioning, such as in the health and education systems of many developing countries and also the US, render such targeting especially problematic.

Moreover, targeting need not imply weak universalism, although in effect, selectivity is usually implemented through segmentation and even segregation of social provisioning systems between different social groups (typically, between poor and middle social strata, or also between different ethnic groups, such as the minority education system in China). Indeed, as noted above, segregation often constitutes much of the political appeal of targeting for middle and upper classes. Esping-Anderson (1990, p. 25) makes a similar point regarding what he calls flat-rate universalism and how this inadvertently promotes dualism within a context of growing working-class prosperity and rising new middle classes because better-off people start to turn to private insurance and to fringe-benefit bargaining to supplement the modest equality promoted in public systems.

Modes of regulation within social provisioning systems also help to distinguish stronger from weaker universalistic principles. Stronger forms of universalism tend to regulate of the quality of service provisioning as a regular part of managing the process of service provisioning (this is also made possible by integrated provisioning), whereas weaker forms of universalism tend to rely more on the measurement of outcomes whilst people exit the system, in part because of an inability to regulate quality within the provisioning. For instance, a high degree of fragmentation in an education system can prevent the ability to regulate and manage quality through the course of education provisioning, and hence such systems usually rely heavily or exclusively on standardised testing as a means to evaluate the quality of learning outcomes in the passage of students to higher levels of schooling.

With regard to social protection, universalism in this dimension mostly applies in the area of social insurance (such as with universal pension schemes or universal health insurance), but much less so with respect to social assistance, as noted above (although there are initiatives in this direction, such as the social protection floor recently mandated by the International Labour Organisation).[27] Certain categories of social assistance are by their nature – often by definition – only destined for certain categories of people deemed to be in need and/or worthy of assistance. Hence, pure targeting is much more common as an exclusive institutional modality in social assistance, which is why it becomes an important issue in poverty-reduction policies. The differentiation between strong and weak universalistic principles within social assistance is more along the lines of whether the provisioning of assistance is based on rights-based criteria or means-tested criteria, with the recent trend of micro-conditionalities (as in conditional cash transfers) constituting a compounded form of means-testing.

Costing/pricing

The second dimension that can help to identify a spectrum from strong to weak universalistic principles in social policy is related to how the costs and prices of provisioning are determined within a system. A strong universalistic principle would imply that costing and pricing are decommodified, meaning that the prices of the provisioning are not determined by market intermediation as if the provisioning is a commodity (i.e., through an auctioning process between supply and demand, or by driving up prices as far as demand continues to allow). Instead, prices are managed through administrative means, and costs are thereby internalised and socialised within the system. As a corollary, users of a universalistic service are not usually faced with the effective price of the service at the time of use, which is discussed in the third dimension below.

Again, the education and health care sectors are the most relevant here, and to a lesser degree social insurance, whereas this dimension is less relevant for social assistance, which by definition is non-contributory and does not impose a monetary price on the recipient. With regard to health care and education, this dimension goes to the heart of the perversities of what Karl Polanyi called 'fictitious' commodification, in this case treating health or education as commodities even though they are not 'produced' for buying and selling on the market (unlike real commodities).[28] Applying market intermediation to the pricing of health services, health insurance or education is problematic not only because markets in these services tend to be highly imperfect given the monopolistic practices that often occur within the provisioning of these goods (such as a locality being serviced by only one hospital, insurance provider or school). It is also problematic because health and education are not alienable or negotiable like commodities (hence the intellectual perversion of the now-dominant 'human capital' discourses). This is particularly the case with health, given that the inevitable human condition of ill health debilitates bargaining power precisely at a time of greatest need, leading to a stark asymmetry in bargaining between user and service provider. This asymmetry can become particularly perverse when applied to a market setting. Similar principles apply in education, particularly given the degree to which schooling can be crucial for reproducing class and privilege (or 'social capital' in the Bourdieusian sense). Hence, in the absence of quality alternatives due to an underfunded and undermined public education system (such as in many parts of the US), the price of private schooling can be well beyond reasonable levels for the norms of a particular community, thereby powerfully reinforcing social inequalities according to means rather than need or merit. To use economics terminology, because health care and quality schooling are to a large degree demand-inelastic, they carry a huge potential for rent-seeking from the cartel-like activities of private profit-seeking actors.

Conversely, a financially sustainable and affordable operation of a health insurance system, for instance, is predicated on a comple-mentary control of costs within the associated health system. This point was noted, for instance, by President Obama himself during the debates over health care reform in the US during his first term, despite his subsequent inability to enforce such control on the US health care system. Similarly, health insurance programmes in India (such as micro-insurance programmes) or in China (such as the rural health insurance system) are only able to make minor dents on large catastrophic health expenditures by households, partly because of the inability to control costs within the effectively privatised health care sys-tems of both countries – a problem that often faces huge institutional barriers to overcome given that it is usually entrenched in a variety of vested interests extending across providers and vying ministries.[29]

Financing

The third dimension of universalism relates to the modality of financing. This is closely related to the second issue of cost and price, although it is distinct because it addresses how users pay for the sys-tem, whether indirectly or directly. In strong forms of universalism, financing generally takes place indirectly (i.e., not at the time of need) through progressive forms of taxation (i.e., progressive income tax, corporate tax or capital gains tax). In weak forms of universal-ism, financing takes place directly (i.e., at the time of need), through often regressive forms of payment (such as out-of-pocket payments for health care, school tuition fees or user fees).

Social insurance is most closely related to this dimension given that the principle operating behind insurance is about making the financing of a service more indirect (hence more universalistic), through socialising the costs of such financing for users. Indeed, pri-vate insurance is no different from public insurance in this respect, except that it operates according to a profit-motive, usually with less regulated prices and with a smaller pool in which to socialise costs, and for these reasons is often less efficient, more costly and more risk-prone than integrated public systems.

Financing is closely related to the cost/price dimension in that direct financing is usually predicated on commodified systems of costing/pricing, whereas decommodified systems mostly operate through indirect forms of financing as this is the most effective way to socialise costs in the widest possible manner. However, as research by van Doorslaer et al. (2005) has analysed with respect to health systems in Asia, the specific balance between these two extremes and along these two dimensions can have a huge bearing on the poverty and vulnerability impacts of out-of-pocket payments in various health systems. Generally, greater reliance on out-of-pocket payments combined with weaker control of costs and prices (or strong commodification) was strongly associated with a much greater poverty impact of catastrophic health expenditures in the cases they studied, circa the year 2000 (and controlling for level of GDP per capita).

Moreover, understanding the interplay of these two dimensions can also help to clarify much of the institutional tensions associated with reforming social policy systems, as mentioned above. Attempts to control costs within a health system that is largely financed directly usually leads to strong resistance to reform because it undermines the financing of provisioning units within the system. Or else shifts towards more progressive indirect forms of financing can be difficult to sustain in financial terms when prices are commoditised. The huge challenge in social policy reform towards more universalistic principles is found in this need for systemically coordinated changes, which at heart is a fundamentally political issue, not a technical one. For instance, while most people agree on the principle of sending all children to school or all people having access to health care, it is clear how the other dimensions of universalism are potentially rife with intense political dispute, as observed in the battles over health care reform in the US.

Additive versus substitutive changes within social provisioning systems

In addition to these three dimensions, for a full appraisal of universalism, it is also important to consider the more systemic interactions across different policies or sectors of provisioning because progressive expansions in some might be cancelled out by regressive retrenchment in others. I refer to this as a distinction between additive and substitutive dynamics within broader social policy systems. This runs against the general consensus in the welfare state and social policy scholarship that universalism should be judged in a sector- or even policy-specific manner, given that universalism might be identified in some policies or sectors but not in others. While this is true, a more systemic view is nonetheless important to assess the equalising or disequalising potentials of changes within a social policy system or regime and whether the overall tendency of change is towards or away from a more universalistic orientation.

The model reference for an additive approach is the case of the Bolsa Familia in Brazil, at least up until the end of the Dilma presidency. The programme was additive in the sense that the expansion of this programme in the formative years of the 2000s supplemented and reinforced other innovations in social, employment and wage policies and was part of a large increase in overall government spending in the social sector. As a result, it is difficult to distinguish the extent to which the positive outcomes associated with the programme were actually due to the programme itself or to other reinforcing and coordinated initiatives, in the absence of which the programme on its own might have had much less effect.

In contrast, the position of the IMF and the World Bank and many donors is explicitly or implicitly substitutive, in the sense that they advocate the expansion of cash transfers conjoined with retrenchment in other areas. Examples include reforming social security or other policies that have social protection functions, such as subsidies, on the basis that these are inefficient and that the money is better spent on transfers. For instance, this position was referred to earlier with respect to the recent IMF framework on social spending (IMF 2017) and was also common in World Bank and IMF positions on poverty reduction in the 2000s, which generally advocated that expansions in targeted transfers to the poor should be financed through fiscal savings in other areas. While it is possibly true that certain policies are inefficient, at least from a particular microeconomic perspective, the broader point is that such positions lead to no net redistributive gain, even though they might involve shifting groups of beneficiaries, given that spending increases in one programme are roughly cancelled out by spending reductions in others.

These questions are important from an evaluative perspective, especially with respect to more macro questions such as the demand effects of cash transfers on local economic activity. The broader question is not whether the income of the person receiving the transfer improved, but whether the net effect on the overall societal income improved as a result. Similarly, the educational or health effects of a cash transfer and its universalistic potential more generally are determined to a much greater extent by changes occurring in the education and health sectors than in the cash transfer *per se*.

Conclusion

Viewed from an institutionalist perspective of social policy, with particular emphasis on the principles of universalism and its dynamic interactions across policy sectors, it is clear how the de-politicising allure offered by various indicators of either poverty or inequality can obfuscate the very political (and politicised) choices about the ways that societies provide public goods and social security to themselves. The allure can also distract from the very political processes of social integration and stratification more generally, which go to the heart of distributive conflicts. The seductively technocratic appeal of the MDGs, for instance, with clear goals and indicators grounded in an authoritative and scientifically informed battery of poverty measures, arguably served to depoliticise these choices and processes among the general lay public, if only through the force of incomprehension and resulting deference to presumably better-informed experts. De-politicisation thus serves to veil underlying agendas, particularly with respect to the normalisation of targeting and segregation within social provisioning systems. This potential is equally present within a revised focus on inequality within the SDGs, if not more so than with poverty because inequality goes to the heart of power relations within and across societies, and yet measures of inequality are potentially less intuitive for general lay comprehension than poverty measures.

The challenge for contemporary development agendas lies in seriously re-engaging development debates with questions about how to create genuinely redistributive structures and institutions at national and global levels. These are political challenges given that they cannot be resolved through technocratic solutions, but require choices to be made about the types of societies we wish to inhabit and how we wish to treat each other within and across these societies.

In this respect, development agendas would carry more political and policy salience for poverty and inequality reduction if they were explicitly anchored within a wider social policy lens. This includes a more comprehensive consideration of the meaning of genuine universalism within social policy as a holistic institutional guiding principle, rather than simply as an indicator to be achieved (such as enrolling all children in schools regardless of the quality of the schools). Given the paramount importance of these social policy modalities in determining patterns of social integration as well as citizenship rights, they should be central concerns in any broader inclusive development agenda. Conversely, insofar as we recognise high levels of inequality as problematic, the censor of universalistic social policy from mainstream agendas implies abandoning at the outset some of our most powerful policy tools to date for dealing with inequality and poverty simultaneously, particularly when combined with developmentalist policy strategies.

If the goal is to return to these more progressive and transformative development agendas, then a holistic understanding of universalism needs to be rehabilitated from decades of neoliberal obfuscation and explicitly presented as a viable policy goal. For this purpose, it would be much more effective to refer explicitly to these politicised policy modalities rather than to rely on the apparently apolitical moral ground of indicators, as has been the case with the MDGs and SDGs. Such explicit anchoring is necessary in order to render more transparent the political choices and institutional trajectories that such development agendas are often used to legitimate. The risk of not explicitly anchoring future development agendas in politicised policy debates is that these agendas can be (and are often being) subverted towards policy agendas that possibly undermine inequality reduction and/or fragment citizenship rights in many contexts, primarily by way of reinforcing social polarisation through processes of stratification, segregation and subordination.

8 | CONCLUSION: POVERTY AS IDEOLOGY IN AN AGE OF NEOLIBERALISM

The first central argument of this book is that the very conception of poverty is inherently ideological. It involves normative judgements that pertain to an exercise of social identification within a vision of what should constitute a just social order. The fact that social identification is usually tied to actual policy and social provisioning means that it also falls into the moral realm of political economy and is conditioned by the power relations that permeate it. This point applies to all social statistics, to the extent that they are contingent on their social and institutional origins. However, poverty statistics are especially ideological given the central role that the idea of poverty has come to play within contemporary ideologies about capitalist development.

The depoliticization of poverty, both within the concepts and measures themselves, and in terms of how they are employed within various development agendas, serves to veil this inherent ideological nature. Moreover, attempts to move away from money-metric lines do not resolve depoliticisation but arguably compound it by adding additional layers of arbitrary complexity and obscurity. The performance of consensus in various global development agendas, in particular the MDGs and SDGs, has also stifled political debate and thereby lent the upper hand to the institutionally and politically more powerful voices within these narrative and policy struggles.

In particular, the project of generating global poverty statistics has been marshalled in various ways to legitimise the recent and especially virulent phase of capitalism variously referred to as 'neoliberalism' or more euphemistically as 'globalisation'. Neoliberalism itself refers to the political project of laissez-faire capitalism, as discussed at the end of the Introduction. However, it has been mixed in with increasing strains of conservative impulse that are almost Victorian in nature, in that they focus on disciplining the behaviour of poor people through segregated (and poor) systems of provisioning, often in a punitive manner (on this last point, see Rodger 2012). While this interventionist and segregationist impulse is not particularly liberal, it somehow fits comfortably with what Kiely (2018) clearly exposes as the ways in which the neoliberal project has been reliant on state power and considerable degrees of state intervention (also see the excellent exposition by Peck 2010). The reason for this is that the neoliberal project has been fundamentally oriented towards the protection of private property rights (and their free creation and use, including financial assets). It thereby also contains a conservative impulse, particularly with respect to protecting the prevailing class order, as opposed to classical liberalism, which was much more revolutionary in seeking to undo the old aristocratic order.[1]

The use of segregated systems to condition the behaviour of poor people also fits with what is considered in Foucauldian terms a form of neoliberal governmentality. This refers to technologies of power for governing populations through discourses and norms of self-regulation or self-discipline, with the aim to make oneself entrepreneurial and fit for engaging in markets. Much of the poverty studies scholarship has been wittingly or unwittingly coopted into the development of such technologies.

The neoliberal period in question witnessed large parts of the Global South being subjected to recurrent deep crises and structural adjustment programmes for well over two decades, until boom-time conditions from about the mid-2000s onwards allowed for some respite, albeit within a transformed setting of fully transnationalised capital and rampant financialisation. It is this new order that the reigning ideology seeks to legitimate with poverty narratives. Poverty data have been used in often dubious ways to reinforce dominant narratives of this recent past as one of tentatively progressive emancipation, and thus the policies that came with it as one of cautious success. The fact that large numbers of people around the world do not feel that this is the case arguably feeds into political reactions against this narrative. However, recent trends suggest that rising right-wing populist movements have been more successful at capturing this sentiment than the Left (with some exceptions). This has the effect of reinforcing the conservative impulse which, as noted above, is ironically aligned with the neoliberal project, even though many claim that it represents the death of neoliberalism based on a misunderstanding of the reactionary element within this ideology.

The other big story of this period has also been the dramatic rise of China, which presents a different ideological narrative. Indeed, poverty statistics are marshalled in China in support of statist developmentalism, as I have analysed in depth elsewhere with respect to minorities in Western China (e.g., Fischer 2005, 2014a). There is some debate about whether China should be considered neoliberal, although this is mostly with respect to the Foucauldian idea of creating neoliberal subjectivities, as mentioned above. It has not had much influence in the more political economy scholarship on actual economic policy, in which China is not considered neoliberal in the conventional sense. Nonetheless, the story of China has been weaved into the dominant narrative on poverty with a large degree of creative license by emphasising its liberalisation from a closed Maoist economy. This narrative generally avoids the legacy and ongoing strong degrees of state control and state-led developmentalism that explain a large part of the poverty-reduction experience in the country, especially but not only on the human development side (although, ironically, state control is brought up when the country is criticised for currency or trade manipulation, as I have discussed in Fischer 2010c, 2012d, 2018b).

The second central argument of this book is more specifically in relation to this orthodoxy. The emphasis of absolute measures in current global development agendas – including so-called multidimensional measures – is both the product of a policy bias towards targeting in social provisioning and, in turn, instils biases towards targeting in a reinforcing manner, as against more universalistic or cross-class solidaristic forms of provisioning. This is partly because many of these measures have been designed as supports for targeting. However, a more subtle reason is that absolute conceptions and measures are poorly suited to reflecting the value of more universalistic forms of provisioning. They also encourage (and are encouraged by) a policy priority of expediency over equality, in terms addressing the poorest first rather than addressing the institutional implications brought into play by such expediency, which tends to encourage segregation at the expense of cross-class solidarities.

These biases might in certain cases appear inconsequential, or expeditious under circumstances of constrained resources and limited capacity, or even logical and equitable. For all these reasons, criticisms of targeting have usually been brushed aside, even despite serious doubts about the efficacy of targeting even from within the ranks of the establishment. But the biases need to be taken seriously because they plant the seeds for possibilities that are much more perverse, given the tendency for targeting to encourage or entrench segregation, as discussed further below.

Indeed, within the current political climate around the world, the risk is that the conservative ideological impulse mentioned above becomes increasingly punitive with its use of targeting devices, many ironically developed by previous 'New Left' governments. There are already signs of this, perhaps most evocatively represented, as in all things, by the Trump administration. By replacing current measures of poverty in the US with 'consumption' measures, i.e., those commonly used in cash transfer programmes in developing countries as discussed in Chapter 3, the administration has recently claimed that no more than 250,000 people are living in extreme poverty in the US, versus an estimate cited in a UN report of 18.5 million, or US census estimates from 2016 of 41 million people living in poverty (not extreme poverty). The move to effectively eliminate the official statistical representation of poverty in the US is part of efforts by Republicans in Congress to add work requirements for recipients of food stamps, Medicaid and housing subsidies, and to make cuts to social assistance more generally (Stein and Jan 2018). In the UK, there is a similar trend to make the Universal Credit, which unified six different benefit schemes into one single monthly payment, increasingly punitive and also a means to effectively cut welfare benefits (e.g., see JPIT 2018; Merrick 2018; NAO 2018). The very fact that 'universal credit' resembles the idea of universal basic income demonstrates the insidious ease by which policy ideas from the social-democratic left can be subverted by the Right (although, of course, it must be remembered that Friedrich Hayek was one of the early supporters of the idea of universal basic income). It is in this sense that the biases within poverty conceptions and measures, which might at times appear innocuous, can quickly turn into slippery slopes when political climates change. We therefore need to take their implicit biases seriously.

The third argument running throughout this book is that absolute poverty measures are poorly suited to reflect dynamic reproductions of poverty within modern processes of structural transformation for several reasons related to the fundamentally relative nature of modern poverty. The result is that such absolute measures have a secular tendency to underestimate the reproduction of poverty over time. This unfitness for purpose is partly related to the inherent arbitrariness of choice that is involved in measuring poverty, as discussed in Chapters 2 to 5, which is an inherent intractable dilemma that must be openly recognised rather than presuming it can be overcome through technical sophistication.

However, even more fundamental is that our current conventions of conceiving and measuring absolute poverty, including multidimensional measures, such as those officially adopted by the MDGs and then the SDGs, are still largely rooted in conceptions of minimal subsistence sufficiency, even despite the inclusion of some inequality indicators in the SDGs. While this remains relevant in certain contexts, especially with reference to contemporary famines (with the caveat that evaluations of hunger are also relative and arbitrary), it is increasingly less relevant in many others. Rather, the profiles of essential social needs have generally changed – often quite radically – within the transformations typically associated with modern capitalist development, demographic transition and other related transformations, alongside rises in associated baseline norms such as literacy and schooling levels, or life expectancy and health profiles. This is not necessarily the same as an upwards shift in subjective preferences, such as when people start to expect more as they become more affluent. Rather, it is a question of the minimum requirements for functioning in modern societies and economies, short of which the options are generally exclusion or exploitation (or both).

One result, for instance, is the persistence of hunger despite rising incomes and falling income poverty, among other manifestations of dissonance that have been recurring subjects of debate in recent decades. Rather than blaming the poor for bad consumption choices, the more straightforward explanation for this dissonance is that the poverty lines are simply not keeping up with the transformations of social need, whereby non-food needs increasingly gain precedence over food needs. Food consumption is therefore repressed, because it is the one need that can be repressed, versus others that are more inflexible, such as transport to be able to work to be able to buy food, etc. This is particularly the case when livelihoods become fully monetised and commodified, as they generally are in urban settings.

As a result, insufficient food consumption can happen in contexts that are far from subsistence and where incomes could technically allow for sufficient food consumption, abstracting from other needs. Poverty lines that are rooted on a conception of food need are therefore prone to underestimate these transformations over time.

In other words, the conventional standards that are currently used for these absolute measures are so minimally defined that they essentially become obsolete over time through the course of the structural transformations that are associated with development, especially but not only urbanisation. Falling poverty rates might therefore, to a lesser or greater extent, actually be a reflection of the fact the standard measures are increasingly falling behind the evolution of the compelling social needs of poor people. This is particularly problematic when these standards are used to determine the thresholds to 'graduate' poor people from support and assistance. Indeed, a similar point might be made with respect to the thresholds that are used to distinguish low- and middle-income countries, that they are too low and, hence, give a false appearance of so-called graduation to lower-middle-income-country status (as discussed in Chapter 2).

Deconstructing for social justice

This deconstruction of prevailing poverty approaches is needed for instilling humility and a healthy dose of scepticism towards any false sense of authority that these approaches might be used to convey. The reality is that we probably do not know, at least not precisely, how poverty is evolving within the volatile and rapidly changing context of contemporary capitalism. The pretence of precision bears a strong propensity for hubris. This realisation is so important in a subject such as poverty because of the power relations involved between the researcher and the researched, in terms of the implications and influence that the former can have on the lives of the latter without any means of contestation, or even without any awareness or comprehension. And the consequences of hubris can be dire for poor people.

This is not to argue against the measurement project, which remains imperative for supporting modern forms of social provisioning and public policy. Indeed, the statistical project needs to remain focused on building up capacity in conventional social-scientific measures that provide valuable and pertinent information for policy-making and social provisioning in a timely manner. This capacity is already weak in so many contexts, even before the addition of extra requirements transposed from every passing fad by successive global development agendas. The statistical agencies of most poor countries submit to these fads, partly out of deference and the ideational influences of so-called 'epistemic communities', but also partly because they remain dependent on donors, both financially and for the human resources required in such technical matters. Yet the direction of many of these transposed or imposed statistical projects is not necessarily the most useful for supporting such government capacities. This is in part because they remain more obsessed with the evaluative aim of building internationally comparative data and indices rather than with the mundane and less-marketable practices associated with conventional but still essential national social statistical collection for governing.

At a more pernicious level, the constant waves of new fads emitting from the centres of knowledge production also reinforce relations of institutional dependency on these centres, as national statistical staff need to be trained in the ways of the latest techniques. Or where there is a lack of capacity or comprehension, they must outsource it to a consultancy or income-earning unit of a university or organisation to do it for them, usually located in the Global North. In this manner, such statistical projects reproduce the dependency associated with the dissemination of technological progress from centres to peripheries, as classically theorised by Latin American structuralist development economists, except, in this case, the progress is often of questionable value or relevance and comes with implicit political and policy agendas. The consumption of such statistical projects emanating from the centre is often driven by things other than need.

Poverty obviously needs to be studied and monitored, although without fetishising the results. The various approaches for doing so remain as rough means to evaluate the evolution of social needs, with the understanding that this can be an erratically moving target, particularly in the contemporary era of rapid and volatile change. Moreover, the aim should be to make such evaluations as available and accessible as possible so that they can become objects of public engagement, scrutiny, contestation, debate and deliberation over their meaning, content and application in policy and social provisioning.

Indeed, this point is shared with Amartya Sen's insistence that functionings should be determined through local-level democratic deliberations, albeit with the qualification that his vision is quite idealised, in an abstract deductive liberal-theoretical sense, especially in the current context of rising right-wing authoritarian populism. Rather, according to a more political economy view, we need to understand such engagement as a field of contest and often conflictive struggle among vying powers, interests and social mobilisations, each supported by various social sources of power (as per Mann 1986, 1993). The outcomes of this contest are not necessarily neatly sorted out through some sort of democratic bargaining equilibrium, as postulated by liberal political theory, but rather as a series of consequences, many of them unintended, driven forward by the constant disequilibria of unresolved and ongoing social and power struggles. Poverty studies is not immune to this, but rather serves as its ideological cannon fodder, in part because poverty is implicated in the narratives of these political economy struggles and is crucially conditioned by the struggles as well.

Poverty measurement in this perspective needs to be understood fundamentally as part of a political project of building state capacity in social provisioning and policy-making, as well as of strengthening processes of accountability with citizens on these matters. This engagement is, in the end, the most important result. After all, in the history of social emancipation, transformative social change has rarely happened through instrumentalised monitoring devices, but instead through active popular mobilisation and engagement, often in the absence of any good data. Mkandawire (2005) has similarly noted, as discussed in Chapter 7, that the past policies in late-developing countries that have been the most successful in reducing poverty generally did not have poverty reduction as a specific or explicit focus, in contrast to state-building or forging strong cross-class support for intensive development endeavours, among other broader objectives.

The poverty of poverty studies

The problem with much of current poverty studies is that it distracts from these broader political economy causal dynamics. Despite the hyperbolic declaration of revolutions within the plethora of poverty approaches and measures in our frenetic age of seeking impact and innovation, an overwhelming emphasis of absolute conceptions of poverty persists, whether income or multidimensional, as was exclusively the case in the Millennium Development Goals (MDGs) and as remains at the core of the Sustainable Development Goals (SDGs). Besides providing a metre that can give some sense of the minimum standards of subsistence and needs that people can be squeezed down to, they are not particularly useful for understanding the broader context that conditions the reproduction of modern poverty. Indeed, even with respect to minimum standards, they are also not very useful given that these change across people, contexts and time.

Contemporary poverty studies have, in this sense, not resolved and to a large extent do not even address the classical debates regarding the creation and division of wealth within and across societies, nor how this is related to social and economic structural transformations associated with modern capitalist development. The elicitation of 'theories of change' that has become popular among certain scholars and the policy and donor communities falls far short of the mark. It also states the obvious given that social sciences have always been centrally concerned about why things happen and change. Moreover, in its common usage, a 'theory of change' is usually used to evoke an individualist ontology of poverty, without considering the poor within their broader social and structural conditions. This insulates the study of poverty from the more uncomfortable questions about whether modern poverty in developing countries is fundamentally due to a lack of integration of poor people into local, national and global socio-economic systems, or whether it is due to the manner by which they have already been integrated.

Hence, our fundamental understanding of the causes of poverty has arguably advanced so little given that so much of poverty research – including that generated under the rubric of the capability approach – has focused on describing poverty rather than on the causal processes that create poverty. These contentions are, of course, disputed given that mainstream approaches to poverty research claim to have made great advances in our understanding of poverty and broadly accept the frames within which poverty has been conceptualised, as led by the World Bank. If critical, scholars in this literature are mostly critical of aspects of methodology, such as with respect to the level of the poverty line, but not with respect to deeper issues regarding political and ideological biases implicit in the operationalisation of poverty studies. (As mentioned in the Introduction, Angus Deaton is one exception in this respect, along with a few other dissenting voices.)

The return of segregation

In the void of this broader consideration of causal dynamics, various policy agendas that have a huge bearing on these dynamics are nonetheless pursued. As noted previously, various critical authors have occasionally made this point, that poverty statistics have been used to legitimise the reigning neoliberal order, such as Wade (2004), Kiely (2007) or Pogge (2010). However, moving forward, the problematic aspects of these agendas are actually becoming more pervasive and diffuse than simply a particular form of capitalist ideology. This can be referred to as the return of segregationism.[2]

Indeed, there is an important social democratic tradition in poverty studies that is explicitly or implicitly critical of neoliberalism, as represented by the work of Amartya Sen. However, whether or not someone ascribes implicitly or explicitly to a neoliberal policy position, the focus on poverty and within this on measuring the poor, through whatever measures, contains within it a tension between identification and segregation, as discussed in Chapter 7. If unchecked, in particular because of de-politicisation, this tension can provide momentum to a much more pervasive intellectual and policy proclivity to single out and segregate the poor from the rest of society as the objects of public (state or non-state) charity. Such tendencies might not necessarily or specifically conform to a neoliberal logic, to the extent that they might advocate for an increased role of the state in providing social welfare to the poor. The question then is whether such public poverty interventions play a role in supporting broader neoliberal processes in society, as argued, for instance, by Lavinas (2013, 2017) or Saad-Filho (2015). (Also, see my discussion of this in Fischer 2010a, 2012, 2014b.) However, even if not clearly neoliberal, the tendencies nonetheless tend to reinforce the more conservative impulses mentioned earlier, which emphasise efficiency and constraint in the use of public resources over concerns of equity and equality.

Accordingly, we have been observing the normalisation of a segregationist approach to social provisioning and welfare systems parallel to the rise of the poverty agenda, and the two have been mutually reinforcing, in both statist and neoliberal regimes. Stratification and segregation have of course been inherent to social provisioning systems since time immemorial, as is a common insight in the field of social policy. Nonetheless, the legitimacy of segregation was on the defensive for several postwar decades and the goal of universalism was at least the target of most countries, even if only achieved by a few. However, more recently there has been a reassertion of segregationism, except within entirely transformed contemporary contexts.

Recent trends have also lent legitimacy to segregation as accepted best practice, to be institutionally strengthened rather than evolved out of over time. For instance, the neoliberal reforms and structural adjustments of the 1980s and 1990s in Latin America exacerbated informality in the economy and served to undermine any embryonic or nascent efforts that could have provided the basis for a universalisation of social security, as in the classic welfare states of Europe. However, this stylised observation is then often used as a reason for the impossibility of universalising social security in such contexts, even though the very retreat from such long-term objectives was arguably a crucial contributing factor for the exacerbation of informality in the first place.

Hence, there is now an accepted conventional wisdom in the ironically austere times of high inequality and fabulous financialisation that large informal sectors cannot be integrated into existing social security systems and/or that the latter cannot be universalised. Social protection for the informal is then turned into an issue of charity or unilateral redistributive transfers, as is suggested by the now-accepted terminology of 'non-contributory' social protection. In effect, the term is factually inaccurate because the poor generally do contribute to state revenues, except not through direct income taxes or social security contributions but through indirect contributions such as value-added taxes, through which much of such 'non-contributory' social protection is actually funded. The non-contribution in this sense is only relevant with respect to specific formal institutions of social security, but not with respect to resource transfers to and from poor people in the overall economy. Nonetheless, these narratives subtly reinforce perceptions that poverty relief or social protection are essentially charity, or at best social assistance. This is in contrast to the perceived deservingness of social security contributors, rentiers or those who make profits, and hence an increasingly smug protectionism from them towards the encroachment of poor people into their benefits. However, the dual pressures to both reform (i.e., retrench) social security systems as well as refine the targeting of social protection for the poorest (e.g., see IMF 2017) reinforces the tendency in most parts of the world for a very large uncovered and unsecured middle, typically the middle 60 percent of the population.

There are still plenty of debates to be had within the accepted frame of charity (or 'non-contributory' benefits). Is poverty relief in fact good policy for growth, versus focusing on employment or productive interventions? Should it be widely or narrowly targeted? Does it induce dependency, or should it be wielded with conditionalities and behavioural nudges? However, the point is that in accepting the frame of these debates, one has already succumbed to a segregationist logic, rather than seeking frames that enhance an understanding of the poor as integrated, integral and interdependent with the rest of society, alongside visions of systems that would come to reflect this overtime.

Such segregationist tendencies cannot be simply explained as part of a neoliberal logic. Indeed, as we ponder the possibilities of post-neoliberal futures within contexts of entrenched high inequality and increasingly reactionary politics, these tendencies may turn out to be far more endemic and long-lasting than neoliberal forms of governance. The appeal is that such segregationist tendencies appear progressive and so-called 'pro-poor', to the extent that the justification for isolating the poor is to better concentrate resources and interventions on them and to filter out the undeserving and the needless.

The political consequences of shifting modalities of targeting

Moreover, the subtle but powerful shift towards top-down technocratically controlled targeting systems as the accepted best practices of contemporary poverty-reduction policy is another instance of how depoliticising tendencies of contemporary poverty studies is, in fact, fundamentally political at the level of actual practice. This is not necessarily an issue about targeting or conditionality *per se*, which receives most of the focus in debates about social protection and social policy more generally (although both practices are fundamentally political as well). Rather, it is about the institutional modalities through which targeting is practiced and their political consequences, which have been hugely neglected by scholarship.

A key point is the severing of practices of rights-claiming and con-testation by beneficiaries from processes of beneficiary selection. This occurs in the shift from classic models of beneficiary-initiated claims-making, wherein even means-testing is initiated by beneficiaries themselves, towards the concentration and control of identification and selection procedures by certain sectors of the state, often quite centralised and distanced from the beneficiaries. In the latter, benefi-ciary selection comes to be determined through surveys and censuses that beneficiaries have little understanding about (especially in the case of proxy means-testing). While this does appear to have an effect in taming disputes (and most cash transfer programmes do implement dispute mechanisms), this is precisely a logical conse-quence of the short-circuiting of contestation and other politicised forms of engagement by the poor, by decentring or obscuring chan-nels of accountability across different state agencies and, in some cases, para-state and non-state entities.

Notably, such modalities have been facilitated by the ease of econometric technologies and their avid uptake in poverty studies, and they are often favoured because they place less pressure on lim-ited local administrative resources, both human and financial. They are also often advocated in the name of empowerment. However, empowerment is mostly evoked with reference to the policy inter-ventions that result from poverty identification. For instance, cash transfers are said to enhance the intra-household bargaining power of targeted women by giving them more money to bargain with. Empowerment is not assessed in terms of how these interventions actually strengthen (or weaken) political systems of representation and accountability.

From a political economy perspective, these current 'best-practice' modes are in fact fundamentally disempowering. They circumvent and short-circuit processes of citizen-led claims-making on the state, thereby undermining the state as a locus of accountability for the poor, as similarly argued by Chandhoke (2003) with respect to the agendas of pluralising the state. For instance, with the accepted best practices of cash transfer policies, the poor themselves generally have no idea how they are being selected or monitored. They often have no means to contest the process or the outcomes, or, if they do, it is towards the end of the process of selection, as part of the verifica-tion of results already generated, in community contexts such as in village committees in which the poor enter as already the weakest player within local power relations. If and when poverty relief arrives, from the perspective of the 'recipients' or 'beneficiaries', it generally arrives with an appearance of a random act of benevolence (as it does to those not selected), rather than as the outcome of a process of asserting entitlement rights.

This is in contrast to the more classical notions and practices of claiming entitlements, whether through means testing or not. However imperfect, these reinforce a process of active rights-claiming by the recipients themselves (or beneficiaries, or citizens). They also serve to reinforce the state as the principle locus of accountability (again, see Chandhoke 2003). These processes are often denigrated as messy and inefficient, while the technocratic processes of selecting beneficiaries despite their incomprehension is celebrated as clean and non-distortionary interventions into the communities of poor people. The latter assessment nonetheless often comes with a dose of naiveté as to the nature of local power relations, and also often ignores many of the large implicit costs for poor people involved in the process, as well as the shift of administrative resources towards monitoring and evaluation, which also becomes the weakest links in such systems. The irony is that such solutions to the messiness of local political economies end out reinforcing the charity view of such forms of social protection, in which the major objective is to devise the best ways of 'us' giving to 'them'. The double irony is that the proponents of such modalities of targeted charity have been almost entirely from non-poor elites and transnational technocrats. They have rarely, if ever, been from popular social movements themselves, or from among the poor and working classes, which generally demand dignity and respect alongside a fairer share of the pie.

Beyond absolute poverty

Returning to the third central argument of the book, to a certain extent the gradual decline in global measures of absolute income poverty, if accurate, can be understood through the massive productivity increases in contemporary agriculture and manufacturing, to the extent that real food prices are at close to an all-time low in historical terms, even despite the recent spike in food prices. Combined with increasingly integrated international markets, it is understandable how the condition of poverty has gradually changed over the last

century from one of food insufficiency to one in which calorie sufficiency is relatively easier to secure (although not necessarily nutrition
sufficiency), while other compelling social needs take over in precedence (or else cause repressed food expenditure). Insofar as absolute
poverty measures are generally designed to reflect food insufficiency,
the long-term secular decline in absolute poverty rates is reflective of
this transformation in the condition of modern poverty.

However, in the face of such global productive capacity, it is surprising that so much of the world's population still subsists under
or just above such minimally defined poverty lines. Part of this is
undoubtedly related to agrarian conditions in much of the Global
South, where peasant farmers struggle to get by on the low food
prices received for their output on shrinking per-person plots of land
(if they produce a surplus), relative to rising prices in the range of
other social needs (such as in health care and schooling, or else in
inputs to production). But much is not related to agrarian conditions. For instance, when we speak of Bangladeshi women factory
workers being 'pulled out of poverty' by working for the equivalent
of 38 dollars a month producing clothing for Western brands (as was
generally cited at the time of the Rana Plaza disaster in 2013), we are
referring to this notion of minimally defined absolute poverty. These
workers and their families subsist only slightly above this absolute
despite being integrated into value chains that generate enormous
value at the retail end. In this sense, such workers are still living under
the predicament posited by classical economists such as Malthus,
Ricardo and Marx, who assumed that workers' wages would always
be squeezed down to a level of subsistence, that is, subsistence minimally defined by the price of food.

In order to move beyond such narrow conceptions of 'achievement',
as enshrined in the MDGs and the SDGs, we need to think about
poverty and vulnerability with a broader and more relative understanding of evolving social needs, particularly in contexts of social
and economic transformation. Such considerations in many cases lie
beyond the space of absolute poverty, whether conceived in income
or multidimensional terms, given that development transitions can
often exacerbate vulnerability and compelling social needs throughout social hierarchies, thereby having very powerful effects on
various dynamics of social stratification, grievance or conflict, which
are relevant for understanding poverty even if they do not necessarily

result in poverty. This more relative approach to understanding poverty and vulnerability within development transformations also helps to shed light on the vital role of redistribution in past and present development as a key mediating factor in cultivating resilience and positive synergies between evolving social needs and human and economic development.

For instance, poverty reduction brought about by targeted cash transfer schemes mostly comes about through lifting the lower tail-end of an income distribution without necessarily effecting the distribution above this tail-end (particularly if the transfers are not funded through progressive forms of taxation). Hence, while producing a reduction in poverty rates and inequality, they can nonetheless leave the broader structure of inequality untouched, or even reinforce it by the manner in which the cash transfers and related policies are institutionally organised. This is important because much of the social dynamics related to inequality, such as stratification, subordination or exclusion, occur above this tail-end or above the thresholds usually used for poverty evaluation (absolute or relative, income or multidimensional).[3] Compulsions that discipline labour can also operate in more affluent conditions, particularly given that social needs evolve relative to context and social status. Hence these social dynamics are not necessarily reflected by conventional poverty or even inequality measures, and they are not considered by policies that target the bottom end of the income distribution. A wider conception of such social needs is therefore needed.

Indeed, as discussed in Chapter 5 on social exclusion, this is a dilemma of social inclusion approaches that treat inclusion as the alter ego of exclusion and, in turn, deals with the identification of social exclusion as more or less the same as relative or capability poverty, or else as horizontal (i.e., group-based) inequality. Beyond the important insight that the problems of poverty are more often the result of exploitative inclusion rather than exclusion *per se*, care must also be taken because inequality measures can mask important exclusionary processes occurring among middle social strata that might be related to inequality even if not reflected by inequality statistics. These can be very politically contentious and can undermine the effectiveness of poverty-reduction strategies predicated on upward mobility (as is the case, for instance, with strategies justified in terms of human capital). It is more important to focus primarily on social processes of stratification and subordination and to use poverty and inequality data as one partial insight into these broader questions of social integration (or segregation).

In this respect, we need to think more broadly about poverty and vulnerability in at least three ways, each of which requires embedding our understanding of poverty and vulnerability within notions of structural transformation. The first is with regard to a more sophisticated understanding of evolving social needs. These include: changing educational needs for employment when the social norm is increasingly based on a floor of full primary enrolment, thereby raising the minimal threshold for socially acceptable schooling qualifications; changing health care needs in a context of rising costs, aging populations or new diseases; or the needs of housing and transport, especially in a context of urbanisation. Remaining within the space of money-metric measures, the thresholds that would allow for a sufficient level of income to meet such needs and that would also offer a substantive sense of inclusion into decent employment (without exploitation or bondage) are generally much higher than those that are currently used in the lower bounds of PPP dollar-or-whatever-a-day poverty measures. (It is not quite clear what the upper bounds refers to, besides convenient cut-off points.) The trends might also be divergent, particularly in a globalising context with generally rising inequality over the last several decades.

Second, it is important to understand that movements out of absolute poverty – and development transitions such as urbanisation more generally – can in many cases exacerbate vulnerability rather than alleviate it, which raises the crucial issue of employment security in a context of labour transitions and the importance of matching such labour transitions with the development of modern social security systems. In other words, movements out of poverty generally involve a streamlining of incomes, such as transitions from diversified, low-productivity but stable and resilient rural livelihoods, to streamlined incomes based on one or two wages, salaries or other sources of income.[4] Indeed, such streamlining is an implication of rising productivity, which generally occurs through specialisation as one of its components, as discussed in Chapter 6. While streamlining generally offers higher returns for labour, it also places employees in a more precarious, all-or-nothing condition, which in turn heightens the imperative for employment security in such contexts, or social security measures such as unemployment insurance. Rather than exacerbating these conditions of insecurity through flexible labour market policies, public policy needs to first focus on creating the conditions that enhance people's ability to transition with relatively secure degrees of autonomy, thereby facilitating their own livelihood strategies in response to socio-economic structural change, as discussed in Chapter 3 in terms of 'subsistence capacity.' This perspective highlights the increasing importance of more universalistic forms of social security and social provisioning as counterparts to the transition of populations out of agriculture and rural subsistence conditions, not simply in preparation for negative economic events, but also for dealing with the increasing structural vulnerabilities that are associated with the disembedding of labour within capitalism.

The dark side of these transitions is that, when they take place through a forced commodification of labour, the resultant insecurity of employment might not even be associated with improved incomes, all considered. This has often occurred in capitalist processes of development whereby labour is forced to become dependent on wage employment through the appropriation or even destruction of their land assets and/or other sources of subsistence. It is often assumed on the basis of classical experiences of capitalist transition that such processes of labour commodification will eventually lead to rising incomes and productive accumulation in the long term, even if the dislocations in the short term can be very disruptive to peoples' livelihoods.

However, we need to be very careful with our evaluation of the value of lost subsistence and of the contingent conditions that allowed for rising wages in the classical cases. As argued by Celso Furtado (1983 [1978]), these contingent conditions included strong working-class mobilisations that were integrated into the broadening social base of nation-states that were, in turn, at the apex of macroeconomic coordination of national economies at the time. These conditions might not apply in contemporary developing countries today, particularly given the increasingly complex coordination of international economic activities that has passed, to a large extent, from nation-states to large private transnational corporations. While this should not be cause for deterministic pessimism, it is also a warning against naïve complacency regarding any natural tendency for wages to rise with productivity, or for a gradual broadening of national social security systems as developing countries become wealthier, as in the classical cases. Rather, intentional and sustained political resolve is required to guarantee such outcomes. Indeed, Furtado himself believed in the role of political activism as 'the necessary condition for the manifestation of creativity in the institutional sphere, in other words, for the creation of new social forms capable of reducing the tensions generated by accumulation' (Furtado 1983, p. 9). Pre-empting the capability approach, he argued from his own structuralist logic that development 'is no more than this: to enlarge the space within which human potentialities can be realised' (ibid., p. 8).

Third, we need to think of vulnerability as a vertically occurring condition experienced throughout social hierarchies at all levels, not merely in the space of poverty or with reference to falling into poverty. This is especially important in a context of rising human development, such as rising schooling levels and rising aspirations for social mobility in a context of urbanisation. New nexuses of vulnerability can be revealed or exacerbated in such contexts further up in a social hierarchy, well above the spaces identified by absolute approaches to poverty, whether income or multidimensional. They might not even be detected by standard inequality measures insofar as they occur in the middle of a social hierarchy. For instance, university graduates, from families that can afford such education, might face exclusionary pressures (such as through racial, cultural, linguistic or gender axes of discrimination) within the types of employment suited to their educational status, such as state-sector or formal corporate professional jobs, rather than in lower strata of employment that would be filled by poorer and/or less-schooled workers. Exclusions in this sense place downward pressures on elite and/or upwardly mobile people within their respective positions in labour hierarchies and, as a consequence, can also create obstacles to the upward mobility of those below them. These processes can be very contentious socially and politically, even though not reflected as increasing poverty or inequality *per se*. As argued in Fischer (2008a, 2009a, 2011a, 2014a), exclusion and vulnerability in this sense need to be understood and evaluated relative to comparable cohorts of people, with similar levels of education and aspiring to enter similar sectors of employment.

This insight is important because vulnerabilities that do not necessarily lead to poverty still have very powerful effects on various social dynamics of social stratification or conflict, among other political economy implications. Indeed, vulnerabilities experienced at the upper end of a social hierarchy are especially potent given that they occur among politically active and powerful classes. Absolute and even relative indicators of poverty often tell us little about these broader processes because they focus our attention towards the bottom of a social hierarchy, which might be normatively justified but analytically partial. Moreover, refocusing our attention towards a more holistic understanding of vulnerability counteracts the tendency to blame poor people for a variety of perverse social dynamics (such as riots, crime, interethnic conflict, civil war, etc.) that emerge across social hierarchies in response to intensifying insecurities, whether due to inequality or other causes. While poverty might play a role in many of these social dynamics, it is important – indeed, it is an ethical responsibility – to also remind ourselves that middle classes and elites are also usually implicated, often in ways that surprise our presumptions, such as when the aggrieved 'poor' turn out to be middle-class activists. Hence, we need social theory to address how middle classes and elites themselves might face various forms of vulnerability that undermine their own perceptions of social need, thereby fuelling politically powerful grievances.

Re-politicising social justice within global development agendas

In sum, the challenge of global development agendas does not lie in the measurement of poverty, however conceived. It certainly should not lie in making poor people work harder, even though this is often implied in many agendas, instead of addressing how their work is valued. Rather, the challenge lies in seriously re-engaging with development debates about how to create genuinely redistributive structures and institutions at national and global levels. These are political challenges given that they cannot be resolved through technocratic solutions, but require choices to be made about the types of societies we wish to inhabit and how we wish to treat each other within and across these societies. Human rights principles might provide some generic ethical guidelines for these choices, although the devil is invariably in the detail of implementation, which is also where the political takes precedence. These choices are being made in any case under the depoliticising guise of various development and other agendas.

In order to avoid the tendency for cooptation into orthodox policy agendas, global development agendas need to be re-politicised through explicit engagement with substantive policy issues. Implicit policy biases and choices need to be made explicit as part of the calculus of public contestation and deliberation, ideally within the domestic sphere of developing countries themselves as a means to strengthen principles of national self-determination and local processes of accountability. Such re-politicisation needs to be backed up by a genuine revival, in research and in practice, of universalistic social policies as viable options for dealing simultaneously with poverty and inequality, if only because real political contestation and deliberation is very difficult to cultivate within a context of starkly unequal, segregated and fragmented societies. If we are to truly embrace an inclusive agenda, it must be more than merely reducing absolute poverty regardless of broader considerations of social integration. Rather, it needs to be based on equitable and even egalitarian sharing without double standards. In failing to assert this, we risk letting others – in particular, an increasingly emboldened, enriched and self-referential transnationalised elite – decide in their own interests and through a veil of depoliticised moral imperatives how we are to best live together.

NOTES

1 Introduction: Poverty, ideology and development

1 Monetisation refers to the increasing use of money in the exchange of goods and services, and hence an economy that is increasingly monetary.

2 Commodification (or commoditisation) refers to an increasing share of consumption and production based on buying goods and services through market transactions rather than producing these goods and services oneself or accessing them through non-market forms of exchange. With reference to labour, it refers to labour itself being treated as a commodity in labour markets.

3 This implies that demographic transition is related to technological changes, such as increased control over mortality and fertility, which are disseminating throughout the world at various speeds and are affecting all societies, rich and poor alike, as part of a global process. On the other hand, the economic growth experiences of countries, while influenced by technological dissemination, are not necessarily determined by it, but rather are ruled by an alternative and overlapping set of parameters related to the global expansion of capitalism. To further paraphrase this (to my own perilous responsibility), the enlightenment is not the same as capitalism. The two are interdependent, but not necessarily in a deterministic causal manner (determinism meaning that technological dissemination will stimulate capitalist growth in the manner that was experienced by the currently advanced industrial economies). This offers a useful perspective to the dilemma faced by many development theorists, as it is often assumed that 'modernisation' in one form or another will ultimately lead to a fairly deterministic economic outcome in the long run. In other words, it is possible to observe societies that modernise without necessarily making their way up the ladder of economic hierarchy.

4 Cf. Spivak (1988), Scott (1998), Harriss (2007), Li (2007, 2017), Ferguson (2015), Flores (2015), Peck and Theodore (2015), Roy (2010) or Roy and Crane (2015), among others.

5 Hickel (e.g., 2016, 2017) is one exception in this respect, although his is mostly a critique of World Bank poverty data based on a rich synthesis of secondary sources. As such, he joins in the tradition of authors such as Wade (2004).

6 I do not mention some of the most egregious recent examples in order to avoid contributing to journal strategies of raising citations and impact factors with such contributions. Moreover, as far as I can tell, these are mostly less-sophisticated variations on some of the earlier positions on this issue, often written from a Marxist perspective, such as Warren (1980).

7 See http://cep.lse.ac.uk/_new/events/event.asp?id=194.

8 Satterthwaite (2004) makes a similar argument with respect to the underestimation of urban poverty.

9 For discussions on universalism, see Fischer (2012) and Sanchez and Martinez (2014, 2016).

2 Unpeeling the politics of
poverty measures

1 Apparently, Thatcher first said this, although I do recall Blair repeating this in several interviews in the mid-2000s. In any case, Thatcher also said that one of her greatest achievements was Tony Blair.

2 Some might argue that Goal 8 provided a list of policies, but these are again better understood as principles, e.g., 'deal exhaustively with the debt problems of developing nations', not *how* to deal with them.

3 Latest data downloaded on 6 March 2017 from Cepalstat.

4 Jerven (2015) makes similar arguments, although looking at different literature.

5 Although, as pointed out by Sumner (2016), the data for the 1980s is so sparse that it is surprising that the World Bank was fine with using it to make estimates or draw trends for this period.

6 See Fischer (2009b, 2015, 2018a) for an explanation of how development itself tends to engender foreign exchange shortages due to the import intensity of modern consumption and investment in peripheral countries, and hence external vulnerability. See Jervon (2013) for a similar reaction to this point made by Collier.

7 Of course, the PPP line was constructed based on the average official poverty lines of a number of poorest countries with available data, and then converted into PPP terms, so we can only assume that they approximate such an absolute poverty line, based on the assumption that these poorest countries were accurately using such a line. See the next chapter for further discussion.

8 For instance, see Fischer (2012) for a discussion of the 2012 WDR on jobs (WB 2012), or Fischer (2010) on the 2004 WDR on services (WB 2003). In a recent presentation at the 2017 conference of the Development Studies Association of the UK and Ireland, Shanta Devarajan, the acting chief economist of the World Bank group and lead author of the 2004 WDR, more or less rehashed many of the arguments and even evidence from the 2003 WDR on services, perhaps demonstrating that they still adhere to the same positions.

9 Personal communication with Andy Sumner, 13 April 2018.

10 As explained further in Chapter 6, the two main tangents of modern neoclassical theory, e.g., the Solow and Arrow-Debreu models, do not actually define labour productivity or bring it into the models, but instead mimic it with endowments. Moreover, capital is treated as a substitutable good, substitutable with consumer goods, e.g., corn for eating or corn for planting. Accordingly, it is not possible to have a conception of labour productivity being enhanced by capital with such a conception of capital. So, in total factor productivity measures, the residual is treated as an amorphous 'efficiency', but not as productivity, whereas the contribution of the factor endowments of land, labour and capital are treated in terms of quantity inputs, but again not in terms of productivity (see Felipe and McCombie 2012 for extensive critiques).

Efficiency and productivity are subtly but fundamentally different. For instance, increasing labour productivity is often predicated on being less efficient with the use of other inputs, such as land being used up for the tire tracks of a combine harvester, versus labour-intensive practices of farming that maximise the use of the land at the costs of lower labour productivity. They only equate in terms of labour productivity being conceived in terms of efficiency in the use of labour inputs, but that is arguably a misleading logic, because the logic of productivity is generally oriented towards using the same amount of labour to produce more rather than just 'being efficient' with its use. In other words, it is not driven by efficiency concerns but by revenue/profit concerns. Again, this is a weakness with the conception and treatment of capital/technology within neoclassical theory.

11 Indeed, as noted above, the tentative *mea culpas* by some IMF staff, e.g., Ostry et al. (2016), generally maintain that the general direction was not wrong and adjustment was in fact necessary for establishing growth recoveries, but that the IFIs had been overly zealous in applying the cure.

12 See a discussion of this by Amsden (2010).

13 In response to these criticisms, Mkandawire (2005, pp. 5–6) notes that the 'most women-friendly' policies are found in societies where universalism is also an integral part of social policies. More generally, he also advocates for the notion proposed by Skocpol (1991) of targeting within universalism as a means to adapt to difference and diversity. As discussed further in Chapter 7, it should be noted that there is a huge degree of difference between targeting within a universalistic system and targeting within a segmented and residualist system of social provisioning. Arguably, it is much more difficult to comprehensively address special needs within the latter, such as learning disabilities among children or sexual and reproductive health issues among women.

3 Money-metric measures of poverty

1 For instance, in many of the country cases that I have researched, proxy surveys are conducted at best only once every five years.

2 She wrote that it is 'the compartmentalism of economic life which partly explains the widespread belief among economists that savings and investment are rare, even as concepts, in indigenous economic life; the economist is so unfamiliar with the forms such savings and investment are apt to take that he does not know where to look for evidence of their existence' (Hill 1966, p. 16).

3 I do not deal here with issues such as adult equivalence scales. For good discussions of this, see Deaton (1997), Hussain (2003) or Saith (2005). On issues of household composition and intra-household allocation and sharing, particularly with respect to gender, see Folbre (1986, 2012), Kabeer (1994) and Folbre and Nelson (2000).

4 At the time of final editing, apparently there have been no new poverty figures – either a poverty line or a survey – since the last data that were derived from the 2011–2012 NSSO survey and that were used to calculate the Tendulkar line. The country is awaiting the results of the 2016–2017 NSSO survey on consumption expenditure (email communication with Jayati Ghosh, 4 February 2018).

5 https://en.wikipedia.org/wiki/Poverty_in_India (last viewed on 2 February 2018).

6 This insight came from a discussion with André Perfeito in Brazil in 2016. For further detail, see the Central Bank of Brazil FAQ document: www.bcb.gov.br/conteudo/home-en/FAQs/FAQ%2002-Price%20Indices.pdf.

7 See Ghosh (2018) for a critique of the use of PPP measures in measurements of inter-country inequality.

8 E.g., the regular flagship reports of the FAO are now presented in terms of food and nutritional security. Also see www.fao.org/ag/humannutrition/nationalpolicies/meetings/en/.

9 See Sathyamala (2016, ch. 4) for an excellent discussion of the debates surrounding the 'small but healthy' hypothesis and the work and influence of P.V. Sukhatme more generally.

10 These involve choices with respect to the use of adult equivalence scales, economies of scale in consumption, the treatment of missing and zero incomes, and the range of possibilities for adjusting household survey incomes for misreporting. They acknowledge that there are at least five other important issues that are also open to assumptions and choices, but they do not deal with these due to data limitations. These include: income adjustments to correct for price variations across regions; the prices used to estimate the value of own-production for self-consumption; the choice of base year in the use of purchasing power deflators; imputed values of public services or subsidies into the definition of income; and the use of the standardised poverty lines across individuals, regardless of differences in person-specific capabilities and needs (Székely et al. 2000, p. 15).

11 Perhaps coincidentally, this line corresponded to a World Bank calculation of a dollar-a-day PPP line for China in 1998, which they estimated at 885 yuan, although this World Bank PPP line was then adjusted downwards to 772 yuan in 2000 (ADB 2003, p. 101). The downward revision was a new line given that the adjustment far exceeded that required to account for deflation (see Fischer 2005, p. 124).

12 Note that the divergence observed in this case would have been even greater had Hussain (2002) indexed the official line to deflation. He did not, presumably to reflect the commonly cited official measures.

13 See Deaton and Dreze (2009) for an alternative interpretation of this incongruence, although it is nonetheless widely accepted that levels of malnourishment in the Indian population have not declined even in the 2000s, despite rapid growth and apparent poverty reduction.

14 Admittedly, as demonstrated above in the case of China from 1998 to 2000, the higher line could have revealed different poverty rate trends despite this indexing issue given that it transects the income distribution data at a higher income stratum in each year. This was probably the dominant concern of Chen and Ravallion in conducting their revision exercise as it would have upset the well-established narrative of the World Bank up to that time. See Himanshu (2008) for a critical discussion of these revised PPP poverty lines, although he does not deal with CPI indexing except with reference to consumption weights (e.g., see p. 40).

15 See the excellent work by Wuyts (2011) on this matter. Also see Günther and Grimm (2007) for an econometric discussion of this point in the case of Burkina Faso.

16 For a discussion on repressed health expenditure in China, see the work of Wang (2004).

17 However, it is not necessarily capitalist if we follow the Marxist schema of the capitalist who purchases commodities with money to make more money (M-C-M'), versus more simple forms of exchanging commodities for money to purchase commodities (C-M-C').

18 A scattering of references to subsistence capacity can be found in the environmental literature, although only as a synonym for carrying capacity, not in the sense used here.

19 E.g., see Satterthwaite (2004) on the underestimation of urban poverty.

4 Multidimensional measures of poverty

1 See Laderchi et al. (2003, pp. 256–257) for a useful discussion of these methods used by the HDI.
2 We have observed this, for instance, in our interviews with various statistical and other government staff, as part of our ongoing research on the external financing of social protection in seven developing countries.
3 Also see Fischer (2014) for further elaboration of this theoretical distinction.
4 For a clear example of this line of reasoning, see Stiglitz (1986).
5 For instance, see Stiglitz (1986) for an example of a convoluted way of explaining why sharecroppers might not act the way theoretical economists think they should act.

5 The social exclusion approach

1 See www.worldbank.org/en/topic/social-inclusion#1 (last accessed 23 July 2018).
2 For instance, see Kingdon and Knight (2007) for a survey of this literature and its relation to poverty.
3 This criticism is addressed in detail in Gore et al. (1995) and Gore and Figueiredo (1997). Hall and Midgley (2004, pp. 10, 54) also mention this criticism in passing.
4 For instance, see the webpage on poverty and social exclusion on the site of the Employment, Social Affairs and Inclusion Department of the European Commission at http://ec.europa.eu/social/main.jsp?langId=en&catId=751 (last accessed on 23 July 2018).
5 Initially, social inclusion was not defined by the World Bank as the terms of participation, although the webpages of the World Bank do not reveal when revisions were made to the text of the website. See: www.worldbank.org/en/topic/social-inclusion (last viewed 23 July 2018).
6 Green (2007, p. 27) makes this same point with regard to poverty discourses of the World Bank.
7 For instance, see Kingdon and Knight (2007) for a survey of this literature and its relation to poverty.
8 This elegant passage nonetheless somewhat contradicts his previous assertion (as discussed in the previous section) that social exclusion should only refer to catastrophic ruptures if it is to be a useful analytical concept.
9 Recall, for instance, the psychological trauma that was unleashed in the US following 9/11 among Americans who were far removed from any threat.
10 See Hussain (2003, pp. 19–21), who finds lower poverty rates among migrants than among local residents in one-third of cities of a 31-city sample in China in 1999.
11 Chant (2007) also makes similar arguments as Jackson, although due to space, I will only deal with Jackson's arguments. Levitas (1996) also explores gender from a similar angle of inequality, which Room (1999, p. 170) suggests as an example of the relational aspects of social exclusion.
12 With respect to churning, Hills (1998) makes the important insight that high mobility is not necessarily contradictory with high levels of inequality.

6 Locating modern poverty within the creation and division of wealth: Towards a structuralist and institutionalist political economy approach in poverty studies

1 For some discussion of this, see Fischer (2008b). I also observed this, for instance, in a lauded income-generation programme run by an NGO in rural India based on selling micro-health insurances, in which the return for the labour time involved in these sales was in effect far below the minimum local wage for women agricultural labourers. The implication was that those who sold the insurances did so for reasons other than earning income, such as the social status or clout that came from representing the NGO locally. They were also only able to do so because they were ironically not very poor, with sufficient resources to afford offering almost voluntary contributions of labour to the NGO and not working at the minimum wage. This obviously leads to sustainability issues, given that it is difficult to maintain incentives for performance on such a basis.

2 Some argue that in Sweden this is at least partly an artifact of the fact that the Swedish accounting for market incomes includes many people who are earning nothing, although the point remains that the redistributive system has been a massive mechanism for instituting some of the lowest levels of inequality outside of some socialist countries.

3 See Fischer (2014b) for detailed discussion of this point.

4 See Cohen and Harcourt (2003) for an excellent discussion of this point.

5 Let us assume that overheads such as expensive lawyers' offices are not part of productive capital but, rather, are part of status-signalling devices (because a lawyer can be equally effective working at home or in a public library).

6 For a good discussion on other related points, see Felipe (2010, pp. 279–288).

7 For instance, see Bernard et al. (2008).

8 See Ndikumana and Boyce (2011) for some interesting estimates of capital flight from sub-Saharan Africa.

9 See Fischer (2010c).

7 Social policy and the tension between identification and segregation within social ordering and development

1 This precise definition of universalism was explained to me by the social protection expert of a country office of the World Bank in Asia during recent fieldwork in March 2018 (country undisclosed for reasons of confidentiality).

2 Again, see Martinez and Sanchez-Ancochea (2016) for some excellent discussion and examples of this.

3 I am grateful for Emma Dadap Cantal, one of my PhD students, for pointing out this distinction to me.

4 For instance, a group of UN independent experts wrote a letter to the UN (www. ohchr.org/Documents/Issues/Development/IEDebt/Open_Letter_IMF_21Dec2017. pdf) and another was signed by 53 economists, myself included (www.networkideas. org/news-analysis/2017/12/53-economists-write-to-imf-directors-on-approach-to-social-protection/).

5   There is little discussion in the 2013 WDR of the relationship between industrial policy and employment besides a few passing and generally derogatory comments (e.g., pp. 37, 217, 218 and 247), although on p. 218 there is favourable mention of the discussion of industrial policy framed within a theory of comparative advantage by Justin Lin, former chief economist of the World Bank. Two other approaches are also briefly considered, although none of the stronger positions in support of industrial policy are presented.

6   I avoid the use of the term 'middle class' because the precise meaning of this term has become excessively nebulous in its recent usage by economists and multilateral institutions, particularly in terms of definitions based on non-poor income status, starting from incomes as low as two PPP dollars per day; e.g., see Ravallion (2010). Any precise sociological meaning is absent from such definitions.

7   Mkandawire (2004, p. 1) defines social policy according to its economic functions, i.e., interventions in the economy to influence livelihoods and income, which is more precisely a definition of social protection. I have expanded this to include the social functions of social policy, such as the provisioning of schooling and health care to effect education and health outcomes in a population, which may or may not have an income effect.

8   See an introductory overview by Hujo and Gaia (2011).

9   For studies on the effect of social policies on women's labour force participation, see İlkkaracan (2012a, 2012b).

10 An example of targeting within universalism would be policies to address learning disabilities within an integrated and publicly funded education system. For one of the classic formulations of 'targeting within universalism', see Skocpol (1991).

11 A strong example of this argument is expressed by Goodin and Le Grand (1987, p. 215) with reference to Northern welfare states. They argue that 'the beneficial involvement of the non-poor in the welfare state is not merely wasteful – it is actually counterproductive. The more the non-poor benefit, the less redistributive the impact of the welfare state will be.'

12 Also see the work of Bob Deacon on this issue (Deacon 2012).

13 See Palacio (2017) for a review of these informality debates and detailed research in Ecuador that demonstrates that these arguments are misattributing tenuous evidence as perverse incentives, when in fact the benefits of going formal and accessing social security are so large that they greatly outweigh the value of the cash transfer in question. She also provides an argument that informality, in the case of the women receiving the cash transfer, is mostly the result of quite rigid structural and institutional obstacles operating in labour markets for these women, thereby questioning whether there is any choice in any case.

14 See an interesting study on this by Brito and Kerstenetzky (2011).

15 Again, see Mkandawire (2005, p. 13, citing various authors) on this budgetary 'paradox of targeting' whereby resources directed towards the (targeted) poor actually fall sharply during or after the shift to a targeting regime is made, thereby undermining the claim that such targeting allows for the *same* amount of resources to be used for greater poverty-reducing impact. As pointed out by Ghosh (2011, p. 5), such reductions can also be partly masked by the shifting of some expenditure items, such as when spending on publicly provided services to poor people is diverted to fund conditional cash transfer schemes.

16 See Kerstenetzky (2011) for some discussion on the role of minimum wages.

17 See Fischer (2009a) for further discussion on this point with respect to Western China.

18 For instance, see Langford (2010) – although, by targeting, he means the use of targets in the MDGs, not targeting in social policy.

19 For instance, this dimension of social policy is entirely absent from the consideration of various criticisms of rights-based approaches by Gready (2008). Gready does discuss how rights-based approaches have re-politicised development, in the sense of bringing attention to disempowerment and of speaking truth to power, but he does not consider the substantive policy dimension of politicisation as discussed here. Exceptions include Langford (2009), who does consider some of these dimensions in his engagement with notions of trade-offs as typically presented in welfare (i.e., neoclassical) economics.

20 I am indebted to numerous discussions and communications on these issues with Carole Samdup, Senior Advisor on Economic and Social Rights at Rights and Democracy in Montreal, Canada.

21 See Anttonen et al. (2012) for an excellent overview of universalism in social policy. The institutionalist political economy approach presented here of conceiving universalism along three dimensions (access/coverage, cost/price and financing), which draws from Fischer (2012), can be seen as complementing their presentation as well as that of Martinez and Sanchez-Ancochea, as noted above.

22 See Mehrotra (2000), Mkandawire (2005) and especially Kwon (2005) and Ringen et al. (2011).

23 See this argument in Fischer (2011b, 2014b).

24 For instance, Stamsø (2009) discusses the segmented nature of social policy in Norway with respect to housing policy in terms of tax benefits for home owners and targeted subsidies for those outside the property market.

25 See www.levyinstitute.org/topics/employer-of-last-resort-elr-policy.

26 For instance, in many Latin American countries, such as Brazil, the tertiary level of education is well subsidised and public universities are some of the best, whereas the opposite holds at the secondary level, with the ironic result that the students who manage to access the affordable and high-quality public universities are those whose families had the resources to pay for private secondary schooling. See Di John (2007).

27 See Bachelet (2011). For an excellent review, see Ocampo (2012).

28 See Mackintosh (2006) for a discussion of health along these lines. Note that this usage of the term 'commodification' is slightly different from the way it is used by Esping-Anderson (1990), as mentioned previously, who uses the term with reference to dependence on labour markets. Here, I am referring more precisely to something being treated (or not) as a commodity. His usage arguably confuses the meaning of commodification, insofar that it is relevant to ask whether labour has ever really been decommodified within capitalist welfare state regimes and whether this was ever the intention of such regimes. This is in contrast to understanding welfare and social security according to their insurance function, which is in effect very much in harmony with commodified labour and very much a counterpart of modern capitalist labour regimes. See Fischer (2014b) for further discussion of this point.

29 See description of this in Lin (2012) and also see a review of prominent debates on health care in China in Chen and Xu (2012). Also see Fischer (2016b).

8 Conclusion: Poverty as ideology in an age of neoliberalism

1 Buğra (2015) also points out that in Friedrich Hayek's conception of economic liberalism, market freedom must be underpinned with strong moral rules. In this sense, there is not necessarily a contradiction, as is often assumed, between the rise of modern and political forms of religious conservatism or fundamentalism and neoliberalism, such as in the US, parts of Latin America, Turkey or India.

2 For an interesting discussion of this in Northern welfare states, see Rodger (2012). See van Gent et al. (2018) for an example of segregationism in the Netherlands.

3 Wilkinson and Pickett (2009) also observe that inequality seems to have an effect not just on the poor but also the non-poor.

4 The understanding of diversified rural livelihoods is one of the generic insights coming out of the literature on livelihoods. The idea of streamlining was classically made by Tony Atkinson and also by Amartya Sen.

BIBLIOGRAPHY

Acemoglu, D., S. Johnson and J.A. Robinson (2001) 'The Colonial Origins of Comparative Development: An Empirical Investigation', *American Economic Review* 91(5): 1369–1401.

ADB (2003) *The 2020 Project: Policy Support in the People's Republic of China, Final Report and Policy Directions.* Manila: Asian Development Bank.

Alkire, S. (2002) *Valuing Freedoms: Sen's Capability Approach and Poverty Reduction.* New York: Oxford University Press.

Alkire, S. and J. Foster (2007) 'Counting and Multidimensional Poverty Measurement', OPHI Working Paper 7. Oxford: Queen Elizabeth House, University of Oxford.

Alkire, S. and M.E. Santos (2010) 'Acute Multidimensional Poverty: A New Index for Developing Countries', Human Development Research Paper 2010/2011. New York: United Nations Development Programme.

Amin, S. (1968) *Les Inegalités dans la distribution des revenus dans le tiers-monde actuel.* Geneva: Institut International d'Etudes Sociales.

Amin, S. (1970) *L'accumulation à l'échelle mondiale: critique de la théorie du sous-développement.* Dakar: Institut fondamental d'Afrique noire.

Amin, S. (1973) *L'échange inégal et la loi de la valeur.* Dakar: Institut fondamental d'Afrique noire.

Amsden, A. (2010) 'Say's Law, Poverty Persistence and Employment Neglect ', *Journal of Human Development and Capabilities* 11(1): 57–67.

Andersen, M.A., J.M. Alston and P.G. Pardey (2009) 'Capital Service Flows: Concepts and Comparisons of Alternative Measures in U.S. Agriculture', Staff Paper P09-8 / InSTePP Paper 09-03. St Paul, MN: Department of Applied Economics and Center for International Science and Technology Practice and Policy, University of Minnesota.

Anttonen, A., L. Häikiö and K. Stefánsson (2012) *Welfare State, Universalism and Diversity.* Cheltenham: Edward Elgar.

Appasamy, P., S. Guhan, R. Hema, M. Majumbar and A. Vaidyanathan (1995) 'Social exclusion in respect of basic needs in India', in G. Rodgers, C. Gore and J.B. Figueiredo (eds), *Social Exclusion: Rhetoric Reality Responses*, pp. 237–250. Geneva: International Labour Organisation.

Appleton, S., L. Song and Q. Xia (2010) 'Growing Out of Poverty: Trends and Patterns of Urban Poverty in China 1988–2002', *World Development* 38(5): 665–678.

Arendt, H. (1951) *The Origins of Totalitarianism.* London: Allen and Unwin.

Arrighi, G. (2003) 'The Social and Political Economy of Global Turbulence', *New Left Review* 20: 5–71.

Arrow, K.J, H.B. Chenery, B.S. Minhas and R.M. Solow (1961). 'Capital-labour Substitution and Economic Efficiency', *Review of Economics and Statistics* 43(3): 225–250.

Atkinson, A.B. (1998) 'Social Exclusion, Poverty and Unemployment', in A.B. Atkinson and J. Hills (eds), 'Exclusion, Employment and Opportunity', CASE Paper 4, January, pp. 1–24.

Atkinson, A.B. and J. Hills (eds) (1998) 'Exclusion, Employment and Opportunity', CASE Paper 4. London: Centre for Analysis of Social Exclusion (CASE), London School of Economics and Political Science.

Bachelet, M. (coord) (2011) *Social protection floor for a fair and inclusive globalization, Report of the Social Protection Floor Advisory Group*. Geneva: International Labour Office.

Bagchi, A.K. (2000) 'Review: Freedom and Development as End of Alienation?', *Economic and Political Weekly* 35(50): 4408–4420.

Banerjee, A.V. (2016) 'Policies for a Better-fed World', *Review of World Economics* 152(1): 3–17.

Banerjee, A.V. and E. Duflo (2007) 'The Economic Lives of the Poor', *Journal of Economic Perspectives* 21(1): 141–167.

Banerjee, A.V. and E. Duflo (2011) *Poor Economics: A Radical Rethinking of the Way to Fight Global Poverty*. New York: PublicAffairs.

Barr, N. (1998) *The Economics of the Welfare State*. Stanford, CA: Stanford University Press.

Barrientos, A. (2013) *Social Assistance in Developing Countries*. Cambridge: Cambridge University Press.

Bateman, M. (2010) *Why Doesn't Microfinance Work? The Destructive Rise of Local Neoliberalism*. London: Zed Books.

Bateman, M. (2012) 'How Lending to the Poor Began, Grew, and Almost Destroyed a Generation in India', *Development and Change* 43(6): 1385–1402.

Bateman, M. (2017) 'Small Loans, Big Problems: The Rise and Fall of Microcredit as Development Policy', *Development and Change* (Virtual Issue): 1–27. DOI: 10.1111/dech.12349.

Baumol, W.J. and W.G. Bowen (1966) *Performing Arts – The Economic Dilemma: A Study of Problems Common to Theater, Opera, Music and Dance*. New York: Twentieth Century Fund.

Beall, J. (2002) 'Globalization and Social Exclusion in Cities: Framing the Debate with Lessons from Africa and Asia', *Environment and Urbanization*, 14(1): 41–52.

Beall, J. and L.H. Piron (2005) 'DFID Social Exclusion Review'. London: Department for International Development.

Berghman, J. (1995) 'Social exclusion in Europe: policy context and analytical framework', in G. Room (ed.), *Beyond the Threshold: The Measurement and Analysis of Social Exclusion*, pp. 10–28. Bristol: Policy Press, University of Bristol.

Bernard, A.B., J.B. Jensen and P.K. Schott (2008) 'Transfer Pricing by U.S.-based Multinational Firms', CES Working Paper 08-29. Washington, DC: Center for Economic Studies.

Besley, T. and R. Burgess (2003) 'Halving Global Poverty', *Journal of Economic Perspectives* 17(3): 3–22.

Bhagwati, J. and T.N. Srinivasan (2002) 'Trade and Poverty in the Poor Countries', *American Economic Review* 92(2): 180–183.

Bhalla, A. and F. Lapeyre (1997) 'Social Exclusion: Towards an Analytical and Operational Framework', *Development and Change* 28(3): 413–433.

Block, F. (2001) 'Introduction', in K. Polanyi, *The Great Transformation: The Political and Economic Origins of Our Time*, pp. xviii–xxxviii. Boston: Beacon.

Brandt, L., J. Huang, G. Li and R. Scott (2002) 'Land Rights in Rural China: Facts, Fictions and Issues', *The China Journal* 47: 67–97.

Braudel, F. (1982) *The Structures of Everyday Life: Civilization and Capitalism, 15th–18th Century*, Volume 1 (original published in 1967, translated by Siân Reynolds). New York: Collins.

Brenner, R. (1998) 'The Economics of Global Turbulence: A Special Report on the World Economy, 1950–98', *New Left Review* I/229 (Special Issue).

Brito, A.S. and C.L. Kerstenetzky (2011) 'Beneficiários do Programa Bolsa Família e Mercado de Trabalho: considerações metodológicas e substantivas', CEDE Discussion Paper No. 21. Rio de Janeiro: Centro de Estudos Sobre Desigualdade e Desenvolvimento, Universidade Federal Fluminense.

Brown, C., M. Ravallion and D. van de Walle (2016) 'A Poor Means Test? Econometric Targeting in Africa', Policy Research Working Paper 7915. Washington, DC: World Bank.

Brys, B., S. Matthews, R. Herd and X. Wang (2013) 'Tax policy and tax reform in the People's Republic of China', OECD Taxation Working Papers No. 18. Paris: Organisation of Economic Cooperation and Development.

Buğra, A. (2015) 'Hayek et Polanyi, sur le destin et le choix', *Sociétés politiques comparées* 37, September–December. www.fasopo.org/sites/default/files/varia3_n37.pdf.

Burchardt, T., J. Le Grand and D. Piachaud (1999) 'Social Exclusion in Britain 1991–1995', *Social Policy and Administration* 33(3): 227–244.

Burchardt, T., J. Le Grand and D. Piachaud (2002) 'Introduction', in J. Hills, J. Le Grand and D. Piachaud (eds), *Understanding Social Exclusion*, pp 1–11. Oxford: Oxford University Press.

Byrne, D. (2005) *Social Exclusion*. Maidenhead: Open University Press.

Chandhoke, N. (2003) 'Governance and the Pluralisation of the State: Implications for Democratic Citizenship', *Economic and Political Weekly* 38(28): 2957–2968.

Chant, S. (2007) *Gender, Generation and Poverty: Exploring the 'Feminisation of Poverty' in Africa, Asia and Latin America*. Cheltenham: Edward Elgar.

Chen, L. and D. Xu (2012) 'Trends in China's reforms: The Rashomon effect', *The Lancet* 379 (March 3): 782–783.

Chen, S. and M. Ravallion (2008) 'The Developing World Is Poorer Than We Thought, But No Less Successful in the Fight against Poverty', Policy Research Working Paper 4703. Washington, DC: World Bank Development Research Group.

Clert, C. (1999) 'Evaluating the Concept of Social Exclusion in Development Discourse', *The European Journal of Development Research* 11(2): 176–199.

Cobham, A. and Sumner, A. (2013) 'Is It All About the Tails? The Palma Measure of Income Inequality', *CGD* Working Paper. Washington, DC: CGD.

Cobham, A. and Sumner, A. (2014) 'Is Inequality all about the Tails? The Palma Measure of Income Inequality', *Significance* 11.1: 10–13.

Cobham, A., L. Schlogl and A. Sumner (2016) 'Inequality and the Tails: The Palma Proposition and Ratio', *Global Policy* 7.1: 201–211.

Cohen, A.J. and G.C. Harcourt (2003) 'Retrospectives: Whatever Happened to the Cambridge Capital Theory Controversies?', *Journal of Economic Perspectives* 17(1): 199–214.

Collier, P. (2007) *The Bottom Billion: Why the Poorest Countries Are Failing and What Can Be Done About It*. Oxford: Oxford University Press.

Corbridge, S. (2002) 'Development as Freedom: The Spaces of Amartya Sen', *Progress in Development Studies* 2(3): 183–217.

Cornia, G.A. (ed.) (2006) *Pro-poor Macroeconomics: Potentials and Limitations.* Basingstoke: Palgrave.

Cornia, G.A., R. Jolly and F. Stewart (eds) (1987) *Adjustment with a Human Face: Protecting the Vulnerable and Promoting Growth, Volume 1.* Oxford: Clarendon Press.

Davis, M. (2000) *Late Victorian Holocausts: El Nino Famines and the Making of the Third World.* London: Verso.

De Soto, H. (1989) *The Other Path: The Invisible Revolution in the Third World.* New York: Harper Collins.

Deacon, B. (2012) 'Shifting Global Social Policy Discourse and Governance in Times of Crisis', in P. Utting, S. Razavi and R. Buchholz (eds), *The Global Crisis and Transformative Social Change*, pp. 81–102. Basingstoke: Palgrave McMillan.

Dean, H. (2009) 'Critiquing Capabilities: The Distractions of a Beguiling Concept', *Critical Social Policy* 29(2): 261–273.

Deaton, A.S. (1997) *The Analysis of Household Surveys: A Micro Econometric Approach to Development Policy.* Washington, DC: World Bank.

Deaton, A.S. (2009) 'Instruments of development: Randomization in the tropics, and the search for the elusive keys to economic development', NBER Working Paper No. 14690, National Bureau of Economic Research, Cambridge, MA, January.

Deaton, A.S. (2010) 'Price indexes, inequality, and the measurement of world poverty', Presidential Address, American Economic Association, Atlanta, 17 January 2010.

Deaton, A. (2013) *The Great Escape: Health, Wealth, and the Origins of Inequality.* Princeton, NJ: Princeton University Press.

Deaton, A. and J. Dreze (2009) 'Nutrition in India: Facts and Interpretations', *Economic and Political Weekly* XLIV(7): 42–65.

Deaton, A. and V. Kozel (2005) 'Data and Dogma: The Great Indian Poverty Debate', *The World Bank Research Observer* 20(2): 177–199.

Devereux, S. (2016) 'Is Targeting Ethical?' *Global Social Policy* 16(2): 166–181.

DFID (2011) 'Cash Transfers', Evidence paper of the Policy Division of DFID. London: Department for International Development.

Di John, J. (2007) 'Albert Hirschman's Exit-Voice Framework and Its Relevance to Problems of Public Education Performance in Latin America', *Oxford Development Studies* 35(3): 295–327.

Dollar, D. and A. Kraay (2002) 'Growth is Good for the Poor', *Journal of Economic Growth* 7(3): 195–225.

Drewnowski, J. (1974) *On Measuring and Planning the Quality of Life.* The Hague: Mouton.

Du, F. (2012) 'Ecological Resettlement of Tibetan Herders in the Sanjiangyuan: A Case Study in Madoi County of Qinghai', *Nomadic Peoples* 16(1): 116–133.

Du Toit, Andries (2004) '"Social Exclusion" Discourse and Chronic Poverty: A South African Case Study', *Development and Change* 35(5): 987–1010.

Dymski, G. (2005) 'Financial Globalization, Social Exclusion and Financial Crisis', *International Review of Applied Economics* 19(4): 439–457.

Dymski, G. (2010) 'Development as Social Inclusion: Reflections on the US Subprime Crisis', *Development* 53(3): 368–375 [8 pages].

Dymski, G.A., J. Hernandez and L. Mohanty (2011) 'Race, Power, and the Subprime/ Foreclosure Crisis: A Mesoanalysis', No. 669, Levy Economics Institute. www.levy institute.org/pubs/wp_669.pdf.

Dyson, T. (1996) *Population and Food: Global Trends and Future Prospects*. London: Routledge.

Dyson, T. (2001) 'A Partial Theory of World Development: The Neglected Role of the Demographic Transition in the Shaping of Modern Society ', *International Journal of Population Geography* 7(2): 67–90.

Dyson, T. (2011) 'The Role of the Demographic Transition in the Process of Urbanization', *Population and Development Review* 37(supplement): 34–54.

Easterly, W. (2000) 'The effect of International Monetary Fund and World Bank programs on poverty', Policy Research working paper, no. WPS 2517. Washington, DC: World Bank.

Easterly, W. (2006a) *The White Man's Burden: Why the West's Efforts to Aid the Rest Have Done So Much Ill and So Little Good*. New York: Penguin.

Easterly, W. (2006b) 'The Big Push Déjà Vu: A Review of Jeffrey Sachs's The End of Poverty: Economic Possibilities for Our Time', *Journal of Economic Literature* 44(1): 96–105.

Economist, The (2012) 'True Progressivism', 13 October.

Economist, The (2018) 'Universal health care, worldwide, is within reach', 26 April.

Edward, P. and A. Sumner (2013) 'The Geography of Inequality: Where and by How Much Has Income Distribution Changed since 1990?', CGD Working Paper 341. Washington, DC: Center for Global Development.

Edward, P. and A. Sumner (2014) 'Estimating the Scale and Geography of Global Poverty Now and in the Future', *World Development* 58: 67–82.

Edward, P. and A. Sumner (2015) 'New Estimates of Global Poverty and Inequality: How Much Difference Do Price Really Make?', CGD Working Paper 403. Washington, DC: Center for Global Development.

Edward, P. and A. Sumner (2016) 'Global Inequality and Global Poverty Since the Cold War: How Robust is the Economic Narrative?', Global Challenges, Working Paper Series No. 1. Bergen: Comparative Research Programme of Poverty, University of Bergen.

Erten, B. (2011) 'North–South Terms-of-Trade Trends from 1960 to 2006', *International Review of Applied Economics* 25(2): 171–184.

Esping-Andersen, G. (1990) *The Three Worlds of Welfare Capitalism*. Cambridge: Polity.

Esser, D. (2014) 'Elusive Accountabilities in the HIV Scale-up: "Ownership" as a Functional Tautology', *Global Public Health* 9(1–2): 43–56.

Esser, D. (2017) 'The Sustainable Development Goals: Elite Pluralism, Not Democratic Governance', BOS Blog, The Business of Society. www.bos-cbscsr.dk/2017/11/13/sustainable-development-goals-elite-pluralism-not-democratic-governance/.

Estes, R.J. (2012) 'Global Change and Indicators of Social Development', in M. Weil (ed.), *The Handbook of Community Practice*, pp. 587–606. Thousand Oaks, CA: Sage Publications.

FAO (2008) 'Methodology for the Measurement of Food Deprivation: Updating the minimum dietary energy requirements', Food and Agriculture Organization of the United Nations, Rome. www.fao.org/fileadmin/templates/ess/documents/food_security_statistics/metadata/undernourishment_methodology.pdf.

FAO (2017) *How Close Are We to #ZeroHunger? The State of Food Security and Nutrition in the World*. Rome: Food and Agriculture Organization of the United Nations.

Felipe, J. (2010) *Inclusive Growth, Full Employment, and Structural Change: Implications and Policies for Developing Asia, Second Edition*. London: Anthem Press.

Felipe, J. and J.S.L. McCombie (2001) 'The CES Production Function, the Accounting Identity, and Occam's Razor', *Applied Economics* 33(10): 1221–1232.

Felipe, J. and J.S.L. McCombie (2003) 'Some Methodological Problems with the Neoclassical Analysis of the East Asian Miracle', *Cambridge Journal of Economics* 27(5): 695–721.

Felipe, J. and J.S.L. McCombie (2006) 'The Tyranny of the Identity: Growth Accounting Revisited', *International Review of Applied Economics* 20(3): 283–299.

Felipe, J. and J.S.L. McCombie (2012) 'Agglomeration Economies, Regional Growth, and the Aggregate Production Function: A Caveat Emptor for Regional Scientists', *Spatial Economic Analysis* 7(4): 461–484.

Felipe, J. and J.S.L. McCombie (2013) *The Aggregate Production Function and the Measurement of Technical Change: 'Not Even Wrong'*. Cheltenham: Edward Elgar.

Ferguson, J. (2015) *Give a Man a Fish: Reflections on the New Politics of Redistribution*. Durham and London: Duke University Press.

Figueroa, A., T. Altamirano and D. Sulmont (eds) (1996) *Social Exclusion and Inequality in Peru*. Geneva/New York: International Institute for Labour Studies and United Nations Development Programme.

Fine, B. (2001) 'Neither the Washington Consensus nor the Post-Washington Consensus: An Introduction', in B. Fine, C. Lapavitsas and J. Pincus (eds), *Development Policy in the Twenty-First Century: Beyond the Post-Washington Consensus*, pp. 1–27. London: Routledge.

Fine, B. (2004) 'Economics and Ethics: Amartya Sen and Point of Departure', *New School Economic Review*, Volume 1(1): 95–103.

Fine, B. and A. Saad-Filho (1975) *Marx's Capital*. London: Pluto Press.

Fischer, A.M. (2005) *State Growth and Social Exclusion in Tibet: Challenges of Recent Economic Growth*. Copenhagen: Nordic Institute of Asian Studies Press.

Fischer, A.M. (2006) 'Subsistence Capacity: the commodification of rural labour re-examined through the case of Tibet', DESTIN Working Paper No. 06–75. London: Development Studies Institute, London School of Economics.

Fischer, A.M. (2008a) 'Resolving the Theoretical Ambiguities of Social Exclusion with reference to Polarisation and Conflict', DESTIN Working Paper No.90. London: London School of Economics.

Fischer, A.M. (2008b) 'Subsistence and Rural Tibetan Household Livelihood Strategies in the Context of Rapid Economic and Social Transition', *Journal of the International Association of Tibet Studies* 4: 1–49.

Fischer, A.M. (2009a) 'Educating for Exclusion in Western China: Structural and institutional foundations of conflict in the Tibetan areas of Qinghai', CRISE Working Paper No. 69. Oxford: Centre for Research on Inequality, Security and Ethnicity.

Fischer, A.M. (2009b) 'Putting Aid in its Place: Insights from Early Structuralists on Aid and Balance of Payments and Lessons for Contemporary Aid Debates', *Journal of International Development* 21(6): 856–867.

Fischer, A.M. (2010a) 'Towards Genuine Universalism within Contemporary Development Policy', *IDS Bulletin* (Special Issue on MDGs and Beyond) 41(1): 36–44.

Fischer, A.M. (2010b) 'The Population Question and Development: the need for a debate in the Netherlands', Final Report on the 2009 SID-WPF-ISS Lecture Series. The Hague: Society for International Development, Netherlands Chapter.

Fischer, A.M. (2010c) 'The Great China Currency Debate: for workers or speculators?' G24 Policy Brief No. 56. Washington, DC: Intergovernmental Group of Twenty-Four.

Fischer, A.M. (2010d) 'Is China Turning Latin? China's Balancing Act between Power and Dependence in the Lead up to Global Crisis', *Journal of International Development* 22(6): 739–757.

Fischer, A.M. (2011a) 'Reconceiving Social Exclusion', BWPI Working Paper No. 146. Manchester: Brooks World Poverty Institute, University of Manchester.

Fischer, A.M. (2011b) 'The Demographic Imperative of Scaling Up Social Protection', paper presented at the conference on Social Protection for Social Justice, Centre for Social Protection, Institute of Development Studies, Brighton, UK (13–15 April).

Fischer, A.M. (2011c) 'Beware the Fallacy of Productivity Reductionism', *European Journal of Development Research* 23(4): 521–526.

Fischer, A.M. (2011d) 'Chinese Savings Gluts or Northern Financialisation? The ideological expediency of crisis narratives', in Peter A.G. van Bergeijk, Arjan de Haan and Rolph van der Hoeven (eds), *The Financial Crisis and Developing Countries: A Global Multidisciplinary Perspective*, Chapter 6, pp. 85–100. Cheltenham: Edward Elgar .

Fischer, A.M. (2012) 'Inequality and the Universalistic Principle in the Post-2015 Development Agenda', official background paper prepared for the global thematic consultation on Addressing Inequalities in the Post-2015 Development Agenda, organised by UNICEF and UN Women (November 2012).

Fischer, A.M. (2013a) 'The Political within the Depoliticised: Poverty Measurement and Implicit Agendas in the MDGs', in M. Langford, A. Sumner and A.E. Yamin (eds), *The MDGs and Human Rights: Past, Present and Future*, pp. 119–142. Cambridge: Cambridge University Press.

Fischer, A.M. (2014a) *The Disempowered Development of Tibet in China: A Study in the Economics of Marginalization.* Lanham, MD: Rowman and Littlefield/Lexington.

Fischer, A.M. (2014b) 'The Social Value of Employment and the Redistributive Imperative for Development', Official Background Paper for the 2014 Human Development Report, UNDP.

Fischer, A.M. (2015) 'The End of Peripheries? On the Enduring Relevance of Structuralism for Understanding Contemporary Global Development', *Development and Change* 46(4): 700–732.

Fischer, A.M. (2016a) 'Aid and the Symbiosis of Global Redistribution and Development: Comparative Historical Lessons from Two Icons of Development Studies', ISS Working Paper No. 618 (AIDSOCPRO working paper No. 1), April 2016.

Fischer, A.M. (2016b) 'On the Macroeconomics of Universalistic Social Policy and Economic and Social Rights', *Global Social Policy* 16(1): 97–104.

Fischer, A.M. (2018a) 'Debt and Development in Historical Perspective: The External Constraints of Late Industrialisation Revisited through South Korea and Brazil', *World Economy* (online, open access. http://onlinelibrary.wiley.com/doi/10.1111/twec.12625/full).

Fischer, A.M. (2018b) 'The Imperial Intentions of Trump's Trade War Babble', ISS Blog, 6 April. Institute of Social Studies, The Hague. https://issblog.nl/2018/04/06/the-imperial-intentions-of-trumps-trade-war-babble-by-andrew-m-fischer.

Fischer, A.M. and A. Zenz (2018) 'The Limits to Buying Stability in Tibet: Tibetan Representation and Preferentiality in China's Contemporary Public Employment System', *China Quarterly* 234: 527–551.

Flores, L. (2015) 'Representation: An Archeology of Poverty for the Present', in A. Roy and E.S. Crane (eds), *Territories of Poverty: Rethinking North and South*, pp. 79–83. Athens, GA: University of Georgia Press.

Foggin, J.M. (2018) 'Environmental Conservation in the Tibetan Plateau Region: Lessons for China's Belt and Road Initiative in the Mountains of Central Asia', *Land* 7(2): 1–34.

Folbre, N. (1986) 'Hearts and Spades: Paradigms of Household Economics', *World Development* 14(2): 245–255.

Folbre, N. (2012) 'Should Women Care Less? Intrinsic Motivation and Gender Inequality', *British Journal of Industrial Relations* 50(4): 597–619.

Folbre, N. and J.A. Nelson (2000) 'For Love or Money – Or Both?', *Journal of Economic Perspectives* 14(4): 123–140.

Fuglie, K.O. and S.L. Wang (2013) 'New Evidence Points to Robust but Uneven Productivity Growth in Global Agriculture', *Global Journal of Emerging Market Economies* 5(1): 23–30.

Furtado C. (1973) 'The Brazilian "Model"', *Social and Economic Studies* 22(1): 122–131.

Furtado, C. (1983) *Accumulation and Development: The Logic of Industrial Civilization.* Oxford: Martin Robertson (translated from 1978 Portuguese version).

Galbraith, James K. (1998) *Created Unequal: The Crisis in American Pay.* New York: The Free Press.

Galbraith, James K. (2012) *Inequality and Instability: A Study of the World Economy Just Before the Great Crisis.* New York: Oxford University Press.

Galbraith, John K. (1992) *The Culture of Contentment.* Boston: Houghton Mifflin.

Gerschenkron, A. (1962) *Economic Backwardness in Historical Perspective.* Cambridge: Harvard University Press.

Ghai, D. and Alcántara, C.H. (1990) 'The Crisis of the 1980s in Sub-Saharan Africa, Latin America and the Caribbean: Economic Impact, Social Change and Political Implications', *Development and Change* 21(3): 389–426.

Ghosh, J. (2011) 'Dealing with "The Poor"', *Development and Change* 42(3): 849–858.

Ghosh, J. (2018) 'A Note on Estimating Income Inequality across Countries Using PPP Exchange Rates', *The Economic and Labour Relations Review* 29(1): 1–14.

GOI (2009) 'Report of the Expert Group to Review the Methodology for Estimation of Poverty', New Delhi: Planning Commission, Government of India.

Goodin, R.E. and J. Le Grand, Julian (1987) *Not Only the Poor: The Middle Classes and the Welfare State.* London: Allen & Unwin.

Goodwin, G. (2018) 'Rethinking the Double Movement: Expanding the Frontiers of Polanyian Analysis in the Global South', *Development and Change*, online early view. https://doi.org/10.1111/dech.12419.

Gordon, D. (2006) 'The concept and measurement of poverty', in C. Pantazis, D. Gordon and R. Levitas (eds), *Poverty and Social Exclusion in Britain: The Millennium Survey*, pp. 29–70. Bristol: The Policy Press, University of Bristol.

Gore, C. (1995) 'Introduction: Markets, citizenship, and social exclusion', in G. Rodgers, C. Gore and J.B. Figueiredo (eds), *Social Exclusion: Rhetoric Reality Responses*, pp. 1–40. Geneva: International Labour Organisation.

Gore, C. and J.B. Figueiredo (eds) (1997) *Social Exclusion and Anti-poverty Policy: A Debate.* Geneva: International Institute for Labour Studies.

Gray, H. (2018) *Turbulence and Order in Economic Development: Institutions and Economic Transformation in Tanzania and Vietnam.* Oxford: Oxford University Press.

Gready, P. (2008) 'Rights-based Approaches to Development: What Is the Value-Added?', *Development in Practice* 18(6): 735–747.

Green, M. (2007) 'Representing poverty and attacking representations: Perspectives on poverty from social anthropology', in D. Hulme and J. Toye (eds), *Understanding Poverty and Well-Being: Bridging the Disciplines*, pp. 24–45. London: Routledge.

Grosh, M. and J. Baker (1995) 'Proxy Means Tests for Targeting Social Programs: Simulations and Speculation', Living Standards and Measurement Study Working Paper 118. Washington, DC: World Bank.

Günther, I. and M. Grimm (2007) 'Measuring Pro-Poor Growth when Relative Prices Shift', *Journal of Development Economics* 82(1): 245–256.

Hall, A.L. and J. Midgley (2004) *Social Policy for Development.* London: Sage.

Hanlon, J., A. Barrientos and D. Hulme (2010). *Just Give Money to the Poor: The Development Revolution from the Global South.* Sterling, VA: Kumarian.

Harriss, J. (2007) 'Bringing politics back into poverty analysis: Why understanding social relations matters more for policy on chronic poverty than measurement', CPRC Working Paper 77. Chronic Poverty Research Centre.

Harriss-White, B. (2005) 'Working Paper Number 134, Poverty and Capitalism', QEH Working Paper Series – QEHWPS134. Oxford: Queen Elizabeth House, University of Oxford.

Haughton, J. and S.R. Khandker (2009) *Handbook on Poverty and Inequality.* Washington, DC: World Bank.

Heintz, J. (2008) 'Revisiting Labour Markets: Implications for Macroeconomics and Social Protection', *IDS Bulletin* 39(2): 11–17.

Helwege, A. and M.B.L. Birch (2007) 'Declining Poverty in Latin America? A Critical Analysis of New Estimates by International Institutions', Global Development and Environment Institute Working Paper No.07-02. Medford, MA: Tufts University.

Heumann, L. (2014) 'The Science Delusion, An interview with cultural critic Curtis White', *Tricycle.* https://tricycle.org/magazine/science-delusion/.

Hickel, J. (2016) 'The True Extent of Global Poverty and Hunger: Questioning the Good News Narrative of the Millennium Development Goals', *Third World Quarterly* 37(5): 749–767.

Hickel, J. (2017) 'Is Global Inequality Getting Better or Worse? A Critique of the World Bank's Convergence Narrative', *Third World Quarterly* 38(10): 2208–2222.

Hickey, S and A. Du Toit (2007) 'Adverse Incorporation, Social Exclusion and Chronic Poverty', CPRC Working Paper 81. Chronic Poverty Research Centre.

Hill, P. (1966) 'A Plea for Indigenous Economics: The West African Example', *Economic Development and Cultural Change* 15(1): 10–20.

Hill, P. (1986) *Development Economics on Trial: The Anthropological Case for a Prosecution.* Cambridge: Cambridge University Press.

Hills, J. (1998) 'Does Income Mobility Mean That We Do Not Need to Worry About Poverty?', in A.B. Atkinson and J. Hills (eds) 'Exclusion, Employment and Opportunity', CASE Paper 4, pp. 34–55. London: Centre for Analysis of Social Exclusion (CASE), London School of Economics and Political Science.

Hills, J., J. Le Grand and D. Piachaud (eds) (2002) *Understanding Social Exclusion.* Oxford: Oxford University Press.

Himanshu (2007) 'Recent Trends in Poverty and Inequality: Some Preliminary Results', *Economic and Political Weekly* 42(6): 497–508.

Himanshu (2008) 'What Are These New Poverty Estimates and What Do They Imply?', *Economic and Political Weekly* 43(25): 38–43.

Himanshu (2010) 'Towards New Poverty Lines for India', *Economic and Political Weekly* 45(1): 38–48.

Himanshu and A. Sen (2004) 'Poverty and Inequality in India: Parts I and II', *Economic and Political Weekly* 39(38): 4247–4263.

Himanshu and K. Sen (2014) 'Revisiting the Great Indian Poverty Debate: Measurement, Patterns, and Determinants', Brooks World Poverty Institute Working Paper No. 203, Manchester.

Hirschman, A.O. (1970) *Exit, Voice, and Loyalty: Responses to Decline in Firms, Organizations, and States*. Cambridge, MA: Harvard University Press.

Hirway, I. (2003) 'Identification of BPL Households for Poverty Alleviation Programmes', *Economic and Political Weekly* 38(45): 4803–4808.

Hujo, K. and E. Gaia (2011) 'Social Policy and Poverty: An Introduction', *International Journal of Social Welfare* 20(3): 230–239.

Hussain, A. (2002) *Poverty Profile and Social Security in China: Final Report*. London: Asia Research Centre, London School of Economics.

Hussain, A. (2003) 'Urban Poverty in China: Measurement, Patterns and Policies'. Geneva: International Labour Office.

İlkkaracan, İ (2012a) 'Why so Few Women in the Labor Market in Turkey?', *Feminist Economics* 18(1): 1–37.

İlkkaracan, İ (2012b) 'Work–Family Balance and Public Policy: A Cross-country Perspective', *Development* 55(3): 325–332.

IMF (2017) *IMF Framework on Social Spending*. Washington, DC: International Monetary Fund.

Jackson, C. (1996) 'Rescuing Gender from the Poverty Trap', *World Development* 24(3): 489–504.

Jackson, C. (1999) 'Social Exclusion and Gender: Does One Size Fit All?', *The European Journal of Development Research* 11(1): 125–146.

Jerven, M. (2013) *Poor Numbers: How We Are Misled by African Development Statistics and What to Do about It*. Ithaca, NY: Cornell University Press.

Jerven, M. (2015) *Africa: Why Economists Get it Wrong*. London: Zed Books.

Jolliffe, D. and U. Serajuddin (2018) 'Noncomparable Poverty Comparison', *The Journal of Development Studies* 54(3): 523–536.

JPIT (2018) 'Universal Credit: increasing hunger by design', briefing released by the Joint Public Issues Team, Churches Working Together for Peace and Justice, London. www.jointpublicissues.org.uk/wp-content/uploads/2018/07/Universal-Credit-Increasing-Poverty-by-Design-Version-4.pdf.

Kabeer, N. (1994) *Reversed Realities: Gender Hierarchies in Development Thought*. London and New York: Verso

Kabeer, N. (2006) 'Social Exclusion and the MDGs: The Challenge of "Durable Inequalities" in the Asian Context', paper presented at the Asia 2015 Conference, London, March 2006.

Kanbur, R. and A. Sumner (2012) 'Poor Countries or Poor People? Development Assistance and the New Geography of Global Poverty', *Journal of International Development* 24(6): 686–695.

Kay, C. (2002) 'Why East Asia Overtook Latin America: Agrarian Reform, Industrialization and Development', *Third World Quarterly* 23(6): 1073–1102.

Kay, C. (2005) 'Celso Furtado: Pioneer of Structuralist Development Theory', *Development and Change* 36(6): 1201–1207.

Kerr, G. (2016) '"Predistribution", Property-owning Democracy and Land Value Taxation', *Politics, Philosophy and Economics* 15(1): 67–91.

Kerstenetzky, C.L. (2009) 'Redistribuição e desenvolvimento? A economia política do programa bolsa família', *Dados* 52(1): 53–83.

Kerstenetzky, C.L. (2011) 'Redistribution and Development? The Political Economy of the Bolsa Família Program', *Dados* 5.

Khan, A.R. and C. Riskin (2001) *Inequality and Poverty in China in the Age of Globalization.* Oxford: Oxford University Press.

Khan, M. (2002) 'Corruption and Governance in Early Capitalism: World Bank Strategies and their Limitations', in J. Pincus and J. Winters (eds), *Reinventing the World Bank*, pp. 164–184. New York: Cornell University Press.

Khan, M. (2006) 'Governance and Anti-Corruption Reforms in Developing Countries: Policies, Evidence and Ways Forward', G-24 Discussion Paper Series No. 42. Geneva: United Nations Conference on Trade and Development.

Kiely, R. (2007) 'Poverty Reduction through Liberalisation? Neoliberalism and the Myth of Global Convergence', *Review of International Studies* 33(3): 415–434.

Kiely, R. (2018) *The Neoliberal Paradox.* Cheltenham: Edward Elgar.

Kingdon, G.G. and J. Knight (2007) 'Subjective Well-Being Poverty vs. Income Poverty and Capabilities Poverty?', in D. Hulme and J. Toye (eds), *Understanding Poverty and Well-Being: Bridging the Disciplines*, pp. 115–140. London: Routledge.

Kobiyama, N. (2013) 'The Obesity-Poverty Nexus in Development', MA Research Paper, Institute of Social Studies, Erasmus University Rotterdam, The Hague.

Korpi, W. and J. Palme (1998) 'The Paradox of Redistribution and Strategies of Equality: Welfare State Institutions, Inequality, and Poverty in the Western Countries', *American Sociological Review* 63(5): 661–687.

Kuznets, S. (1955) 'Economic Growth and Income Inequality', *American Economic Review* 45(1): 1–28.

Kwon, H.J. (ed.) (2005) *Transforming the Developmental Welfare State in East Asia: Social Policy in a Development Context.* London: Palgrave Macmillan.

Laderchi, C.R., R. Saith and F. Stewart (2003) 'Does It Matter that We Do Not Agree on the Definition of Poverty? A Comparison of Four Approaches', *Oxford Development Studies* 31(3): 243–274.

Langford, M. (2009) 'Social Security and Children: Testing the Boundaries of Human Rights and Economics', in S. Marks, B. Andrassen and A. Sengupta (eds), *Freedom from Poverty as a Human Right: Economic Perspectives*, pp. 193–217. Paris: UNESCO Publishing.

Langford, M. (2010) 'A Poverty of Rights: Six Ways to Fix the MDGs', *IDS Bulletin* 41(1): 83–91.

Lavinas, L. (2006) 'From Means-Test Schemes to Basic Income in Brazil: Exceptionality and Paradox', *International Social Security Review* 59(3): 103–125.

Lavinas, L. (2013) '21st Century Welfare', *New Left Review* 84 (Nov–Dec): 5–40.

Lavinas, L. (2017) *The Takeover of Social Policy by Financialization: The Brazilian Paradox.* New York: Palgrave MacMillan.

Lenoir, R. (1974) *Les Exclus: Un Français Sur Dix.* Vol. 13. Seuil.

Levien, M. (2018) 'Reconstructing Polanyi?' *Development and Change*, 49: 1115–1126.

Levitas, R. (1996) 'The Concept of Social Exclusion and the New Durkheimian Hegemony', *Critical Social Policy* 16(46): 1–20.

Levitas, R. (2006) 'The Concept and Measurement of Social Exclusion', in C. Pantazis, D. Gordon and R. Levitas (eds), *Poverty and Social Exclusion in Britain. The Millennium Survey*, pp. 123–162. Bristol: Policy Press.

Levy, S. (2006) *Progress Against Poverty: Sustaining Mexico's Progresa/Oportunidades Program*. Washington, DC: Brookings Institution Press.

Lewis, W.A. (1954) 'Economic Development with Unlimited Supplies of Labor', *Manchester School of Economic and Social Studies* 22(2): 139–191.

Lewis, W.A. (1978) *The Evolution of the International Economic Order*. Princeton, NJ: Princeton University Press.

Li, T.M. (2007) *The Will to Improve: Governmentality, Development, and the Practice of Politics*. Durham and London: Duke University Press.

Li, T.M. (2017) 'After Development: Surplus Population and the Politics of Entitlement', *Development and Change* 48(6): 1247–1261.

Lin, V. (2012) 'Transformations in the Healthcare System in China', *Current Sociology* 60(4): 427–440.

Lipton, M., S. Maxwell, J. Edström and H. Hatashima (1992) 'The New Poverty Agenda: An Overview', IDS Discussion Paper. Brighton: Institute of Development Studies.

Lu, C. (2010) 'Who is Poor in China? A Comparison of Alternative Approaches to Poverty Assessment in Rural Yunnan', *The Journal of Peasant Studies* 37(2): 407–428.

Mackintosh, M. (2006) 'Commercialisation, Inequality and the Limits to Transition in Health Care: A Polanyian Framework for Policy Analysis', *Journal of International Development* 18(3): 393–406.

Maddison, A. (2001) *The World Economy: A Millennial Perspective*. Paris: Organisation for Economic Co-operation and Development, Development Centre.

Mader, P. (2015) *The Political Economy of Microfinance: Financializing Poverty*. Basingstoke: Palgrave Macmillan UK.

Mader, P. (2018) 'Contesting Financial Inclusion', *Development and Change* 49(2): 461–483.

Mann, M. (1986) *The Sources of Social Power: Volume 1, A History of Power from the Beginning to AD 1760*. Cambridge: Cambridge University Press.

Mann, M. (1993) *The Sources of Social Power: Volume 2, The Rise of Classes and Nation States 1760–1914*. Cambridge: Cambridge University Press.

Mann, M. (2005) *The Dark Side of Democracy: Explaining Ethnic Cleansing*. Cambridge: Cambridge University Press.

Martinez Franzoni, J. and D. Sanchez-Ancochea (2014) 'Should Policy Aim at Having All People on the Same Boat? The Definition, Relevance and Challenges of Universalism in Latin America', desiguALdades.net Working Paper Series 70, International Research Network on Interdependent Inequalities in Latin America, Berlin.

Martinez Franzoni, J. and D. Sanchez-Ancochea (2016) *The Quest for Universal Social Policy in the South. Actors, Ideas and Architectures*. Cambridge: Cambridge University Press.

Meenakshi, J.V. and B. Vishwanathan (2003) 'Calorie Deprivation in Rural India: 1983–1999/2000', *Economic and Political Weekly* 38(3): 369–375.

Mehrotra, S. (2000) 'Integrating Economic and Social Policy: Good Practices from High Achieving Countries', Innocenti Working Paper No. 80. Florence: UNICEF Innocenti Research Centre.

Merrick, R. (2018) 'Ministers have shelved a plan to cut benefit sanctions, sending poorest to food banks', *The Independent*, 3 March 2018. www.independent.co.uk/news/uk/politics/benefits-sanctions-cut-number-dwp-department-work-pensions-hunger-home-eviction-a8237131.html.

Milanovic, B. (2011) 'More or Less', *Finance and Development* 48(3): 6–11.

Mkandawire, T. (2001) 'Social Policy in a Development Context', Social Policy and Development Programme Paper No. 7, June. United Nations Research Institute for Social Development, Geneva.

Mkandawire, T. (2004) 'Social Policy in a Development Context: Introduction', in T. Mkandawire (ed.), *Social Policy in a Development Context*, pp. 1–36. New York: Palgrave Macmillan.

Mkandawire, T. (2005) 'Targeting and Universalism in Poverty Reduction', Social Policy and Development Programme Paper No. 23. Geneva: United Nations Research Institute for Social Development.

Mkandawire, T. (2014) 'Can Africa Turn from Recovery to Development?' *Current History* (May): 171–177.

Morris, M.D. (1979) *Measuring the Condition of the World's Poor: The Physical Quality of Life Index*. New York: Pergamon Press.

Moyo, D. (2009) *Dead Aid: Why Aid Is Not Working and How There Is a Better Way for Africa*. New York: Farrar, Straus and Giroux.

Mukerjee, M. (2010) *Churchill's Secret War: The British Empire and the Ravaging of India during World War II*. New York: Basic Books.

Mukherjee, R. (1974) *The Rise and Fall of the East India Company: A Sociological Appraisal*. New York: Monthly Review Press.

Myrdal, G. (1957) *Economic Theory and the Underdeveloped Regions*. London: University Paperbacks, Methuen.

NAO (2018) 'Rolling out Universal Credit: Report by the Comptroller and Auditor General', HC 1123, Session 2017–2019, 15 June 2018, National Audit Office, London.

Ndikumana, L. and J.K. Boyce (2011) 'Capital flight from sub-Saharan Africa: linkages with external borrowing and policy options', *International Review of Applied Economics* 25(2): 149–170.

Nicholas, H.V.B. (2011) *Marx's Theory of Price and its Modern Rivals*. Basingstoke: Palgrave Macmillan.

Nishida, C. and P. Mucavele (2005) 'Monitoring the Rapidly Emerging Public Health Problem of Overweight and Obesity: The WHO Global Data-base on Body Mass Index', *SCN News* 29: 5–11. Geneva: United Nations System Standing Committee on Nutrition.

North, D.C. (1990) *Institutions, Institutional Change and Economic Performance*. Cambridge: Cambridge University Press.

North, D.C. (1995) 'New Institutional Economics and Third World Development', in John Harriss, Janet Hunter and Colin Lewis (eds), *The New Institutional Economics and Third World Development*. London: Routledge, pp. 17–26.

O'Brien, D., J. Wilkes, A. de Haan and S. Maxwell (1997) 'Poverty and Social Exclusion in North and South', IDS Working Paper 55. Brighton: Institute of Development Studies.

Ocampo, J.A. (2012) 'Review of M. Bachelet (coord.), *Social protection floor for a fair and inclusive globalization, Report of the Social Protection Floor Advisory Group*', *International Social Security Review* 65(4): 107–111.

O'Neill, M. and T. Williamson (2012) 'The Promise of Predistribution', Policy Network.

Ostry, J. D., Loungani, P. and Furceri, D. (2016) 'Neoliberalism: Oversold?' *Finance and Development* (June): 38–41.

Palacio Ludeña, M.G. (2017) 'A matter of choice? Cash Transfers and Narratives of Dependence in the Lives of Women in Southern Ecuador', PhD Thesis, Institute of Social Studies, Erasmus University Rotterdam, The Hague.

Pantazis, C., D. Gordon and R. Levitas (2006) 'Introduction', in C. Pantazis, G. David and R. Levitas (eds), *Poverty and Social Exclusion in Britain. The Millennium Survey*, pp. 1–28. Bristol: Policy Press.

Parker, J. (2015) 'Why don't households smooth consumption? Evidence from a 25 million-dollar experiment', NBER Working Paper Series No. w21369. Cambridge, MA: National Bureau of Economic Research.

Pasinetti, L. (2007), *Keynes and the Cambridge Keynesians: A 'Revolution in Economics' to be Accomplished.* Cambridge: Cambridge University Press.

Peck, J. (2010) *Constructions of Neoliberal Reason.* Oxford: Oxford University Press.

Peck, J. and N. Theodore (2015) 'Paying for Good Behaviour: Cash Transfer Policies in the Wild', in A. Roy and E.S. Crane (eds), *Territories of Poverty: Rethinking North and South*, pp. 103–125. Athens, GA: University of Georgia Press.

Piketty, T. (2014) *Capital in the Twenty-First Century.* Cambridge, MA: Belknap Press.

Plotnick, R. (1982) 'The Concept and Measurement of Horizontal Inequity', *Journal of Public Economics* 17(3): 373–391.

Pogge, T. (2010) *Politics as Usual: What Lies behind the Pro-Poor Rhetoric.* Cambridge: Polity Press.

Pogge, T. and S.G. Reddy (2002a) 'How *Not* to Count the Poor' (Version 3.0). New York: Barnard College (mimeo).

Pogge, T. and S.G. Reddy (2002b) 'How Not to Count the Poor! A Reply to Ravallion'. www.columbia.edu/~sr793/poggereddyreply.pdf (last accessed November 2009).

Polanyi Levitt, K. (2000) 'The Right to Development', Fifth Sir Arthur Lewis Memorial Lecture, Eastern Caribbean Central Bank, St Lucia (8 November).

Polanyi, K. (2001 [1944]) *The Great Transformation: The Political and Economic Origins of Our Time.* Boston: Beacon Press.

Prasad, E., K. Rogoff, S.J. Wei and M.A. Kose (2003) 'Effects of Financial Globalization on Developing Countries: Some Empirical Evidence', International Monetary Fund, 17 March 2003. www.imf.org/external/np/res/docs/2003/031703.pdf.

(Prebisch) United Nations Economic Commission for Latin America (1950) *Economic Development of Latin America and Its Principal Problems.* Lake Success, NY: United Nations, Department of Economic Affairs.

Ptackova, J. (2016) 'Making Space for Development: A Study on Resettlement from the Longyangxia Water Reservoir Area of Qinghai Province', *Inner Asia* 18(1): 152–166.

Putzel, J. (2000) 'Land Reforms in Asia: Lessons from the past for the 21st Century', Working Paper no.4, Working Paper series, LSE Development Studies Institute, London School of Economics, London.

Randall, S. and E. Coast (2015) 'Poverty in African Households: The Limits of Survey and Census Representations', *The Journal of Development Studies* 51(2): 162–177.

Ravallion, M. (1992) 'Poverty Comparisons: A Guide to Concepts and Methods', LSMS Working Paper No. 88. Washington, DC: World Bank.

Ravallion, M. (2002) 'How Not to Count the Poor? A Reply to Reddy and Pogge' (mimeo).

Ravallion, M. (2010) 'The Developing World's Bulging (but Vulnerable) Middle Class', *World Development* 38(4): 445–454.

Reddy, S.G., S. Visaria and M. Asali (2006) 'Inter-Country Comparisons of Poverty Based on a Capability Approach: An Empirical Exercise', Boston University – Department of Economics Working Paper No. 038. Boston, MA: Boston University.

Ringen, S., H.J. Kwon, I. Yi, T. Kim and J. Lee (2011) *The Korean State and Social Policy: How South Korea Lifted Itself from Poverty and Dictatorship to Affluence and Democracy*. Oxford: Oxford University Press.

Robinson, J. (1936) 'Disguised Unemployment', *The Economic Journal* 46(182): 225–237.

Rodger, J.J. (2012) '"Regulating the Poor": Observations on the "Structural Coupling" of Welfare, Criminal Justice and the Voluntary Sector in a "Big Society"', *Social Policy and Administration* 46(4): 413–431.

Rodgers, G. (1995) 'What is special about a "social exclusion" approach?', in G. Rodgers, C. Gore and J.B. Figueiredo (eds), *Social Exclusion: Rhetoric Reality Responses*, pp. 43–55. Geneva: International Labour Organisation.

Rodgers, G., C. Gore and J.B. Figueiredo (eds) (1995) *Social Exclusion: Rhetoric Reality Responses*. Geneva: International Labour Organisation.

Roelen, K. (2017) 'Monetary and Multidimensional Child Poverty: A Contradiction in Terms?', *Development and Change* 48: 502–533.

Room, G.J. (1994) 'Poverty Studies in the European Union: Retrospect and Prospect', paper presented at a meeting on Understanding Social Exclusion: Lessons from Transnational Research Studies. London: Policy Studies Institute (24 November).

Room, G.J. (1995a), 'Poverty in Europe: Competing Paradigms of Analysis', *Policy and Politics* 23(2): 103–113.

Room, G.J. (ed.) (1995b) *Beyond the Threshold: The Measurement and Analysis of Social Exclusion*. Bristol: The Policy Press, University of Bristol.

Room, G.J. (1999) 'Social Exclusion, Solidarity and the Challenge of Globalization', *International Journal of Social Welfare* 8(3): 166–74.

Rosenstein-Rodan, P.N. (1956–1957) 'Disguised Unemployment and Underemployment in Agriculture', *Monthly Bulletin of Agricultural Economics and Statistics* 6(7–8): 1–7.

Rothstein, B. (2001) 'The Universal Welfare State as a Social Dilemma', *Rationality and Society* 13(2): 213–233.

Roulleau-Berger, L. (1999) *Le travail en friche. Les mondes de la petite production urbaine*. La Tour d'Aigues: Editions de l'Aube.

Rowntree, B.S. (1901) *Poverty: A Study of Town Life*. London: Macmillan and Co.

Roy, A. (2010) *Poverty Capital: Microfinance and the Making of Development*. London: Routledge.

Roy, A. and E.S. Crane (eds) (2015) *Territories of Poverty: Rethinking North and South*. Athens, GA: University of Georgia Press.

Saad-Filho, A. (2015) 'Social Policy for Neoliberalism: The Bolsa Família Programme in Brazil', *Development and Change* 46(6): 1227–1252.

Sachs, J.D. (2005) *The End of Poverty: Economic Possibilities of Our Time*. London: Penguin.

Saith, A. (2005) 'Poverty Lines versus the Poor: Method versus Meaning', *Economic and Political Weekly* 40(43): 4601–4610.

Saith, A. (2006) 'From Universal Values to Millennium Development Goals: Lost in Translation', *Development and Change* (37)6: 1167–1199.

Saith, R. (2001) 'Social Exclusion: The Concept and Application to Developing Countries', QEH Working Paper Series No. 72. Oxford: Oxford: Queen Elizabeth House, University of Oxford.

Samuelson, P. (1966) 'A Summing Up', *Quarterly Journal of Economics* 80(4): 568–583.

Sathyamala, C. (2016) *Nutrition: Contested Meanings, A Theoretical and Empirical Enquiry*. PhD thesis, Institute of Social Studies, Erasmus University Rotterdam, The Hague.

Satterthwaite D. (2004) 'The Under-estimation of Urban Poverty in Low and Middle-income Nations.' Human Settlements Working Paper Series Poverty Reduction in Urban Areas No. 14. IIED, London.

Schulte, B. (2002) 'A European definition of poverty: the fight against poverty and social exclusion in the member state of the European Union', in P. Townsend and D. Gordon (eds) *World Poverty: New Policies to Defeat an Old Enemy*, pp. 119–145. Bristol: The Policy Press, University of Bristol.

Scott, J.C. (1976) *The Moral Economy of the Peasant: Rebellion and Subsistence in Southeast Asia*. New Haven, CT: Yale University Press.

Scott, J.C. (1998) *Seeing Like a State: How Certain Schemes to Improve the Human Condition Have Failed (1st edn)*. New Haven, CT, and London: Yale University Press.

Sen, A. (1977) 'Starvation and Exchange Entitlements: A General Approach and Its Application to the Great Bengal Famine', *Cambridge Journal of Economics* 1977(1): 33–59.

Sen, A.K. (1983) 'Poor, Relatively Speaking', *Oxford Economic Papers* 35(2): 153–169.

Sen, A.K. (1985) 'A Sociological Approach to the Measurement of Poverty, a Reply to Professor Peter Townsend', *Oxford Economic Papers* 37(4): 669–676.

Sen, A.K. (1999) *Development as Freedom*. Oxford: Oxford University Press.

Sen, A.K. (2000) 'Social Exclusion: Concept, Application and Scrutiny', Social Development Papers No. 1. Manila: Office of Environment and Social Development, Asian Development Bank.

Shorrocks, A. (1995) 'Revisiting the Sen Poverty Index', *Econometrica* 63(5): 1225–1230.

Silver, H. (1995) 'Reconceptualizing Social Disadvantage: Three Paradigms of Social Exclusion', in G. Rodgers, C. Gore and J.B. Figuerido (eds), *Social Exclusion: Rhetoric, Reality, Responses*, pp. 57–80. Geneva/New York: IILS/UNDP.

Skocpol, T. (1991) 'Targeting Within Universalism: Politically Viable Policies to Combat Poverty in the United States', in C. Jencks and P.E. Peterson (eds), *The Urban Underclass*, pp. 411–436. Washington, DC: The Brookings Institution.

Skoufias, E. (2005) 'PROGRESA and its Impacts on the Welfare of Rural Households in Mexico', IFPRI Research Report No. 139. Washington, DC: International Food Policy Research Institute.

Soares, S., P.H.G. Ferreira de Souza, R.G. Osório and F.G. Silveira (2010) 'Os Impactos Do Benefício Do Programa Bolsa Família Sobre a Desigualdade e a Pobreza', in J. Abrahão de Castro and L. Modesto (eds), *Bolsa Família 2003–2010: avanços e desafios, Volume 2*, pp. 25–52. Brasília: Instituto de Pesquisa Econômica Aplicada.

Sodnamkyid and E.R. Sułek (2017) '"Everything Costs Money": Livelihood and Economics in the "New Resettled Village" of Sogrima, Golok (Qinghai Province)', *Nomadic Peoples* 21(1): 136–151 (16).

Solow, R.M. (1957) 'Technical Change and the Aggregate Production Function', *Review of Economics and Statistics* 39(3): 312–320.

Souza, C. (2006) 'Evaluation of the National Human Development Report System: Case Study, Brazil'. New York: Evaluation Office, United Nations Development Programme.

Spivak, G.C. (1988) 'Can the Subaltern Speak?', in C. Nelson and L. Grossberg (eds), *Marxism and the Interpretation of Culture*, pp. 66–111. London: Macmillan.

Stamsø, M.A. (2009) 'Housing and the Welfare State in Norway', *Scandinavian Political Studies* 32(2): 195–220.

Stein, J. and T. Jan (2018) 'The Trump administration has a new argument for dismantling the social safety net: It worked', *The Washington Post*, 14 July 2018.

Stewart, F. (2002) 'Horizontal Inequalities: A Neglected Dimension of Development', CRISE Working Paper No.1. Oxford: Queen Elizabeth House, University of Oxford.

Stewart, F., M. Barron, G. Brown and M. Hartwell (2006) 'Social Exclusion and Conflict: Analysis and Policy Implications', CRISE Policy Paper. Oxford: Queen Elizabeth House, University of Oxford.

Stiglitz, J.E. (1986) 'The New Development Economics', *World Development* 14(2): 257–265.

Sukhatme, P.V. and S. Margen (1978) 'Models for Protein Efficiency', *The American Journal of Clinical Nutrition* 31: 1237–1256.

Sukhatme, P.V. and S. Margen (1982) 'Autoregulatory Homeostatic Nature of Energy Balance', *The American Journal of Clinical Nutrition* 35(2): 355–365.

Sumner, A. (2010) 'Global Poverty and the New Bottom Billion: What if Three-Quarters of the World's Poor Live in Middle-Income Countries?', IDS Working Paper. Brighton: IDS.

Sumner, A. (2016) *Global Poverty: Deprivation, Distribution, and Development Since the Cold War*. Oxford: Oxford University Press.

Sumner, A. (2017) 'The Developer's Dilemma: The Inequality Dynamics of Structural Transformation and Inclusive Growth', ESRC GPID Network Working Paper. London: King's College London.

Székely, M., N. Lustig, M. Cumpa and J.A. Mejía (2000) 'Do We Know How Much Poverty There Is?', Inter-American Development Bank Working Paper No. 437. Washington, DC: Inter-American Development Bank.

Tauger, M.B. and A. Sen (2011) 'The Bengal Famine', *The New York Review of Books*, 12 May 2011. www.nybooks.com/articles/2011/05/12/bengal-famine/.

Titmuss, R.M. (1968) *Commitment to Welfare*. New York: Pantheon.

Townsend, P. (1979) *Poverty in the United Kingdom: A Survey of Household Resources and Standards of Living*. Harmondsworth: Penguin.

Townsend, P. (1985) 'A Sociological Approach to the Measurement of Poverty: A Rejoinder to Professor Amartya Sen', *Oxford Economic Papers* 37(4): 659–668.

Townsend, P. (1993) *The International Analysis of Poverty*. Hemel Hempstead: Harvester Wheatsheaf.

Townsend, P. (2002) 'Poverty, social exclusion and social polarisation: the need to construct an international welfare state', in P. Townsend and D. Gordon (eds), *World Poverty: New Policies to Defeat an Old Enemy*, pp. 3–24. Bristol: The Policy Press, University of Bristol.

Townsend, P. (2006) 'Introduction', in *Compendium of Best Practices in Poverty Measurement*, pp. 15–28. Rio de Janeiro: Expert Group on Poverty Statistics.

Triplett, J.E. and B.P. Bosworth (2003) 'Productivity Measurement Issues in Services Industries: "Baumol's Disease" Has Been Cured', *FRBNY Economic Policy Review* (September): 23–33.

Ul Haq, M. (1976) *The Poverty Curtain: Choices for the Third World*. New York: Columbia University Press.

UNDG (2003) *The Human Rights Based Approach to Development Cooperation: Towards a Common Understanding Among UN Agencies*. New York: United Nations Development Group.

UNDP (2013) *Human Development Report 2013, The Rise of the South: Human Progress in a Diverse World*. New York: United Nations Development Programme.

UNESCO (2015) *Global Education Monitoring Report 2016 – Education for People and Planet: Creating Sustainable Futures for All*. Paris: United Nations Educational, Scientific and Cultural Organization.

UNRISD (2010) *Combating Poverty and Inequality: Structural Change, Social Policy and Politics*. Geneva: United Nations Research Institute on Social Development.

Van Doorslaer, E. (2005) 'Paying Out-of-Pocket for Health Care in Asia: Catastrophic and Poverty Impact', EQUITAP Project Working Paper No. 2. Equity in Asia-Pacific Health Systems.

van Gent, W., C. Hochstenbach and J. Uitermark (2018) 'Exclusion as Urban Policy: The Dutch "Act on Extraordinary Measures for Urban Problems"', *Urban Studies* 55(11). https://doi.org/10.1177/0042098017717214.

Wade, R.H. (2004) 'Is Globalization Reducing Poverty and Inequality?', *World Development* 32(4): 567–589.

Wade, R.H. (2014) 'The Piketty Phenomenon: Why Has Capital Become a Publishing Sensation?' *International Affairs* 90:5 (2014): 1069–1083.

Wagner, D.A. (2018) *Learning as Development: Rethinking International Education in a Changing World*. New York and London: Routledge.

Wang, S. (2004) 'China's Health System: From Crisis to Opportunity', *Yale-China Health Journal* 3(Autumn 2004): 5–49.

Warren, B. (1980) *Imperialism: Pioneer of Capitalism*. London: Verso.

Warren, E. and A.W. Tyagi (2004) *The Two-Income Trap: Why Middle-Class Mothers and Fathers Are Going Broke*. New York: Basic.

WB (1990) *World Development Report 1990: Poverty*. Washington, DC: World Bank.

WB (2003) *World Development Report 2004: Making Services Work for Poor People*. Washington, DC: World Bank.

WB (2005) *World Development Report 2006: Equity and Development*. Washington, DC: World Bank.

WB (2011) *Learning for All: Investing in People's Knowledge and Skills to Promote Development. World Bank Education Strategy 2020*. Washington, DC: World Bank.

WB (2012) *World Development Report 2013: Jobs*. Washington, DC: World Bank.

WB (2013) 'Inclusion Matters: The Foundation for Shared Prosperity', *New Frontiers of Social Policy Series*. Washington, DC: World Bank.

WB (2015) 'FAQs: Global Poverty Line Update'. Washington, DC: World Bank. www.worldbank.org/en/topic/poverty/brief/global-poverty-line-faq (last accessed 29 May 2017).

WB (2017a) *Monitoring Global Poverty: Report of the Commission on Global Poverty*. Washington, DC: World Bank.

WB (2017b) 'Monitoring Global Poverty, A Cover Note to the Report of the Commission on Global Poverty, Chaired by Prof. Sir Anthony B. Atkinson, October 18, 2016'. Washington, DC: World Bank. http://pubdocs.worldbank.org/en/733161476724983858/MonitoringGlobalPovertyCoverNote.pdf.

Weeks, J. (1977) 'The Sphere of Production and the Analysis of Crisis in Capitalism', *Science & Society* 41(3): 281–302.

White, C. (2013) *The Science Delusion: Asking the Big Questions in a Culture of Easy Answers*. Brooklyn: Melville House.

Wilkinson, R. and K. Pickett (2009) *The Spirit Level: Why More Equal Societies Almost Always Do Better.* London: Allen Lane.

Wrigley, E.A. (1999) 'Corn and Crisis: Malthus on the High Price of Provisions', *Population and Development Review* 25(1): 121–128.

Wrigley, E.A. (2004) *Poverty, Progress, and Population.* Cambridge. Cambridge University Press.

Wuyts, M. (2002) 'Aid, the Employment Relation and the Deserving Poor Regaining Political Economy', in V. FitzGerald (ed.), *Social Institutions and Economic Development: A Tribute to Kurt Martin*, pp. 169–188. Dordrecht: Kluwer Academic Publishers.

Wuyts, M.E. (2011) 'The working poor: a macro perspective', Valedictory Address. Institute of Social Studies, The Hague, The Netherlands, 8 December. http://hdl. handle.net/1765/104231.

INDEX

r